# PRAISE FOR FULFILLING A PROMISE

"This book follows the author's journey from a young boy in Cambodia into manhood in the United States. It is a remarkable description of his transition from rural life in his native land to the abundance of opportunities in his new one. Chamroeun has described well the difficulties in mastering a new language, as well as the educational and cultural challenges. The reader will cheer as he meets his goals with the help and support of his own family and the U.S. family that considers him one of their own, too, and I look forward to reading more of his experiences in the future."

—Judy Cummings

"Chamroeun tells an extraordinary story about the unlikely journey of growing up in poverty in Cambodia and coming of age in the United States. His memoir will not only bring hope to many young people in Cambodia seeking a better life, but also inspire greater understanding and empathy for the hardships and struggles suffered by so many people around the world and in our own families. Chamroeun's memoir teaches us about loyalty, kinship, and unconditional love, while shedding a critical light on U.S. intervention in Southeast Asia, the Khmer Rouge genocide, and the educational system in post-conflict Cambodia. I am grateful to have learned about Chamroeun's families in Cambodia and in the United States, and I am eager to see how he will continue to fulfill his promise to achieve a full and happy life wherever he goes."

—Jesse Nishinaga,
Program Director, Human Rights and
Business Initiative, UC Berkeley

"Chamroeun Pen has written an engaging, personal account of his search for education. Encouraged by his father who survived the Pol Pot regime of the 1970's and sponsored by an American family, Chamroeun left the security of his family and community to pursue an education in the United States. His bravery and hard work led him from an impoverished background where achieving any kind of education was almost impossible to a completely different culture where he earned an education far beyond his boyhood dreams."

—Michael Marquardt

"From his humble beginnings in Cambodia to his graduation from an American university, Chamroeun takes the reader on an inspiring and triumphant journey. His story is one of adversity, good fortune, perseverance, love, and determination. Given his rise from extreme poverty to success in the United States to the fulfillment of his noble promise, the book serves as a reminder that with passion and hard work, even a seemingly impossible goal is achievable. The next chapter of his story, fully fulfilling his promise, is one I hope to someday also read."

—Michael Pierce,
Director of Admissions, Bishop
Blanchet High School

"*Fulfilling A Promise* is a tremendous achievement. This true story of Chamroeun Pen's remarkable journey from a seriously impoverished childhood in rural Cambodia, to graduating with a business degree from the University of Washington in Seattle, is both heartbreaking and heartwarming. Courage, perseverance, love, and sheer intensity of effort just jump off the pages. And it is so beautifully written, it is difficult to take a break from turning the next page."

—Randall K. Gould, M.D

"It was one thing to watch Chamroeun's experience as a teacher. It was an entirely different experience to read about Chamroeun's first-hand experiences as the student I knew during his time in high school. The grit and determination it took to navigate the familial, social, and political boundaries of his family's story and history are inspiring, let alone doing so while also navigating the dynamics of American high school life, which are complicated enough for most teens. Chamroeun's story is a story filled with hope, authenticity, and a honest look at some of the successes and shortcomings of the "American Experience." Chamroeun's honesty and candor should inspire others to speak up about their own experiences, their own truths, and to be agents of change in their families and communities."

—Kristin Kuzmanich,
English Teacher, Holy Names, Academy

*Fulfilling a Promise* is a fascinating memoir about Chamroeun Pen's unshakeable determination to learn and pursue the best education possible. From the obstacles of growing up in poverty in Cambodia to the difficulties of adjusting to life and scholastic study in the United States, the book unveils a life lived with unwavering purpose. Chamroeun's incredible work ethic, and fierce loyalty to his family and his country carries him through personal, economic, and academic challenges. Readers are inspired to help Chamroeun fulfill his promise of commitment to education in his community."

—Rachel McGovern,
English Department Chair, Bishop
Blanchet High School

# FULFILLING
# A PROMISE

A MEMOIR

———————— ◆ ————————

LIFE AFTER THE KHMER ROUGE

## CHAMROEUN PEN

978-1-7350678-1-0 (Print Book ISBN)
978-1-7350678-0-3 (Ebook ISBN)

*A portion of the proceeds will be donated to buy school supplies for impoverished children in Cambodia.*

# CONTENTS

# A Promise Made

*"If you let me go, I learn as much as I can about the world I know nothing about. And I come back and help teach other students what I learn. I do as much as I can to help. I promise."*

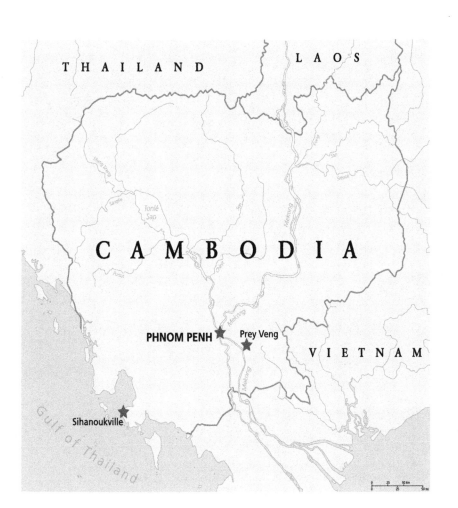

# CAMBODIA

WHEN PEOPLE THINK about Cambodia, they may imagine the incredible architecture of the Angkor region or the exotic beaches of the Southern coast. With roots in the ancient Angkor civilization, the Cambodian people still carry on many traditional practices. Modern citizens, known as Khmers, often perform the famous *robam apsara* dance and the martial arts known as *pokator*. Traditional music is performed with percussion, string, and woodwind instruments in a style known as *pin peat*. Many learn to use natural remedies like tree roots, herbs, and leaves to cure diseases. Furthermore, artisans are able to reproduce the elaborate Angkor sculptures and paintings found in ancient temples. Theravada Buddhism is the most widely practiced religion in Cambodia. Many Khmers, like my family, go to the temples during religious holidays, and donate food to the monks to receive good karma. We believe that doing good will allow us to reincarnate into a better life.

If its progress had been uninterrupted, Cambodia could potentially be as economically and socially advanced as its neighboring countries, Thailand and Vietnam. Most importantly, Cambodia would have more educators to guide the younger generations. Unfortunately, this nation has also suffered a brutal history of genocide, which has made life difficult and at times unbearable for the Khmer people.

# PREFACE

EVERYONE COMES FROM a different place. Everyone has a story. This is a story of how an opportunity changed my life.

My name is Chamroeun Pen (pronounced CHAHM-RON PEN). Born in Prey Veng Province, Cambodia, I am the youngest son of an impoverished family. My siblings were forced to drop out of school early to help support our family. I am the only one that was lucky enough to stay in school.

I was born after my country had suffered great devastation under the Khmer Rouge, an army led by the dictator Pol Pot. The Khmer Rouge carried out devastating purges in Cambodia at the end of the Vietnam war. These included some of the most brutal mass killings of the twentieth century. This genocide amounted to the slaughtering of roughly two million men, women, and children from 1975 to 1979. Pol Pot wanted to destroy the middle class, empty the cities, and establish an agricultural utopia.

I hope this book allows you to better visualize what life is like growing up in Cambodia today and better understand my emotional journey, through vacillating successes and struggles. Most importantly, I hope you will come to appreciate the value of education the way I have. In my experience, without it, life is very limited. It's like living in a dark world with no hope. Lastly, I hope my story inspires those around the world who are in the position where I began. My aspiration is to motivate people to pursue and finish their education.

This is my story.

# FAMILY STRUCTURE

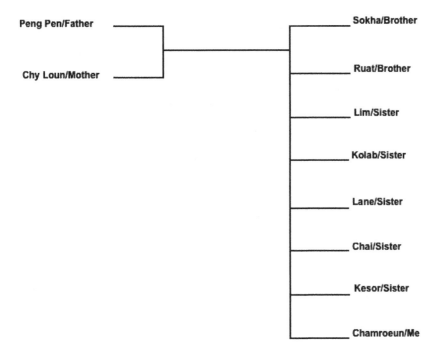

Peng Pen/Father

Chy Loun/Mother

Sokha/Brother

Ruat/Brother

Lim/Sister

Kolab/Sister

Lane/Sister

Chai/Sister

Kesor/Sister

Chamroeun/Me

# 1

# THE STRUGGLE

I REMEMBER WAKING early one morning as a breeze cooled my body. I wrapped my arms around my chest as goosebumps rose all over me. As usual, I was sleeping in between my parents on thin grass mats that lay directly on top of the wooden floor. Being the youngest, I always wanted to be near them, especially Mother.

Mother pulled our thin blanket over me.

"Are you feeling warmer?" she whispered in Khmer, the language of the Cambodian (or Khmer) people. Everyone else was asleep.

"Not really," I mumbled.

"Come here." She wrapped her arms around me, hugging me tight. Her body heat warmed me. "I love you more than you could know, my last one." She kissed me softly on my head. Mother frequently called me, "last one." She went on, "don't forget about me when you grow old, okay?"

"I won't, Mother." I hugged her, resting my head on her chest.

Our conversation was interrupted when Father put his arm around us. "Why are you awake?" he spoke. "It's too early. The roosters haven't even crowed yet."

"Chamroeun got cold. I have to keep him warm," said Mother.

Father scooted closer. I could hear him breathing. "What are we going to do with you?" he said, putting his arm on my stomach. "You're getting bigger every day. We have to sign you up for school soon."

"Why do I have to go to school?"

"Because school will give you a bright future. It will help you find a good job that will save all of us."

"I can tell that you will be one of the smartest in our family," said Mother.

"Oh, he will be more than that," Father added, "he will be one of the smartest in his class and anywhere he goes." He chuckled.

His comments warmed my heart. I knew I had to make them proud. "When I get bigger, I'll find a good job. I'll take care of both of you."

They laughed quietly. "Very good, Son." Father tapped me on my back.

At that point, I had no idea of what kind of job I needed to rescue my family. Since I was the youngest in a family with seven siblings—two brothers and five sisters—my life was fairly easy. My sisters, Lim, Chai, and Kesor were frequently there to look after me. Lim was responsible for helping Mother cook, while my brothers Sokha and Ruat, and my sisters Lab and Lane, had to help my parents farm. They worked long hours and did not return home until evening.

I lived in Kouk Kong village, Prey Veng Province. Unlike other farmers, my family was one of the poorest households in the village. My eldest three siblings, Sokha, Ruat, and Lim were forced to drop out of school to work on the family farm and do chores. Sokha and Ruat left school at grade seven. Lim stopped in grade three. Abandoning school did not bother Sokha and Lim much. They never liked classes and were happy to hear my parents' decision. Ruat had the desire to learn. Yet, he had no choice but to obey my parents' words. Fortunately, the rest of my siblings were able to continue their schooling. Lab was in grade seven, Lane was in grade five, followed by Chai in grade four, and Kesor in grade three. Despite our struggles, Father would never allow all of my siblings to drop out of school. He believed in the value of education. To him, knowledge was key to escaping poverty.

At the age of six, I occasionally had to help my family with the rice crops too, by carrying the green tender stalks across the muddy ground.

Our rice field was roughly 1 hectare (2.5 acres), with narrow walking paths cutting through the farm to form a rectangular land shape. There, my sisters Chai, Kesor, and I transferred piles of rice stalks from the edge of the field to my mother, who planted them in the middle with my other sisters: Lim, Lab, and Lane. They placed them one by one into the soft wet soil in straight lines, allowing room for the rice to grow. Walking in the sticky sludge with a big pile of stalks in my arms was difficult.

One morning, I lost my balance and fell into the rice plants, their sheaves covering me.

"Chai and Kesor! Help your brother up!" Mother yelled. My sisters hustled, picking the plants off me.

"Are you okay, Chamroeun?" Chai asked, hoisting me up.

"Yeah, I'm fine."

Kesor scowled at me, then grabbed some crops from my load.

"Hurry up, Chramouh Thom! Mother is waiting," she said. "Chramouh Thom" meant "Big Nose." I had a big flat nose, wider than most people in my family, but I didn't think it was that big. Most Khmers also had flat noses, black hair, and brown skin. But I was the color of charcoal because I often played outside under the sun.

I got up, now carrying fewer crops, and followed my sisters at a quicker pace.

"The crops are all dirty!" said Mother, shaking her head. She had short black hair, hanging at the sides of her oval face beneath a *kroma* (scarf) tied around her head. Her scarf had red and white checks. "Give them to Lim and Lab." We placed the crops near Lim. "You shouldn't let your brother carry that much. I don't want him to drop the crops. I don't want the crops to be ruined."

"I tried to tell him, Mother, but he didn't listen," said Kesor.

Mother was quiet and continued planting. She didn't want to waste time talking to us. Those rice crops were soaked with water. We had to plant them before they died off.

"Because of you, Mother's mad at us," said Kesor, glaring at me. She walked past Chai and me to get more crops.

"Come here, Chamroeun," said Chai, "you still have some mud on your face." She wiped my cheeks gently. "Are you thirsty? Let's go get some water."

We sat on the walk path, covered with grass. The heat caused sweat to drip down my forehead. I swallowed, watching Chai pour me a small pot of water.

"Here you go," she said. I smiled, then gulped it down.

The landscape of Prey Veng was breathtaking. It was dominated by green rice fields spreading as far as my eyes could see. Tall palm trees grew individually alongside the walking paths. Every morning, people woke up early and headed to their rice fields. Farmers bent over their crops, singing and conversing as they began the day's work. Others stayed home, feeding their animals: cows, water buffalos, chickens, and ducks. Villagers preferred working in the cool morning breeze as the temperature increased in the afternoon, reaching over 100 degrees Fahrenheit. The majority of villagers relied on rice farming as their main source of income while others worked in rubber tree plantations throughout the province. Villagers prepared their fields using cows and water buffalos to plough the wet soil and transfer crops. Kids searched for crabs and fish near the edges of the fields or sauntered on walk paths, pulling ropes attached to farming animals. Large bells were strapped around the animals' necks.

"Woo . . . Woo . . ." A voice called from a distance away. I got up searching but couldn't tell where it came from. "Woo . . . Woo . . ." I heard it again. This time, the voice was much closer as my sister, Lim, stood tall, repeating it. This was a traditional way of calling for wind. Quite often, when it got so hot, farmers yelled, "woo," begging the gods for a cool breeze.

Jingling noises were traveling on as a light breeze approached; it sounded like instruments were playing. The tinkling noise was getting closer and closer. I looked to my right and saw a white cow, mostly covered with brown soil, approaching our field.

"Chamroeun! Chase that cow away from the crops!" Chai yelled. "Do something! Don't just sit there!"

I skipped across the muddy ground, heading toward the cow, screaming at the top of my lungs.

"Hey! Hey!" I shouted. "Go away, you stupid cow!" But the cow continued forward, staring straight at our crops. Chai appeared, holding a stick, and it ran off.

"Take this," Chai gave me the tree branch. "Hit it if it comes back."

The cow returned after seeing Chai walk away. I realized that it was not afraid of me.

"If you come back, I'll hit you!" I yelled. The cow did come back. I raised the stick over my head and went after it. The cow ran into another rice field and was chased by three of the neighboring kids. They grabbed handfuls of mud and threw at it fearlessly. I joined them. Chasing cows and water buffalos alongside the walk paths was always fun. We often played together, searching for fish and frogs hidden underneath the shallow water.

"There's a frog!" Bona pointed, then dove into the water. The frog escaped, jumping to me. "Get it, Chamroeun!"

I squatted and grabbed it with both hands, but the frog's skin was too slippery. It slid out of my palms and skipped toward the walk path. Another village boy, Chan, dove over and gripped it tight. "I got it!" he said with a big smile.

"Good job, Chan!" said Bona, "we caught one."

The frog opened its mouth repeatedly, like it was begging for mercy.

"We have to kill it so it won't get away," said Chan. He smashed its head against the dirt until it stopped moving.

One of my favorite dishes was fried frogs mixed with lemongrass. Mother always made it a little spicy. Whenever the neighboring kids and I found a frog, we tried to catch it, and we always ended up with our bodies covered with sludge. Mother would get mad at me for playing in the mud. She hated washing my dirty clothes, which was why she rarely took me to the rice fields. Regardless, I knew Mother loved me dearly and would do anything to protect me.

Rice farming was not enough to sustain our family. This convinced Father to buy an outdated tractor to help villagers prepare their farm lands. Father and both of my brothers had to work long hours, ploughing soil in rubber tree plantations to receive a small payment of roughly 1 dollar (4,000 *riel*) a day. This rusty tractor frequently broke down, and Father had to borrow an enormous amount of money from villagers to fix it. Tremendous debt finally forced my parents to sell the tractor and our worn A-frame wooden house, which had tall stilts underneath and long stairs in the front. Most of the money was used to pay off the arrears.

I did not want to leave Kouk Kong and was doleful knowing that my family had sold our house. This was my birthplace. My siblings and I had many friends here, but our financial struggle required us to move to the village of Entha Jeng. Grandmother Louk, who was my only living grandparent, had given my parents a piece of property near her house in front of a number of banana trees. There, we built a wooden home directly on the ground, without stilts, and covered it with a thatched grass roof.

Since we had no money to buy new furniture, Father assembled beds and tables from pieces of used wood. Unlike the neighbors' houses, our house was one small room full of shabby furniture: grass mats for sleeping and small derelict clay stoves. Our neighbors' homes were traditional A-frames like our last house, with tall stilts and stairs underneath. This was a typical house for the majority of people throughout the provinces. Because it got so hot in Cambodia, people liked to sit in the shade below the first floor. Most people in the village had newer furniture and television sets.

Living in Entha Jeng was even more challenging for us. Once again, my family was one of the poorest in our community. While most families in the village kept livestock, we did not have farm animals or a fenced enclosure. Cows and water buffalos helped farmers to efficiently work their crops. Selling eggs from chickens or ducks was a convenient way for villagers to generate more income. My parents knew that not owning domesticated animals was a disadvantage, but there was nothing we could do since we were not able to afford them.

My father was a hard worker and a doer. He bought wholesale rice cakes and sold them around the village to earn more money on top of long hours farming.

Some of our neighbors treated our family as pariahs due to our extreme poverty. The neighborhood kids didn't dislike us, but they were trained by their families to look down on us. I remember so well, a moment when I was playing with one of my next-door friends, Bora, in front of my home. His mother saw us. She marched out of her house with her hands on her hips screaming, "Bora! Come back to our house now!" Bora immediately got up and sprinted barefoot back to his mother. "I told you not to go over to that house," she said, making sure I could hear. She glared at me, then grabbed Bora's hand, dragging him toward their house. I was disheartened hearing her words. I stood there quietly staring at the ground with shame. But there was nothing I could do to change my family's reputation.

Since my family couldn't afford a TV, my sisters and I had to go across the dirt street to one of our neighbor's houses if we wanted to watch a movie. The owners frequently rejected us. Their front doors were intentionally locked if they saw us coming. Yet, we continued to sit on the wooden stairs, peeking through small holes in the doors, trying to see the bright screen.

"Go away!" the owner shouted, pounding on the door to scare us. "Stop coming to my house, I don't want you here!"

Going down the stairs, I asked Lane, "why do people hate us so much?"

"I don't know," she said, "maybe because we don't have anything."

We walked back home in silence, embarrassed for being poor.

Because of my family's poverty, my parents had to find other ways to sustain us. Father would regularly borrow other people's money to buy food. Villagers trusted him because he had a reputation as an honorable man and was born in the same village they were. However, we were not able to pay off what we owed. This put us in even greater debt than before. I remember villagers coming to our house to ask for their hard-earned money back. They often left disappointed. Sometimes, they even threatened to take our farming equipment.

"If you don't have my money by the next time I come, I will take everything you have," said an elderly lady. Others would publicly embarrass us in front of my grandmother and our neighbors by calling us offensive names and cursing. Neighbors across the street would laugh at us. People sat in the shade of their tall wooden stilt homes, gossiping about my family. What was worse, my aunt Len, Mother's older sister, who lived with Grandmother, ridiculed us.

"Why did you let them live near us?" Aunt Len asked Grandmother Louk with anger. "Loun is embarrassing us. She is a disgrace to our family."

Grandmother Louk did not reply and decided to distance herself from us, but the sorrow on her face gave her feelings away.

As I was getting closer to the age of seven, a common time to start school, my parents took me to the registration office to enroll me in the first grade. Primary education in Cambodia is first through sixth grade. Up until then, I was never interested in school. I enjoyed spending time at home with my older siblings and especially my mother. Being a mama's boy, I always wanted to go wherever she went. I could not live one day without her presence. I begged my parents to wait until I was a little older to enroll me. Of course, they didn't listen. They knew I was trying to avoid school. When we arrived home from the registration office, I was crying and shaking because I was afraid to start classes. I was also scared of being away from my family for the first time. I groveled at Father's feet with tears on my face, trying to convince him to cancel the school's registration. "Father, please, I beg you, please cancel school." I looked up, seeing him staring hard at me through his glasses.

"No Son, school is very important. Everyone has to attend school to have a successful future. School will help you find a good job when you are grown. You have to do this for your own sake," he said.

# 2

# FIRST DAY OF SCHOOL

WHEN THE FIRST day of school arrived, I was afraid and ran to the back of my grandmother's house, where I hid behind the banana trees. I saw Mother bustling around the house, trying to find me. "Chamroeun, where are you?" she yelled. "Chai and Kesor, help me find him." Kesor and Chai ran to our neighbors' house to inquire.

"Chamroeun, come out! It's time to go to school!" Mother yelled, walking toward my location. She was so mad, she continued to shout for a while. As Mother and my sisters got closer to my hiding place, I started running. I tripped over a tree root and fell face first into the packed dry dirt.

"Mother! There he is!" Kesor screamed. She sprinted to grab me, then picked me up and dragged me back into the house.

"Let me go! Let me go!" I twisted my arms, trying to escape.

"Stop it, Chamroeun," Mother said. She spanked me hard on my lower back with an open hand. I was shocked to be treated this way. Mother rarely hit me because I was her "last one." Mother then broke a branch off a small tree and whipped me in the back several times.

"Why do you have to make it so difficult?" Mother asked. "I don't want to hit you, but you leave me no choice." She threw the stick away. "Take him inside," Mother said to Chai and Kesor.

I cried as my mother dressed me in Ruat's old ripped and dirty school uniform. The white shirt and blue pants were mostly covered with dust and brown soil.

"It's going to be okay," said Chai, as she came and wiped my tears. "Most of your friends will be in the same classroom and you will have plenty of fun. Besides, my class is right across from yours, so if anything goes wrong, you can always come to me."

"But I don't like being away from Mother," I mumbled.

"Mother will be home waiting for you when you're done with school." She patted me on my back.

The first day of class was nerve-racking. I remember the frightening feeling of hearing the intimidating voice of my forty-five-year-old teacher for the first time. His name was Mr. Charya. He seemed so tall, wearing a dark blue polo shirt along with black trousers and brown flip-flops. The scariest thing about him was his tone of voice: a clear deep baritone. He spoke very loudly to students. While he took roll call, I sat at my desk distracted. I was thinking about being home with Mother.

"Pen, Chamroeun!" he shouted and looked around the room. I was too afraid to raise my hand. "Pen, Chamroeun!" he repeated. I finally raised my hand, doing so timidly. He looked at me angrily. "Why didn't you raise your hand the first time?" he asked. I was frozen, startled by his aggression. He walked closer to my desk. "Can you hear me? Are you okay?"

I forced myself to look at him, my hands shaking, and answered, "yes sir. I am just a bit nervous."

He laughed at my comment. "You are nervous? I thought you were deaf!" He turned to the class. "Everything is going to be fine, kids. School is fun. Education is a special tool that will guide every one of you toward success."

As I looked around the classroom, I saw partially torn paintings of past Khmer students hanging on the dark yellow cement walls. Our brown wooden desks were about five feet long, with small storage compartments underneath for students to keep their backpacks. There were thirty-five students in the classroom. The front two desks of each row were filled with students who were well dressed, each wearing brand-new school uniforms. Behind them, I sat alone in the rear, at the fourth desk in the far-right corner of the room.

"Everyone, listen up!" Mr. Charya screamed to get the attention of the class after he wrote the Khmer alphabet on the blackboard. "There are many letters in the Khmer alphabet. There are subscript consonants and independent vowels. The alphabet contains thirty-three consonants, thirty-two subscript consonants, and fourteen independent vowels. When you get home, make sure you practice reading these letters. Moving forward, I will call for volunteers to come up and read in front of the class. You better know how to read."

I was intimidated by his comment. I didn't even have the confidence to make eye contact with him. In Khmer culture, it was considered rude to look at elders in the eyes. But I wasn't alone. Other students were staring at their desks, afraid to look up. "Everyone!" he shouted, "stand up and repeat after me." We all stood and loudly repeated after him in unison one letter at a time.

Toward the end of this first class, I looked outside the window and saw Chai in front of my classroom, waiting for me. Finally, the teacher made the announcement. "That's it for today. I will see you all tomorrow." Most students stayed and tried to make new friends, while I quickly walked out to meet Chai.

"How was it?" Chai asked, smiling slightly.

"It was great!" I lied, not wanting to share my real feelings.

"See, I told you that it's going to be fine."

During dinner that evening, Father asked me, "so Chamroeun, how was your first day of school?"

I paused from eating *prahok chien* (fried fermented fish) and rice. "It was okay," I said.

"Oh, he had a great time," Chai added. "He told me so with excitement when he first got out of class."

Father looked at me and smiled. "Good! I am so glad you liked it. Education will definitely help you later on," he said.

After we had finished eating, surrounded by the darkness of night, my sisters worked on their homework near a dimly lit candle. There was no electricity in the province. Villages used candles and lanterns to light their houses. Some people used batteries as a source of power to run their televisions. I knew the brightness of the light glowing from a family's house was reflective of their wealth. Richer households could afford to buy more candles and lanterns.

Our home was dark. We had roughly two candles and one lantern placed in the middle room and near the walls. I sat nearby my sisters, watching them do their homework. Lane, Chai, and Kesor talked quietly among themselves as they browsed through their class lessons. Lab, however, was reading her textbook in silence. She was a hard worker and always took school seriously. Despite failing a few classes, Lab was recognized in our family as the first person that truly had the potential to finish school. She had reached one of the highest grade levels in the family and visualized herself as the first person to graduate from secondary school (grades seven to twelve). Lab was a role model. I wished to be just like her.

When I looked across the room, I saw Sokha and Ruat lying on their faded wooden beds beside a yellow candle. Father was sitting next to an open window. He was smoking a cigarette as he always did when he had a moment to rest. He didn't like to smoke near us because he knew we didn't like the smell. Mother made this especially clear as she would always cough after breathing in the smoke. Father and my brothers were exhausted. I couldn't imagine what they had to go through each day at work. I knew that farming must be extremely difficult because growing rice was physical work.

The next morning, before my sisters and I left for school, my mother gave us 500 riel (approximately 12 cents) to split among us.

"Is that going to be enough for the five of us?" I asked Lab on the walk to school.

Her eyes narrowed. "No, but it's better than nothing. We should be happy that she gave us some money for snacks. Sometimes, she doesn't have anything to give us and there's nothing we can do about it." I didn't say a word for the rest of the way.

When we got there, we parted ways, heading toward our separate classes. Chai suddenly turned around and yelled, "Chamroeun! I'll wait for you at the same spot. See you after class."

"Okay! See you," I yelled back excitedly.

Mr. Charya continued the previous day's lesson about learning the Khmer alphabet. "Who here wants to come up in front of the class to read the alphabet?" He challenged us with his aggressive tone. A boy sitting in the front of my row raised his hand. Mr. Charya pointed at the boy with surprise. "Yes! You, come up here." The boy stood up from his desk and walked toward the blackboard.

When he got there, he read the alphabet at a fast pace with apparent ease.

Mr. Charya tapped the boy on his back. "Wow! I'm impressed," he said, then turned around to face the class. "See class! This boy right here is brave. He is also smart. By reading all the letters correctly, it indicates that he is a good student." He looked at the boy. "What's your name?"

"Rei," said the boy.

"Take a good look at Rei," he addressed the class. "He should be a role model to all of you. I bet Rei will end up living a successful life and will have a good job when he grows up."

I remembered looking at Rei's smiling face as he returned to his desk. I visualized myself being him. I imagined how proud my parents would be. This was what they wanted for me.

"I need another volunteer," Mr. Charya boomed as he was searching around the classroom. No one raised their hand. Most students including myself stared down at our desks, afraid that he would call on one of us. "So, no one else wants to come up here to read?" He scanned around the room. "Fine! Then I will call on one of you."

My palms sweated as I nervously stared downward, closing my eyes and hoping that he would not call on me.

"You there in the middle row," he said. I looked up and saw him pointing at a student who sat near me. He wore brown pants, ripped on the sides, with a dirty white shirt. "Yes, you. Come up and read," Mr. Charya continued.

The boy slowly got up from his desk and made his way up to the blackboard. "Hold up!" Mr. Charya approached him. "What color are your pants?" The student froze. "Did you hear what I asked?" he yelled. Suddenly, the student started to cry, his hands reaching up to cover his face as tears flowed through his fingers. "Do you think crying will prevent you from answering my question?" He grabbed the student's wrists and ripped them away from his face. "Answer me!"

"I'm sorry sir, my parents couldn't afford a pair of blue pants. This is the only good pair that I have," the student mumbled.

"If your parents are too poor, then what are you doing in my class? Shouldn't you be at the farm helping them? Being poor is not an excuse for wearing the wrong uniform," he continued berating the boy. "Next time, don't even bother showing up to my class." Mr. Charya walked away from the boy. "Go ahead, read!" He pointed at the board.

I felt so awful for the boy. I couldn't imagine how embarrassed he must have felt standing there in front of the class.

The student wiped off his tears and read quietly. After stating the first three letters, he took a long pause.

"What is the matter?" Mr. Charya asked.

The boy looked to the teacher, "I don't know how to read this letter," the boy said softly.

"You don't know how to read? Did you not pay attention to Rei when he was reading?" Mr. Charya walked closer to the student.

"I did sir, but I forgot how to pronounce it." He looked down at the ground. His hands were shaking.

"You forgot how to pronounce it? What do you normally do at home? Did you not practice reading these letters at home?"

"I did sir, but I don't know how to say them correctly."

"Did you ask your parents or siblings to help you at all?"

"My parents are always busy. Even if they were available, they can't help because they can't read."

"How embarrassing is that." Mr. Charya turned toward the class with a chuckle. "He is telling me that his parents can't read Khmer letters. I can't believe it." He stared intently at the student's face. "Well then, you better pay closer attention in class and listen to others when they come up here, so you won't end up as dumb as your parents." He walked away then sat in his desk. "Go back to your desk, farm boy," he added.

The boy immediately walked back to his desk. He placed his face down over his arms and cried. My heart dropped to the floor as I listened to his sobs. I wished I could go check on him but doing so could only get me in trouble. Looking at him, I could visualize myself being the next victim. I knew I would have to practice to avoid being in that position.

Toward the end of class, Mr. Charya asked us to spell the alphabet. Students had to write letters with white chalk on small rectangular blackboards. Everyone brought out their board, preparing to write the letter called out by the teacher. I did not have mine with me. Kesor had borrowed it from me earlier for her class. I didn't know what to do and continued to sit at my desk in silence. The teacher started calling out letters. Students wrote on their boards, then showed it to him. He walked around the classroom to make sure everyone wrote correctly. A student would be whipped on his or her hand for misspelling a letter. Mr. Charya soon noticed that I did not have my board. He scowled at me.

"Where is your writing board?" he asked.

"Sorry sir, I don't have it."

"What do you mean you don't have it? You have to bring your writing board with you to class every day. Where is it?"

"I forgot it at home. Sorry sir," I lied. I didn't want to tell him that my sister borrowed it. I didn't want him to know that my family was too poor to afford a new writing board. My sisters and I had to share school supplies: writing boards, pencils, erasers, and notebooks.

Mr. Charya didn't believe me. He thought that I didn't know how to write the alphabet and was trying to come up with an excuse. To prove it to him, I opened my backpack, pretending like I was double-checking, so he would forgive me. My mouth was dry and my hands were beginning to shake as I shuffled through my bag. "I don't have it, sir."

"Let me see." He grabbed my school bag from me then quickly checked it. "Yeah, I don't see it either. But that's your fault." He hit me in the back with my bag. He hit me so hard, I slid off the seat as my chest banged against the wooden desk. I wanted to cry, but I knew he would punish me more. But no matter how hard I tried, I still was not able to control my emotions. Tears fell down my cheeks, dripping onto the scratched wooden desk. I saw the whole class staring at me with pity. "From now on, you need to bring a writing board to class every day. Do you hear me?"

"Yes, sir." I forced myself to reply.

He tossed my backpack to the side of my desk. Books poured out and lay on the dirt. I wiped the tears off my cheeks then picked up my books. I spotted Kesor near the window staring at me. She looked heartbroken after witnessing this punishment. Yet, there was nothing she could do besides stand there, speechless.

The class continued on with the writing activity. For the last few minutes, I sat there quietly, face down at my desk. I was humiliated and did not have the nerve to look at my classmates, especially my teacher.

After that, I always brought my blackboard to class and didn't allow Kesor to borrow it ever again. I consistently double-checked my school bag to ensure that I had everything before coming to class.

To avoid the wrath of my teacher, I was forced to become a better student. I also knew this would cheer up my parents in their miserable situation. In order to achieve this, I knew I had to work harder and pay more attention in class. From then on, I was inspired. When I got home that day, I practiced reading the alphabet for hours. When I got stuck, my sisters were there to help. I practiced and practiced until I was dizzy. But I was able to learn most of the letters.

As I made progress, I participated more in school. Sometimes, I raised my hand to go to the blackboard and read the assignment for the class to follow. The teacher would compliment me when I read it correctly. "Good job," he'd say and pat me on my shoulders. He would, however, embarrass me if I made a mistake. "Stupid boy! Next time, study more before you volunteer," he would shout. Other times, he would make fun of my dirty uniform, calling me, "stinky boy" or "garbage boy." Despite all of this, he knew my reading skills were improving.

As life went on throughout this first school year, my family's financial standing continued to worsen. My parents couldn't provide enough money to feed our large family. Kesor was taken out of school and sent to live with my aunt Lam in Kampot, located in the middle of Southern Cambodia. Aunt Lam was opening a coffee shop at the time and needed Kesor's assistance. Sokha married and moved to a distant village to live with his wife. Without Sokha, Father was shorthanded on the farm. This meant that Lim had stopped helping Mother with chores and started farming instead. Mother decided to sell homegrown vegetables, including lettuce, eggplant, and peppers, around the village to help support our family.

As the end of the school year approached, Mr. Charya stood in front of the class to make an announcement. "Okay, there are thirty-five of you here. After grading your assignments and your participation, only twenty of you are qualified to pass. I can't announce who those people are yet, since we still have two more weeks of school left. But to those of you who are working hard and have made progress since day one, you will have a good chance of passing my class." He smiled directly at Rei.

I was convinced that I was also going to be one of those twenty students.

When the last day of class was finally upon us, I arrived to class thirty minutes earlier than usual. I witnessed some other students arrive accompanied by their parents. My fingers tapped the desk repeatedly until the teacher walked in. I could feel my heart racing, like it was about to jump out of my chest. The teacher pulled out the list of who had passed his class. He called the first name on the list, Rei. Other students that always sat next to him were also called. Name after name was called. But I waited. When he reached the seventeenth student, my hands were shaking. By now I was worried that I might not pass. He called the last student's name, "number twenty, Channary." He then folded the sheet and congratulated Channary, a girl who sat two desks in front of me.

I was shocked and disappointed. I did not believe that some students who passed were smarter than me. A few of those kids often struggled with reading the alphabet. Yet, they were richer than me and had much cleaner uniforms. At the time, I didn't think that wealth was a factor that helped them pass the class. But it was definitely a key to earning the teacher's acknowledgment. He was always nicer to richer students and sometimes refused to hit them for their mistakes. Numerous thoughts raced through my mind. I sat speechless. I watched the students exiting the class, smiling and waving to their parents.

The teacher then reopened the grade sheet and called the remaining names, the names of the kids who didn't pass the class. My name was called twenty-first. After hearing my name, I was so emotional that tears started slowly rolling down my face. I was ashamed. I had let my family down. I was embarrassed about wasting all the hard-earned money that my parents had invested in my school supplies and especially the money that Mother had given me for snacks. Even worse, I didn't know how I was going to explain this to them.

After the teacher was done reading the names, he folded his paper and put it in his briefcase. "Since the rest of you are stupid, you can't move on to second grade," he said. "You will have to repeat my class next school year." He picked up his suitcase and left the class.

I did not understand how I had failed first grade. I thought that I was becoming a good student. My reading was improving daily especially toward the end of the school year. In Khmer schools, even smart students had failed classes due to the placement grade system. Only a certain number of students are allowed to move up, leaving the rest to repeat until they pass. This rule is caused by limited classrooms and class size, which means the school only accepts a small number of students in certain grades.

I continued to sit alone with my tears, replaying in my head being called, "stupid." I started to doubt myself, thinking *maybe he's right, maybe I am stupid. Maybe my stupidity made me misread those letters.* I thought about the small mistakes that might have prevented me from passing. The more I thought about it, the more upset I became.

When I got home, Lab, Lane, and Chai were all celebrating inside the house. They had all passed their classes. But I couldn't celebrate with them. I went outside and sat underneath a Star Apple tree in front of the house. In the background, my sisters were laughing while jumping up and down.

They were hugging each other and my mother. I looked at them, wishing so badly that I could be with them. My family would have been so proud of me.

Suddenly, Father walked up to me. "Did you pass your class?" he asked.

I looked up. "I did not. I'm sorry." As I scanned his face, he took a deep breath. I could tell he was disappointed.

He pushed his glasses up slightly on his nose. "It's okay. Now you know that you will have to work harder to pass your class."

Father looked me in the eyes, showing deep concern. He knew I was upset and wanted to leave me alone. He sighed, then walked away, going back inside the house.

I felt dejected. My failure isolated me from all the happiness in the world. I kept replaying my teacher's comment in my head, "stupid boy!

You should have studied harder." Eventually, a calm came over me. At that moment, I made myself a promise. I told myself, *I would never fail a class ever again.* Failure had lit a fire in me. From then on, I was determined to work harder than ever before.

# 3

# EMERGING HOPE

ONE AFTERNOON, LANE, Chai, and I sat on pieces of bricks, eating the remaining burned rice from the bottom of the pot for a snack. I loved chewing on the crispy dry rice mixed with salty fish sauce. It almost tasted like rice cake. Father frequently told me leftover rice was the best. To him, nothing was better than cold rice with smoked fermented fish, wrapped with banana leaf.

One of my favorite places to be was outside. After finishing the snack, I squatted, drawing cartoon figures in the soft brown soil. Tom and Jerry were my favorites. Whenever I saw the show streaming on the neighbor's TV, I would sprint there, crawl in, and sit at the door quietly so they wouldn't kick me out.

A light breeze hit me, carrying the sounds of instruments playing at people's weddings far away. I enjoyed listening to *pin peat*, a traditional music played on percussion, string, and woodwind instruments. It was Father's favorite.

Sketching the mouse, I heard Lab speak to my other sisters. "Our parents have sold our house." Shocked, I hustled to listen.

"When are we leaving?" Lane asked.

"Father didn't say, but I think we are moving out soon." She glanced at us. "We all should start packing."

She turned to me. "Chamroeun, start gathering all of your stuff. Say goodbye to your friends. We could be leaving any day."

After hearing the news, I went inside to pack my clothes for the big move.

The next morning, while I was playing with my friends underneath the Star Apple tree, Chai told me, "Mother has to go to Kampot to get Kesor."

I was excited to hear that Kesor would be returning, but a part of me was afraid to be at home without Mother there.

I headed inside to watch Mother get ready for the trip. "When are you coming back?" I asked.

She looked down, seeing right through me.

"I can't take you, Chamroeun. I'm going alone. I'll only be gone for a day. I need to get your sister. I'm worried about her." Mother did not say anymore, but the distress on her face gave it all away. I stood there quietly but there was nothing I could do to change her mind.

Shortly, Father returned home from the fields. He sat on his dirt encrusted motorbike, waiting for Mother, ready to take her to the taxi driver's house. People normally took a taxi if they were traveling far away. There were very few taxis in our village. Drivers had to put many passengers in their vehicles before departure.

Mother then walked out holding a small black bag and climbed on the back of the motorbike. They disappeared down the rutted dirt road.

I was unsettled being home without Mother. Lim and Lab had to play the role of Mother: doing chores, cooking, and preparing meals. Unlike Mother, Lim and Lab didn't have time to please me. They would whip me if I didn't obey their words.

The next day, we gathered around the table for lunch, eating rice with boiled eggs and fish sauce. Suddenly, I heard a motorbike approaching. I dropped the spoon, sprinted toward the door and saw Mother and Kesor carefully dismounting an unfamiliar bike.

"Mother's here!" I yelled at the top of my lungs with pure joy. We ran out the door to meet them.

"Thank you so much for bringing us home," Mother said to the man who drove them.

My sisters ran up and hugged Kesor. We were all so happy to see her. Kesor looked healthier. Her face was fuller. She had had more to eat while living with Aunt Lam. Together, we went inside the house to hear about Kesor's time away.

"Kesor," said Father, setting his spoon down. "It's been almost six months since you left. We missed you." He pushed his glasses up lightly. "Part of the reason that your mother and I decided to get you back is to ensure you will be able to focus on school. It's our responsibility to look after you and see that you do well in class."

"Yes, Father," said Kesor quietly.

Kesor continued to eat with a melancholy expression. I could tell she had felt betrayed when my parents sent her away. Kesor never wanted to live with Aunt Lam. She enjoyed going to school in Prey Veng and had many friends in our village. Because of our financial struggle, she had no choice but to move to Kampot. Nonetheless, I knew Kesor was relieved to be back with us and so was I. Like Chai, Kesor was always nearby. It was strange living without her. Kesor and I often fought about random things, competing to be Mother's favorite child. I was thankful to have her reunited with us once again. Kesor living with us also meant that she would continue pursuing knowledge. Without Father's guidance to watch over her, she could easily drop out of school.

That evening Sokha arrived home on a bicycle. This was strange since he rarely visited us from his village. We gathered together on one of the wooden beds inside the house. I sat near Mother, listening to my family talk.

"Father came by our house yesterday and told me that you were all moving out of Prey Veng. I want to go with you," Sokha said.

"What about your wife and Puana?" Ruat asked. Sokha's son, Puana, was roughly eight months old.

"Well, they can either come with us, or I will have to come back and visit them."

"We don't even know where we are going yet. Father hasn't told us anything," Ruat said as he glanced at my father.

"Sokha, Ruat is right. Your mother and I haven't decided where to go or when we are leaving. I don't think that it's wise for you to leave your wife and child behind. You should stay with her and look after your child," Father said.

"Father!" he raised his voice. "I am sick and tired of farming. I want to make more money at a better job. I will come back to visit them. And I will bring them with me when I find a sustainable job."

"Let your mother and me chat about it more. We'll think about it." My parents got up and walked to the back of the house. They stood there and talked for nearly an hour as the rest of us quietly waited inside the house.

Finally, I heard Father call out, motioning his hand, "Sokha, Ruat, come out here." My brothers looked at us uncertainly as they walked out the backdoor. Ruat took a candle with him as night was approaching. They continued to talk calmly in the darkness.

After dinner, I stood near the backdoor to listen. I could still hear soft talking. I peeked my head out and saw they were standing in a circle near a banana tree. The light of the candle was glowing. I saw my parents and Sokha speaking and gesturing. Ruat stood there in silence, staring at the pitch-black ground. The despair on his face told me that something was wrong.

I looked up and saw thousands of bright stars spread across the sky. Nighttime in Prey Veng was magical, especially in the summer. The stars were shining so close to each other, there was barely room for darkness. I stared up for a short while, wishing for my family to stay together no matter where we went.

"Chamroeun! What are you doing there? Go to bed, it's late," Lim called. I walked back and lay on the bed next to my sisters. I closed my eyes and dreamed of a new home. I fantasized about my family living together with no more worries. I drifted off to sleep.

At around four in the morning, I heard footsteps nearby. A voice softly whispered in my ear, "Chamroeun . . . Chamroeun, wake up . . ."

I opened my eyes and blurredly saw Chai looking down at me, hair hanging at the sides of her face. "We have to go . . . We are moving out. Get ready." She crawled away and started folding her clothes.

I got up, rubbed my eyes, and saw everyone packing in the candle light. The entirety of the family was in a scramble to gather their things. We were making so much noise that our neighbors' dogs started barking.

"Chamroeun, pack your stuff. The taxi will be here any minute," said Mother as she folded the sleeping net to stack with the pillows and blankets. I walked into my dimly lit corner of the house to finish organizing my clothes. Sokha was helping Father collect the remaining farm equipment, making me think he was coming too.

The barking eventually woke up the village. I looked out the front window to see neighbors standing in the dark, holding lanterns and candles underneath the stilts of their houses. Some men were shirtless, wearing kroma on their waists. They were staring at us. Others were in small groups of three or four. The light revealed they were pointing at us. A number of families were gossiping.

While I was looking around, I spotted Father and Ruat preparing for an early departure. Ruat had to stay in Prey Veng to help other farmers. Ruat's skills, in particular repairing and engineering, had become a major asset to other successful farmers in Prey Veng.

Father put on his hat and pushed his motorbike toward the road in the dark. He climbed on and waited for my brother.

No one could keep from crying, especially my mother. "Take care of yourself, Son. Your father and I will come visit you soon." No one really knew when we would see Ruat again.

The motorbike rumbled to life. "Ruat, it's time to go," said Father.

Ruat ambled slowly toward the bike. But before he climbed on the back, we all hugged him one last time. He sat behind Father, a pained look on his face. Father patted Ruat's leg, looking at Mother as he spoke.

"I'll be back in a while. I have to go pay off our debts. I'm giving this bike to people we owe. It's the only way to settle the debt." He drove off into the darkness.

I went back to packing. I tried to think of memorable moments of my time with Ruat. I could hardly think of any. He had always been away from home, farming with Sokha and Father. But one memory did stick with me.

I remembered helping him carry some small rusty farm equipment across the muddy trails between rice fields. As I followed him, I tripped on a rice plant and fell face first in the mud. I sat up, mud dripping down my face, the smell of rot burning my nostrils. Ruat laughed so hard that he snorted. He picked me up and wiped the dirt from my face using the bottom of his shirt to clean me off. He walked by my side the rest of the way, pushing away the rice plants to clear the path. We chatted and laughed the whole time.

Fun times together with Ruat were rare because he was always exhausted from work. That and he was much older than me.

As we continued to pack, the neighbors started to realize we were leaving. A few of them walked across the dark street with lit candles to get a closer look. I spotted my grandmother walking inside our house with a blue blanket wrapped around her.

"Loun, what's going on? Are you moving away?" she asked.

Mother paused collecting our equipment. "Yes, we are heading to Kompong Som."

Grandmother stood there speechless and did not have the nerve to look Mother in the face. Grandmother wasn't alone. Others were stunned to hear the news. They looked at each other with wide-eyed, shocked expressions. They did not see this coming. Some people crossed the street, asking if they could help. They gathered around Mother to assist her with gathering our meager kitchen supplies: blackened cookware, rusty pans and silverware, and dented metal plates.

"Loun, I'm so sorry that you have to leave. If I'd known, I would've spent more time with you." Tears poured down my grandmother's cheeks.

"It's okay, Mother. We will come back to visit you."

Mother gently rubbed Grandmother's back in an effort to calm her down. I was both saddened and surprised to see Grandmother cry. I never actually thought that she cared about us. Nevertheless, we all loved and respected my grandmother.

My father was sitting in the front passenger seat of the taxi. It approached our house, headlights ablaze. It was an old Toyota pickup truck, accented with rust and caked with dirt. There were two rows of seats installed in the truck bed, covered by a canopy, but open on the sides. We quickly loaded our luggage into the back. By now, it seemed as though the whole neighborhood had come to help us move the last of our things into the taxi. Perhaps, this was their way of saying sorry.

With nine of us trying to fit into a little Toyota truck, there was limited space. Kitchen utensils and small farming tools were brought along, as well as our small collections of personal items. Father quickly sold the larger pieces of farming equipment to our neighbors at steep discounts.

It was time to say our last goodbyes. The crowd of people, including Grandmother, watched us with their candles and lamps in the darkness. We sat there quietly, heavyhearted. It was especially hard leaving Ruat behind. People waved and called as the taxi slowly pulled away.

"Good luck," they said, waving and smiling. "Don't forget to come visit us."

Our life in Prey Veng was over. A new journey had begun.

Mother, my sisters, and I sat on the metal seats in the back of the truck with our luggage, while Sokha and Father were in the front with the driver. Since this was my first time riding in an automobile, I was excited, bouncing up and down in my seat. The youngest of us sang and laughed as the engine roared, accelerating onto the dirt streets. As the sun crept up, we drove up the road and out of town.

I looked out the open canopy, watching the sun rise. Wind whipped my face as the light shone bright on the green rice paddies, reflecting onto intermittent tall palm trees. The day grew brighter and soon the sun stood above the horizon, a brilliant orange sphere. Taking in the beauty of this new day, I couldn't help but smile. In the distance, farmers walked the paths between the rice fields. As the taxi sped on, I realized I might never come back. I whispered to myself, *goodbye Prey Veng.*

Mother saw me looking out of the open canopy. "What's the matter?"

"I'm just nervous." I rested my head softly on her chest.

"Don't be, everything is going to be fine." Mother reached her arms around me, kissing my forehead. "If you weren't so difficult at the rice field, I would take you anywhere I go," Mother continued. "I love you so much. I wouldn't trade you for anything." She slowly rubbed my arm. This is among my favorite memories of my mother. I didn't say anything back, but I felt so thankful that I had a mother like her.

Three hours into the journey, we reached Phnom Penh. There were more people than I had ever seen living in one city. The chaos of so many street vendors alongside heavy traffic was overwhelming. The roads were jammed with fancy motorbikes and cars, their drivers angrily waiting for the traffic light to turn green. They honked repeatedly as their exhausts rumbled. Children my age and older walked from car to car, selling flowers and snacks.

The driver continued deeper into the city. Father called to me over the noise of the windy truck bed. "Chamroeun! Pretty soon, we will cross Chroy Changvar Bridge. It's the longest bridge in Cambodia. It crosses over Tonle Sap River."

I had never heard of the bridge nor the river, but seeing Father's excitement, I couldn't wait to see for myself. I peeked my head out of the open side of the canopy to look ahead. Soon the bridge came into view. There were two long bridges, parallel to each other, with lanes divided by white lines, allowing room for people to drive. Vehicles were traveling in both directions, crossing over the massive river. I turned my head and saw the dark and muddy water flowing for miles into the distance. Small boats were moving slowly with the current. I looked behind the taxi and saw motorbikes following us in a cloud of dust. Up ahead, I saw a number of buildings squeezed together along the shore. All of this made me feel optimistic for a better life. I felt a sense of hope.

"Chamroeun, on the other side of the river is the royal palace, the place where the king lives. Your grandfather and I visited it once. It was incredible!" Father wrapped his left arm around me. "It's over there." He pointed toward the shore of the river. "If you look close enough, you might be able to see its golden roof." My sisters and I searched for the Royal Palace but couldn't spot it. We had no idea what to look for.

We then approached a strange hill. It was covered with tall trees, and there was a large, round clock made out of foliage in the center. A huge pointed cement monument was at the top of the hill. "Chamroeun, this place is called Wat Phnom. Khmer people consider it a magical place. It's where they come to worship," Father said, smiling.

As I continued scanning the city, I saw a unique building surrounded by a tall black metal fence. There were police guarding it. I tapped my father's arm.

"Father, what's that place with the security guards and the fence?" I pointed toward the building.

"Oh, that's the embassy of the United States of America."

"What's the embassy of the United States of America?"

"The United States of America is the most powerful country in the world. And that is its embassy. People have to go through that building if they want to go to America."

I didn't understand the concept. All of this newness was too much for me to absorb. Nonetheless, I was grateful that Father was there to tell me about what we were seeing.

After four more hours of semi-flat tires bouncing over rutted, pothole-laden roads, we reached Kompong Som. While entering the province, we saw beautiful beaches covered with pure white sand. The gulf water was royal blue and speckled with small islands. As the horizon stretched into the gulf, the shining water seemed to melt into the blue sky. The current created little waves that washed softly against the seashore while the warm breeze gently touched my face. It was the prettiest place I had ever seen. My siblings were all amazed by the natural beauty. We had never seen beaches or the sea. Kompong Som was an absolute paradise.

While taking in these incredible views, I thought of Ruat. I felt guilty that he wasn't able to share this with us. I knew that if he were here, he would be happy.

We soon arrived at my aunt's house, located in a village called Oue Muoy (Oh-Moy), which roughly translates to "One Water Stream." Her house was a big rectangular cement structure surrounded by tall jackfruit and mango trees. As the driver parked the truck, I saw my aunt walking out with a kroma wrapped around her head, wearing a *sarong* (a traditional long skirt) and a t-shirt. She was waving and smiling.

Aunt Lou walked toward Mother and grabbed her hands. She had tears in the corners of her eyes. "How have you been my little sister?" They embraced.

I had never seen Mother this excited to see anyone before. She talked calmly with a big smile on her face. I was surprised to know that Mother had a sister who loved her. Unlike Aunt Len, Aunt Lou was kind and thrilled to see Mother. It had been a long time since they last met.

We all went inside the house. My sisters helped Aunt Lou prepare dinner while everybody else sat on the shiny tile floor in the TV room. The room was furnished with a wooden desk with a radio, VHS player, and big

TV on top of it. There were some blue plastic chairs near the white wall. This province had electricity. Aunt Lou turned on a fan to keep us cool.

"So, I understand that you all came to Kompong Som to find jobs, correct?" Aunt Lou asked.

Mother glanced at Father. "Yes," she said. "You told us on your last visit that there were more jobs here than in Prey Veng. We were hoping that you could help us find jobs for some of our daughters."

Aunt Lou turned to my sisters then looked at Lim and Lab, cooking in the kitchen. "My daughter, Srey, is working at a factory not too far away from here. I can ask her to help when she gets back. But the factory won't accept people younger than sixteen."

"Lim and Lab are old enough, but Lane is only fifteen," Father said.

"She's too young. What about school? Were they in school in Prey Veng?"

"Lim had to drop out of school in third grade. The rest of them failed a few classes, but fortunately Lab and Lane passed sixth and seventh grade," Mother answered, then looked at Chai and Kesor. "Chai is now in fifth grade, and Kesor is going to repeat third grade since she didn't get to finish class and went to Kampot."

"I'll ask Srey to help your daughters, but this means that only Lim and Lab can get hired. Lane is too young."

"If that's the case, then we'll have to push Lane's age a bit," said Father.

"You can try, but looking at her, she seems too young. I don't know if they'll accept her." Aunt Lou looked at Lane with regret. She sighed. "I'll tell my daughter to put in a good word so they'll be generous. If they work, it means that they won't be able to continue school."

"We don't really have a choice. We need them to contribute to the family," said Father as he scratched his head. "We have to do what's necessary in order for all of us to survive. Even if we wanted them to continue school, we wouldn't be able to afford their school supplies, anyway."

Mother looked at Father with shame. "I'll talk to them. They'll understand."

I knew this news would severely affect Lab's chances of ever being able to pursue her goals. She had dreamt of being the first person to finish secondary school. I knew my parents' decision would crush her.

That evening, Aunt Lou's daughter, Srey, and her husband, Thom, arrived home from work. Just like Aunt Lou, they were pleased to see us. We all settled down for one of the most peaceful dinners we had had in a long time. We sat on the floor, legs crossed, eating sweet and sour fish soup, while cheerfully telling Aunt Lou and Srey about our journey from Prey Veng.

In the morning, Srey and Thom went to work on their motorbike. My parents asked my elder sisters to come into the TV room and sit next to Aunt Lou. I sat near Mother on the tile floor, listening.

"We have asked Srey to find jobs in the factory for the three of you," said Father.

"What about school?" Lab asked.

"You and Lane will not be able to continue school any further." Lab was speechless. I could tell she was distraught, but she knew that she could not refuse my parents.

"It was a difficult decision, but we need the three of you to help support the family," Father continued.

Mother rubbed Lab's arm. "Lab, my dear, I know that you have always been passionate about school, and I know this is tough on you . . . but you need to understand that we don't have any other option." Lab then took a deep breath and wiped away tears. It was hard seeing Lab cry, but it was also difficult to see my parents' tortured faces as they delivered the message. I knew this was a difficult decision for them. Lab was the family's first hope to finish school.

After a short silence, Father reached over to hold Lab's hands. "We need to take advantage of this opportunity. This job will help provide income to sustain our family," he said.

"I'll do it," said Lab, still tearful. "But you need to keep Chai, Kesor, and Chamroeun in school."

"There is a school in Oue Pir where we can enroll them," said Aunt Lou. Oue Pir (Oh-Bee) meant Two Water Streams. "It's not too far from here."

"So, when will we start work?" Lim asked.

"Srey said that the factory is hiring, but she will have to take you there first in order to apply for the jobs," said Father.

"We asked Srey to bring the three of you to work with her tomorrow. You will get a chance to see the factory," said Mother.

No one discussed what kind of factory or the types of jobs that would be available. I would find out later from Aunt Lou that the factory was owned by a Chinese company. It was a clothing manufacturer specializing in t-shirts, jackets, and sweaters.

The next day, after my elder siblings dispersed, Mother and Aunt Lou took me, Chai, and Kesor to register for school. We met the principal of Mittapheap, a public school. He told us tuition was free, but we would have to buy our own uniforms and supplies. He signed Chai and Kesor up for fifth and third grade. He even enrolled me in second grade because the placement grade was higher, taking the top thirty to thirty-five students. I was elated.

We walked out of the office, and I appraised the school grounds. It was a much bigger school than the one in Prey Veng. A smile crossed my face. I was delighted that I would be attending school with my sisters. I couldn't wait to start.

When we got home, we found out that only Lim and Lab had gotten hired. Lane was denied because of her age. My parents were disappointed to hear the news. They both took Lane back to the factory the very next day and begged them to take her. This time the manager finally relented. Apparently, workers were in sharp demand.

A week later, we moved out of Aunt Lou's house. My parents rented a blue A-frame house with tall stilts, and a kitchen underneath. This house was roughly five minutes away from my aunt's house. There was a deep well in one of the front corners. Most importantly, the house was big enough for us all. Father bought an old TV so we wouldn't have to go to our neighbor's house. He also bought Sokha a motorbike so that he could become a *motodop* (motorbike-taxi driver). For their part in supporting the family, my parents brewed rice alcohol at home to sell to our neighbors. They also started raising a pig in hopes that it would generate profit by the time they could sell it. Everyone was pitching in to help our family. We felt a sense of hope for our future.

# 4

# THE SPARK

EVERY NIGHT, CHAI and Kesor had to help my older sisters stick brown labels from the factory into small notebooks. This was how they recorded the quantity of clothing they had manufactured on a given day. My sisters came home with piles of labels, one for each piece they had completed. Sometimes, it took them hours to align the labels neatly. At the end of each month, the management from the factory would check the notebooks and pay a bonus to the high producers. Chai and Kesor were often rewarded with 1,000 riel each from my elder sisters for sticking in the labels.

My parents were initially able to gain a little profit from the sales of their brewing. Many people in the neighborhood enjoyed the taste. They came to our house and bought one or two liters of rice beer daily. With the help from my elder brothers and sisters, our situation finally started to improve. My parents could now afford school supplies for me and my sisters.

One week before school started, Mother took Kesor and me to the market to buy uniforms. Chai had to stay home, helping Father brew. Chai and Kesor wore almost the same size so anything that fit Kesor would work for Chai.

We walked along a narrow path across the village, passing coffee shops and cement and wooden houses. People were examining us with curious faces: some smiled, others stared. We had been living in Kompong Som for one-and-a-half months now, yet most people still did not know who we were.

After a ten-minute walk, we encountered something I had never witnessed before. Roughly fifteen to twenty kids around my age were sitting in groups on the side of the street putting their faces into plastic bags and sniffing with their eyes closed. They were skinny and dirty. I could see the bones under their brown skin. It seemed like they hadn't eaten in days. Seeing their suffering made me feel guilty. I wanted to go talk to them, but Mother pulled me by the neck of my t-shirt.

"Why are they smelling the plastic bags?" I asked Mother.

"Don't look at them, Chamroeun. Those street kids are orphans. They're glue-sniffers. They're bad kids. Last week, one of them tried to steal the bowl in the water container. I had to chase after him to get it back. These kids have no future. You don't want to end up like them," Mother said. "Kesor, stop looking at them and follow me quickly!" Mother grabbed my hand, pulling me ahead at a faster pace.

"Are all of them orphans?" Kesor asked from behind me.

"I don't know. Lou told me that some of their parents abandoned them and some passed away long ago."

"Why aren't they in school? The principal said it was free."

"Enrolling students is free, but school supplies are expensive. You need notebooks, writing boards, pens, pencils, and more. Much like the experience of me and your father, most parents can't afford school. You need to understand that." We walked in silence the rest of the way.

It seemed reasonable for Mother to get angry. Occasionally, our plastic buckets or metal pots would get stolen by street kids who were walking through our neighborhood. Mother always ran out to get our supplies near the well every time these kids came around. She often yelled at them, telling them to go away. They were carrying big plastic bags and searching for plastic bottles or metal items to sell to dealers near the market. A pound of plastic or metal was worth 500 to 1,000 riel.

Collecting and stealing were common ways for some of them to earn money. But not all street kids were bad. Some attempted to sell newspapers or shine shoes to buy food and school supplies. But most Khmer people normally wear flip-flops, not shoes, and they don't buy newspapers. This made it especially difficult for them to earn money, giving them no choice but to steal and collect. Glue sniffing made them less hungry so they wouldn't have to buy meals consistently. It was a typical life for many street kids throughout Cambodia. They did what was necessary to survive.

About five minutes later, we reached the edge of the market. We immediately smelled a revolting mix of fish entrails, mud, and sewage puddled on the ground. Potholes were filled with black sludge with garbage floating on top. We couldn't handle the stench, so we lifted the necks of our shirts to cover our noses.

Once we got inside, things were much cleaner. People sat on the ground alongside the walkways, selling all kinds of goods: fresh fruit, rice cakes, flowers, raw meat, and even live chickens. People were buying and selling groceries directly off the wet concrete ground in busy aisles. The market was covered with rusty corrugated metal roofing with small sky lights of dark stained-yellow plastic. Spider webs hung from rafters that had not been cleaned in decades. The densely packed shops blocked any potential breeze, making the still humid air stiflingly hot. Worse, motorbikes overloaded with groceries, drove chaotically through the packed aisles. Some people heading toward the exits toted huge bags of rice over their shoulders. Sellers were persistently calling across the aisles to attract customers. I was completely overwhelmed.

"There are a lot of people here," Mother said over the noisy crowd. "You two need to follow me closely. I don't want either of you to get lost." We followed tight on her heels as we explored the rest of the market.

After squeezing through a crowded and noisy section, we approached a much calmer area: the clothing booths. Small square stalls without any walls were connected in long rows. Each shop had a variety of children's and adult's clothes around the perimeter. There were so many fascinating and exotic looking items, but I didn't want to bother Mother because I knew that we couldn't afford them. Kesor looked at the items with an open jaw. She was amazed too.

I felt ashamed. Growing up, I never had any new clothes. Mother rarely bought me secondhand pants and shirts. I normally had to wear Ruat and Sokha's old clothes.

In short order, a salesperson came up to Mother. "Hello Aunt! Can I help you all find anything?" the seller asked in a friendly tone. Khmer people called elders Aunt or Uncle.

"I'm looking for school uniforms. Do you have them in your shop?" Mother politely asked.

"Yes, of course! Come on in." The saleswoman walked inside and pulled out a pile of blue pants, blue skirts, and white button-down shirts. "Here, try these on."

I carefully put my dirty feet into the pant legs, not wanting to get mud on the clean blue silk. Mother would have to buy it if it got filthy. After putting the uniforms on, we looked at each other and smiled. It was our first time trying on new clothes. I was so happy and was bending my knees up and down.

"How much is each one?" Mother asked.

"The boy's uniform is 20,000 riel [5 dollars] and the girl's uniform is 24,000 riel [6 dollars]. The total is 44,000 riel."

"That's really expensive. Could you give us a discount? We just recently moved here from Prey Veng. We don't have much money. I still need to buy them notebooks, pens, pencils, and backpacks. If you could discount them, I'll get another uniform for my other daughter at home."

"Okay, I'll make you a deal. If you buy all of those items at my store, I will discount the three uniforms to 55,000 riel."

"Yeah, I can do that."

The seller grabbed the school supplies out of a display case. Meanwhile, I looked at Kesor with relief. We were so glad that the seller understood our budget. I could not thank my mother enough for buying new school supplies. Kesor and I couldn't contain how thrilled we were to start school.

Khmer schools in Kompong Som had two semesters in each academic year, the first ending in April around the time of the Khmer New Year. All students had to attend class Monday through Saturday. There were two schedules: morning classes and afternoon classes. The morning schedule was from seven o'clock to noon, and the afternoon was from one o'clock to five o'clock. Students only had to attend school once a day. My sisters and I had a morning schedule.

On the first day of school, we headed off down the narrow dirt road in front of the house. Neighborhood dogs barked at us as we passed houses surrounded by barbed wire fences. It took approximately twenty-five minutes of walking before we finally reached the school's entry gate. After agreeing to meet Chai and Kesor after school, I entered the classroom. I noticed it had a similar setup to the one in Prey Veng. It was rectangular and on the cement walls were paintings of Khmer students holding books. The room was bigger, with three open windows on the sides. There were five rows of wooden desks and each row had five to six desks with narrow aisles between each row. Every desk was roughly five feet long and accommodated two or three students. While taking in the classroom, I spotted a student sitting by himself in the fourth row. I joined him.

"Hi, my name is Borey," he said. "What's your name?"

"I'm Chamroeun." I put my backpack on the desk and sat down.

"Do you want to be my friend?"

"Uh, sure." Borey seemed really friendly, but I didn't want to talk too much. I wasn't there to make friends. My goal was to do well in school. Shortly after I sat down, the teacher entered, followed by multiple students carrying textbooks. She wore a long black skirt with a blue blouse and black high heels. She was talking to the students behind her while carrying a navy-blue purse and a black suitcase.

"Put the textbooks on the ground underneath the blackboard, then take your seats," said the teacher.

Each student carefully set the books on the cement floor.

The teacher set her purse on her desk then moved toward the blackboard. "Hello students! My name is Chanda," she said as she wrote her name on the board. "Before I get started with the lesson, I want to inform you all about class policy." She pulled out a piece of paper from her suitcase and read. "There are certain rules you must follow in this classroom. You must show up on time. You all must dress in appropriate school uniforms. Boys must have short hair, no longer than three inches. Girls cannot paint their fingernails, and everyone must have short fingernails. If any one of you violates any of these rules, I will whip you with this wooden stick on the hands or back."

She lifted up the wooden stick to show the class. It was roughly thirty inches long. I looked at some of the students' faces next to me while listening to the rules. Some appeared scared, and a few seemed to be shaking.

"I will be teaching you two subjects: Khmer reading and writing and mathematics. I will show you all how to add and subtract, which are valuable skills for you to use throughout life. One last thing—if you receive a bad grade on an assignment, you will also be whipped. In fact, I will hit you the same amount of times as the number of mistakes you've made."

Many students, including myself, were intimidated by the prospect of corporal punishment. I could still remember the pain from when my teacher in Prey Veng hit me with my own backpack.

She began with a review of first grade, starting with simple greetings. She wrote multiple individual words and several sentences on the blackboard. When she finished, she wandered around the classroom. "Who here wants to come up and read this lesson to the class?" she asked, still holding the wooden stick. No one raised their hands. I looked around and then slowly put up my hand. "Okay, you there, come up here." She pointed at me with the stick. I stood up and walked to the blackboard. I knew that I had to read well or be punished.

"Here, use this and point to each letter as you read it," said the teacher, handing me the stick. I cautiously took it from her hand. It was a thick, round dowel covered with a smooth dark brown layer of stain and lacquer. She seemed eager to hit students, and I couldn't imagine how painful it would be to get whipped.

I read the words slowly, the teacher standing over me. Her presence made me stutter during a few syllables. I read each letter of each word and kept glancing back and forth between the teacher and the stick, pointing toward the board. While reading the last sentence, I sped up my pace then quickly handed the stick in her direction.

"Not bad," said Ms. Chanda with a smile as she grasped it. "What's your name?"

"Chamroeun," I said, looking down at the ground.

She patted me on my shoulder. "Good job, Chamroeun. You did great. You can return to your desk. Keep up the good work."

Ms. Chanda's compliment felt amazing, but I was mainly relieved that I didn't get whipped in front of the class. I smiled as I headed back to my desk. I saw the other students' faces staring at me. It reminded me of when I looked at Rei's face as he walked back to his desk in Prey Veng. I knew how it felt to be them.

The teacher searched the room for another reader. Suddenly, I heard a thunderous sound of a jet engine roaring from a distance away. Everyone looked up, staring at each other with curious faces. Students who sat near the windows, peeked their heads out, searching into the bright sky.

"It's an airplane! I can see it. It's right there!" said a boy, yelling at the top of his lungs, and pointing up behind the building. All students, including myself, hustled out of our desks, disobeyed the teacher's words, and sprinted outside to explore the airplane.

I stared at the shiny plane as it slowly left sight. Airplanes rarely flew over our village. I considered airplanes a symbol of the outside world, the world I knew nothing about. I was not alone. Many kids in my class and other grades above us were thrilled to see an airplane flying high in the air. Some kids even attempted to chase after the plane until it was absorbed into the clouds. Aircraft intrigued many Cambodian children. We loved watching something so far from our reality.

The second half of the class was mathematics. The teacher started explaining addition and subtraction. She later wrote problems on the blackboard for students to practice.

"Here is an exercise that you all need to solve. Work with the other students at your desks to answer each problem. I will be assigning homework, so you'd all better understand how to solve these," Ms. Chanda said as she leaned on top of her desk. She then waited for groups to find solutions. Meanwhile, I transcribed the problems in my notebook. I started counting in my head, once again afraid I would get an answer wrong. I glanced at Borey, who was using his fingers to count out loud. I thought this was brilliant, so I scooted over to him. "Hey, can I join you?" I asked.

Borey paused, but smiled, "yeah."

"What problem are you on?"

"The third one, the adding problem. Twenty-three plus seventy-four is such a big number. It's taking me a while because I only have ten fingers. I'm getting a little mixed up."

"If we use my fingers too, it will help us count higher."

Borey's face lit up. We counted our fingers one by one starting from seventy-four. Seventy-five . . . seventy-six . . . seventy-seven . . . but then I realized that we would need three more fingers than we had in order to count twenty-three times. I raised up my feet and rested them on the seat next to Borey.

"What are you doing?" Borey asked.

"We both only have twenty fingers, so we are going to use three of our toes to help us count up to twenty-three."

"That's a really good idea." Borey laughed. We continued to count out loud until we reached the answer.

"Ninety-seven. The answer is ninety-seven," I said. We both quickly jotted down the answer. At the time, we both thought this was an efficient way of solving the problem. For the rest of the class time, we counted together using both our hands and feet.

"Okay everyone, it's time to go. See you all tomorrow," said Ms. Chanda. Everyone stood up from their desks and gathered their things. I grabbed my backpack and walked across the schoolyard to meet my sisters.

That day, I stopped to watch a crowd of students playing volleyball and ended up being late to meet my sisters for the walk home.

"Next time, we will leave without you," Kesor fumed then took off ahead of Chai and me.

After a short distance walking on the dirt road full of potholes, she was able to calm down. She looked at me and asked, "Chramouh Thom, how do you like your teacher?" I hesitated. When I think of my teacher, I visualized her smiling cruelly and holding her wooden stick.

"She was nice but scary," I said.

"How come?" Chai asked.

"She has this wooden stick that she uses to punish students. I don't want to get beaten with her stick. It looks like it'll be painful." Chai and Kesor laughed.

"Don't worry, as long as you study hard, the teacher won't be hitting you," said Chai. "Besides, the punishment encourages you to become a better student. I had to deal with punishment in my class as well. In fact, my previous teachers have whipped me on my hands, back, and even my legs many times. It hurts really bad, but it will make you study harder, trust me." Chai looked at me genuinely.

Chai had been right about school before, but it still seemed terrifying. I didn't understand how whipping students was supposed to encourage them. I thought to myself, *how could we get good grades if no one wanted to come up and read? Was this the only way for a student to show the teacher that he or she was learning?* Everyone, including myself, was terrified by the wooden stick.

When we got home, Chai and Kesor headed upstairs to get changed out of their uniforms. I set my backpack down and drank from a red water cooler sitting on the table. Father was brewing beer. He was scooping liquid out of a large black wok into small white plastic bottles resting on the ground. Meanwhile, Mother was cooking in the kitchen, preparing the lunch that she would bring to my sisters at the factory. Every day, Mother fed the pig, helped Father with brewing, and packed lunches for my sisters. She picked up the soup pot and carefully set it on the kitchen counter. Then she scooped the fish soup into a metal lunch box. She usually packed rice, soup, and fried fish in those metal containers. She'd stack them in a metal carrier with a cover. It was a difficult task for her to manage. If they were not secured well, the food could be spilled while traversing the bumpy roads on the motorbike on the way to the factory.

Mother looked exhausted. Sweat was slowly falling from her forehead, wetting her cheeks. She smelled like a mix of fried fish and sweet sugar.

She wiped her face. "Chamroeun! You should go upstairs and get changed," said Mother. "Food is ready, and you need to take care of your school uniform. It was really expensive." I did what she asked then settled for lunch.

We ate white rice mixed with fried eggs and fish soup.

"Chamroeun said that he was intimidated by his teacher," said Kesor with a laugh. "He said he was afraid of getting whipped by her."

I sneered at her, but I held my tongue. I hated it when she tried to embarrass me in front of our parents.

My father chuckled. "Don't be scared. Most teachers use punishment to make students try harder. When I was in the second grade, my teacher forced me to run five laps around the school property whenever I made a mistake on my homework. I got so sick and tired from running, I put more effort into school instead." He lightly pushed his glasses up. "My hard work led me to become one of the best students in my class."

"I will work harder, Father," I said.

"Then there's nothing to worry about."

Sokha showed up on the motorbike. He parked in front and walked over to us. "Mother, it's time to bring lunch to the factory," he said.

That day Kesor and I asked to go along, and Mother agreed.

I put on my yellow flip-flops and grabbed some water bottles from Kesor. We hopped on the motorbike and set off down the narrow dirt road. In Cambodia, it was common to have multiple people on a motorbike as long as there was room for people to sit.

After a fifteen-minute ride, we climbed a steep hill to reach the factory. The place was crowded. Vendors were selling food and snacks outside for the workers who were on break for lunch. Motodops were aligned in rows, waiting to take workers to other places to eat. Other families like us were waiting for their family members with meals. Sokha parked the bike on the side of the road near a tall tree. I looked across the street at the factory and saw many white cement buildings with blue roofs surrounded by a tall cement fence topped with barbed wire. There were security guards standing at the front gate, each man holding a black walkie-talkie.

"Mother, I'm going to be a motodop while you guys are waiting for them," said Sokha.

"Okay, go ahead, we'll wait for you here."

Workers soon exited one by one. I saw my elder sisters walking across the crowded street toward us. When they arrived, they took off their flip-flops and carefully sat on them. Lab and Lane opened the metal lunch boxes, and hastily devoured the meal. Meanwhile, Lim sat resting.

"How are you all doing?" Mother asked. Lane and Lab didn't reply and kept eating. Lim sighed but didn't say anything. "How's work?" Mother continued.

"Exhausting," Lim said as she reached over to grab a bottle of water.

"Lab, my dear, please take your time," said my mother, watching as Lab shoveled food into her mouth.

"I have to eat quickly. I don't have much time. I want to go back in early to talk to the manager. I messed up sewing some garments earlier."

They seemed so tired. They worked Monday through Saturday from seven o'clock in the morning to eight o'clock in the evening. I felt terrible for my sisters as I watched them eat their meals. After a few more bites, Lab wiped her lips and prepared to head back. She glanced at me and Kesor.

"Did you like your school?" Lab asked, putting her flip-flops back on.

"Yes, I volunteered to read some letters in front of the class today," I said with a smile.

"How about you, Kesor?"

"It's okay," said Kesor, staring down at the grass.

"Well, good. Keep pushing yourselves so you won't end up working in a place like this." Lab walked back toward the gate. The rest of us sat in silence. I didn't say anything back.

"Thanks for the food, Mother," said Lim as she finally ate. "She's right you know," she continued as she casually chewed her meal. "It is really tough working here. Every day, Chinese managers yell at me for any small sewing mistake. I barely have time to breathe."

"Staring down all day while sewing those clothes really hurts my neck," said Lane.

As a kid, I didn't fully understand the struggle of sweatshops, but after listening to my sisters, I couldn't imagine the hardship they experienced. Working in sweatshops was one of only a few regular jobs available in Kompong Som. Tens of thousands of Khmer women and men worked in sweatshops across the country. Furthermore, factories didn't require a diploma. As long as you were a hard worker, you could get hired. My sisters only earned between seventy to eighty-five dollars a month, but it was better than nothing.

"Okay, we're going to head back to the factory. Thanks for the food," said Lane. They both got up, put on their flip-flops and walked off toward the green entry gate. We moved back toward the crowded street and waited for Sokha to return.

We stood next to many workers who were talking with their families before they too headed back. I looked up at Mother, her face sorrowfully staring at the factory's white fence. Kesor reached out and gripped Mother's hand. Mother looked down at Kesor with a smile. I watched them for a moment and then looked down at a pothole filled with rocks and dirt. I watched an ant trying to climb out.

Shortly, Sokha arrived. We got on the motorbike. I wrapped my arms around Sokha.

"We're ready," Mother said as she put her right arm around me and Kesor. Sokha drove down the hill.

When we got home, I hustled off the bike to grab my school bag. I opened up my textbook and began reading letters. My mind kept wandering to images of the factory, the wooden stick, and even my previous teacher calling me "stupid." I had to find a way to become educated, so perhaps one day, I could escape working in a sweatshop.

Every day in class, I forced myself to pay close attention to the teacher. Each time she looked for volunteers to read an assignment, I raised my hand. I would go to the blackboard and read out loud. When I misread the letters, she stared coldly and snarled, "let me see your hands." I reached out slowly and exposed my palms. She hit me twice on each hand, hard. Dark red welts raised up on each of my palms. No matter how much I shook them, the work of the wooden stick remained.

My worst beating came when I made seven mistakes on a math assignment. My teacher whipped my hands so badly I couldn't make a fist. I could barely hold a spoon to eat. I tried gingerly grasping it with the tip of my right thumb and pointer finger and softly scooping the food.

The teacher's punishment was cruel, and yet, it didn't dissuade me from achieving my goal. If I got whipped, I knew what to work on as soon as I made it home. When I struggled, I would ask my father to explain. Then I would return to the table to try the assignment on my own.

My struggle with pronunciation made me extremely frustrated. I repeated the word out loud, over and over again, until I could do it correctly. My father applauded my hard work. "Good job, Son," he said, clapping. I didn't stop there. When I finished my homework, I would read the next chapter before the teacher had even started to teach it. I needed to get ahead so I could read smoothly in class. Most importantly, I wanted to be the best student in the class.

As I made progress, the teacher took notice of my effort. She was quick to compliment me in front of the class with, "excellent job." Sometimes she gave me bonus points for my willingness to volunteer. The more effort I put into school, the fewer beatings I received. By the end of the year, I rarely got hit. Quite often, I would receive good or even perfect scores on my assignments. It seemed that all of my hard work was finally starting to pay off. When the teacher announced the placement grades on the final day of school, I didn't have to wait long to hear my name.

"Seventh place, Pen Chamroeun," my teacher announced, standing in front of the blackboard. This time, I walked up to her with a smile on my face.

"Thank you so much," I said.

"Good luck in third grade." She patted me on the shoulder. I sprinted out of the classroom and ran home. I was so happy that I didn't even bother waiting for Chai and Kesor. Along the way, I was jumping and yelling. I couldn't believe what I had accomplished. People gave me strange looks as I was running by. They probably thought I was crazy.

When I made it home, I sprinted to Father to hug him. "I'm seventh in my class. I passed second grade!"

"Really? I'm so proud of you, Son." He hugged me tight and lifted me up. When he put me down, he reached into his pocket and pulled out 100 riel (2.5 cents). He gave it to me as a reward. It may not have been much to other people, but in our family, it was a tremendous gift.

"Loun, Chamroeun got seventh place!" Father yelled. My mother came out of the kitchen and kissed my cheek.

"I knew you could do it," she said with joy. "Good job, my last one." I was so grateful to see the pride on my parents' faces. Most importantly, earning seventh place gave me a taste of success. It was the spark that fueled me to push myself further.

Soon, we found out that Chai and Kesor had also passed their classes. Everyone was proud. As for me, this time I could celebrate with them.

# 5

# FROM DESPERATION
# TO POTENTIAL

KHMER SCHOOLS GAVE students a two-and-a-half-month break after each school year. "Vakong Tom" ran from August through mid-October. My sisters and I stayed home and helped my parents by doing chores. Sometimes, I would go to the market with Mother to help her carry groceries. In Cambodia, people go to the market every day for fresh food.

One Sunday, my sisters and I were sitting on the outdoor wooden dining table while Mother was making *nom banh chok* (fish soup with white rice noodles) for dinner. She made it special by adding red curry. This was an unusually expensive meal. The aroma of warm curry burned my nose. I kept walking to the kitchen to check on the food. Breathing in the pungent variety of spices made me so hungry.

Mother picked up the steaming black pot and set it on a wooden placemat on the table. We gathered in a circle and enjoyed slurping up the meal together. The curry was so tasty, we were going for seconds and even thirds.

Suddenly, I heard the sound of a motorbike approaching. I looked and it was Sokha, but his clothes were ripped and dirty, and the bike had scrapes on the side. His arms and legs were bleeding.

"What happened?" Lim asked, rushing to him.

"I got in an accident," said Sokha, looking ashamed.

"You got in an accident with whom?" Father asked.

"I was taking a customer home from the market. A dog ran across the street. I swerved and hit a lady on the side of the road." Sokha limped over and took a seat on the table.

"Is that person okay?" Father persisted.

"She was hurt. She wanted me to pay for it." Sokha looked directly at Father. "She wants 250 dollars."

"What? We don't have 250 dollars! We barely have enough money to pay the rent this month."

"Father, if we don't pay her, she will ask the police to take me to jail. She told me, we have one week to come up with the money."

My father stared at the dirt in silence.

Accidents in Cambodia could be devastating, since people don't wear helmets or other protective gear. Many people die from accidents every day throughout the country. Victims might demand money from the person at fault, with the price varying depending on their injuries or the amount of damage to their vehicles.

I hated watching my family suffer. I knew if we paid off this ridiculous charge, it would put us in a desperate place once again. But my parents did not want Sokha to be in jail.

"Sokha, why don't you eat first. We can discuss this later. I saved some curry for you," Mother said.

"I'm not hungry." Sokha gingerly made his way upstairs, noticeably wincing with pain. Seeing Sokha in this position reminded me of Ruat when we had left him behind. He had been deeply pained when we left.

Since we had very little time to come up with enough money, my parents sold our pig and the brewing equipment. My parents looked hopeless as they stood watching people carry away what had been improving our lives. They really enjoyed brewing and raising animals. They put their hearts and souls into it. But selling them was possibly the only way to keep Sokha out of jail. Still, the amount of money that my parents raised wasn't enough. My sisters' salaries were needed to reach 250 dollars. With that money gone, there was less money for food, electricity, and rent.

Some days, Mother had to buy pig's skin for lunch and dinner because it was one of the cheapest available meats at the market. A kilogram (about two pounds) of pig's skin was 1,000 riel. Mother would stir-fry it with palm sugar, so we could eat it with white rice. Lab always complained that this oily meal made her feel nauseous.

"Pig skin for lunch and dinner again. Are you kidding me?" Lab pushed her rice plate away. "I can't eat this! The last time I ate it, I almost threw up." She pulled 200 riel out of her pocket. "Chamroeun, go buy me a bag of noodles." She handed me the money and went upstairs.

Mother watched Lab leave. She stared at Lab's plate for a few seconds before taking a small bite.

We couldn't afford to continue living in the same rental house. My parents searched for and found a cheaper place. It ended up being only a five-minute walk to the new house. Similar to the place we were giving up, it had a well in front and a steep staircase to get to the living quarters. However, the tall stilts of the house were surrounded by a cement wall which had a small entry door. Near our new rental was a small river. The muddy water was surrounded by garbage, creating a rotten smell. It stretched for miles all the way to the beach.

Living in the new rental house was difficult. Most of my sisters' salaries went directly to paying off debt, rent, and electricity. If we decided to buy food, we didn't have enough money to pay rent. The landlord would cut off the electricity for a few days as a warning. The money ran out before payday every month. The only way for us to eat was to borrow.

When Sokha couldn't provide enough money for food, Father sent Chai next door to see if we could borrow money from the neighbors. The family was fairly wealthy. They sold seafood including crab, lobster, and fish for a living. They lent us about five to ten dollars each time and we had to pay them back when we could.

To feed everyone, Mother had to continue making cheaper meals, like watery porridge with boiled eggs and fish sauce. She did her best to avoid pig's skin. What was even worse, my parents kept on getting into arguments. Mother often blamed Father for poorly managing our food budget. She didn't like seeing him wasting money on cigarettes and betting in the lottery which Father often did.

I remember one afternoon, when I was alone with my parents. While drawing cartoon figures outside, I could hear Mother cursing loudly. She sat on the bed downstairs and kept swearing and swearing. I had no idea who Mother was cursing at. I then heard footsteps on the thin wooden floor. I looked up and saw Father coming down the stairs.

"Who are you cursing at?" he asked, glaring at Mother.

"At you, you stupid dog!" Mother raised her voice. "We are in such a terrible condition because of your terrible money management."

Father slapped her hard enough to knock her off the bed.

I stood up and saw Mother cry as she held her face. "You crazy dog! Why did you hit me?"

He kicked her on her hips. I could hear the sound of his foot crushing her skinny body. She screamed even louder.

I ran over and grabbed his leg tightly. Tears fell on my cheeks.

"Father, please! Stop this! Don't hit her!" I begged, trying to push him away. I wasn't strong enough. He looked down at me with regret.

"I'm tired of her treating me this way. I'm her husband! She has no respect for me!" I didn't say anything and continued holding his leg. Mother kept on sobbing. I could see red finger prints on her cheek. My heart dropped to my toes. I gripped onto Father's leg even tighter. "Let me go!" he said.

"No!" I mumbled. "Don't hit Mother anymore, please . . ."

"I'm done. Let go." I slowly let go, hoping he would keep his word. Father walked away. "Mother," I touched her gently, "get up."

"Get away from me!" she shouted and continued to cry. I felt helpless. I sat there by her side, watching tears fall on her cheeks. I was disgusted by Father's use of violence. I closed my fists. I wished I could stand up for my mother. But I was too small to defend her.

I admired my father for his knowledge and leadership, but he was not perfect. I loved Father dearly, but I abhorred him when he chose violence over words. Mother had said terrible things, but she didn't deserve a brutal beating.

My experience taught me that domestic violence could never solve any problem.

In an effort to dig us out of our hole, Chai helped one of our neighbors sell traditional Khmer rice donuts called *nom kong*, *nom pong sorng*, and *nom kroch*. The owner gave my sister a small percentage of the profits. Chai would carry a full tray to sell around the village. Sometimes, she would walk all the way to the beach where there were more tourists, foreigners, we all called *barang*. This term really meant a French person, but it was broadly used to describe anyone who was white. Cambodia was heavily influenced by the French. Before gaining independence in the early 1950s, it was part of the colony of French Indochina.

There were days Chai couldn't even cover the cost of production. But on a good day, she could earn as much as seven dollars in profit. She figured out that if she sold to barangs, she could charge 1,000 riel each, about 800 riel more than the locals would pay. Chai was able to learn English while selling to them. However, she had to stop selling when school started.

When the first day of the next academic year arrived, my sisters and I had a morning schedule once again. We wore the same uniforms since we couldn't afford new ones. Fortunately, we were given new notebooks.

Chai brought a small bag of leftover rice donuts for the walk to school because Mother didn't have any money to give us for snacks.

When we reached the school's entry gate, we separated, heading toward our respective classes. I entered my classroom and saw the teacher, Mr. Heng, already sitting in his desk chair, reading from the class textbook.

There were lots of open spots in the front two rows. I wanted to be brave, so I sat alone at a desk in the middle of the front row.

As I looked out the door, I saw a brand-new motorbike with a student sitting on the back. He jumped off, waved at his father, then jogged into the classroom. He was different. He wore fancy sandals with a black rubber strap wrapped around his ankles, new blue shorts, and a white shirt. He looked rich, not just because of the bike that dropped him off, but also because he had lighter skin than the rest of us. He walked toward me after noticing the open seat at my desk. The bell rang. It was time to begin day one of third grade.

As usual, the teacher started class with roll call. "Boul, Chamroeun!" Mr. Heng shouted. The boy next to me raised his hand. Another person with the same name surprised me. I had always thought my name was rare. "Chamroeun," meant prosperity.

Mother told me that my name was chosen by my grandmother a few days after I was born. On the night before Mother gave birth, Grandmother

Louk stayed at our house to support her. Grandmother had a clear dream of two Chinese people giving her a new cement water container as a gift. Such a dream had persuaded her to bet 1,000 riel in the lottery. In Cambodia, people would predict numbers based on their dreams. Results were broadcast daily, and people could bet from two to four digits. The winning number might win as much as ten dollars or more based on the amount of money a person bet and the digits. Grandmother won the lottery and received roughly fifty dollars.

Exactly one day after I was born, she had a similar dream and continued to bet, and by some miracle, she won the lottery again. This prosperity convinced her that I was a lucky child and she later named me, "Chamroeun."

The teacher continued to take roll call, and mine popped up after multiple names had gone by. "Pen, Chamroeun," Mr. Heng said. I raised my hand. "Hold on, you're both named Chamroeun?"

"I guess so." Everyone laughed, including the teacher.

"Great, you are both named Chamroeun, and you're sitting at the same desk. How strange is that?" The class laughed.

Mr. Heng finished roll call before discussing class policy. The rules were basically the same as second grade. However, we had to stand up every time he entered or exited the class. All students needed to say in unison, "*chom-reap-sueh*, Teacher," meaning "hello, Teacher" when he entered and "*chom-reap-leah*, Teacher," meaning "goodbye, Teacher" when he left. Additionally, everyone had to gather at the center of the school property at seven in the morning to raise the flag.

This year had more reading and writing assignments. Mathematics would introduce multiplication and division. Social studies would cover Khmer history, including moral and civic norms. Specifically, Mr. Heng would explain socially acceptable conduct within the Khmer culture, covering the proper way to behave around elders. We would also study the ancient Khmer empire, how each king came to power, and how each temple was established. Physical education was also added to the curriculum. However, it ended up being basically a period where we were required to pick up garbage around the school grounds. We had to do it once a week.

The teacher informed us that there would be two exams during the school year. He called them, "Bralang Choumeas Te Muoy and Te Pir."

One would happen at the end of each semester. These were essentially final exams, which would play a major role in placement grades.

During recess, most kids played outside. Some bought snacks sold by the relatives of the faculty, who had set up small wooden stores behind the school grounds. Since Mother couldn't give me any money, I stayed in the classroom and practiced reading. Mostly, I didn't want people to know that I was poor.

While reading, I saw two boys were chasing each other around the classroom. One boy took off his sandal and threw it at the other boy. It ended up hitting me in the chest, leaving a dirt footprint on my white shirt.

"Hey!" I shouted. "You got my shirt dirty, come clean it now." The boy picked up his sandal but didn't do anything else. "Did you hear me?"

"You can't tell me what to do," he smirked.

I shoved him. He fell butt first on the cement floor. He got up and pushed back. Students gathered around us. I kicked him. He kicked me back. Behind him, I saw Kesor standing outside the window. While I was distracted, he raised his hand and punched me in the eye socket. My vision blurred as the pain kicked in.

Our fight was reported to Mr. Heng. He whipped me twice on my hand. However, the other boy got hit four times for punching me in the face. The boy's fist left a black ring around my eye socket as it swelled up. Worse, Kesor told Mother about the fight when we got home, causing Mother to whip me yet again.

"I didn't send you to school so you could become a gangster," she said, after hitting me a few times on my back. "Why did you get in a fight?"

Both of my eyes were bright red as tears fell. I had never cried this much in one day. My nine-year-old mind couldn't stop cursing Kesor. I thought she had tried to turn Mother against me.

"You're not a gangster!" Mother continued. "If I hear that you've gotten into a fight again, I will hit you more than this. You hear me?"

"Yes, Mother," I wiped my runny nose.

Chamroeun and I ended up helping each other with assignments. He was proficient in math and I was solid at reading. Helping each other meant less punishment for both of us. One day during recess, he approached me. "Chamroeun, why do you always sit here? Don't you want to go play outside?"

"I like sitting here. It's cooler," I lied. I enjoyed watching kids chase each other and play hopscotch. But if I joined, I knew I would end up thirsty.

"I'm thirsty, do you want to go buy water with me?" Chamroeun asked.

"No, I'm not thirsty."

"Would you come with me anyway?"

"Sure. I'll come along." I got up from the desk and walked with him to the back of the building. There were a bunch of wooden shops all lined up. In fact, each school building had small shops directly behind them. The teachers and their families were selling a variety of snacks such as apples, candies, beef sticks, and even fried rice. When we reached our teacher's store, Chamroeun pulled 1,000 riel out of his pocket. He bought an apple and a bag of dark yellow iced tea. Most teachers added sugar to make the water tastier.

Chamroeun quickly put his lips on the straw and sucked down the cold water. He then took a big bite from the apple. I was so hungry watching him eat.

"It's really good, you should take a bite," he said handing it to me.

I sunk my teeth into a big chunk of the crispy apple. "It's really yummy," I mumbled while chewing.

"Yeah, the teacher's wife always sells tasty snacks. Especially rice with fried pork. You should buy it sometime. It's only 500 riel." I didn't reply. I continued to walk. "How come you never buy anything? Teacher told me that he will give students a better score on their assignments if they consistently buy his snacks."

"I don't have any money. My parents can't give me money for snacks. That's why I never buy anything."

"Is that why you always sit at the desk during recess?"

"Yes."

"Well, here, have 200 riel." He handed me paper bills. "My father always gives me 1,000 or 1,500 riel for school every day. Tell you what, if you come out and play with me during recess, I will give you some money for a snack."

"Okay, I can do that." I grinned. Our friendship continued to grow. Occasionally, he would visit me at my house later in the afternoon. He often brought small colorful marbles. We would play a game on the dirt where we would try to hit each other's marbles from a few feet away. Other times, he brought playing cards, and we would play War and *See-Kou* for hours. However, I never let this prevent me from finishing my homework. After Chamroeun left, I would practice the lessons in the textbook. I would read a few pages before switching to math. Most days, I sat alone on the balcony near the stairs. It was brighter here than inside. It was my favorite study area because Father was always lying in the hammock nearby.

If I was stuck, he was quick to come up with precise answers. Better yet, he consistently explained each step until I understood fully. Father was proficient at solving division and multiplication problems. He frequently showed off his math skills by reciting the times table for the numbers one through ten. He went through the numbers so fast, it was obvious he had memorized them. At the time though, I didn't realize he was forced to remember the multiplication table and knew them by heart.

"When I was in school, my teacher asked students to come and multiply these numbers out loud in front of the class. Students would either be whipped or be forced to kneel in front of the board for an hour if they messed up," he said in a serious tone.

I never understood why Father always tried to make it seem like school had been so difficult when he was younger. Nonetheless, I understood that he recounted these stories as encouragement rather than fear.

Three months into the school year, Chai and Kesor began selling bracelets on the beach after school. Chai noticed that many foreigners were purchasing bracelets, chips, and fruit while she was selling rice donuts. Chai convinced Father that it was a way to earn money and learn English. Mother bought them twenty-five to thirty bracelets each from the market. From then on, my sisters went to the beach every day after school. On Sundays, they were gone all day, departing around eight in the morning and not returning home until five or six in the evening.

They barely had time to do their schoolwork. Sometimes, Chai had to wake up as early as five in the morning to do her homework. One time, she stepped on my ankle while trying to quietly open the front door. I woke up startled. Rubbing my eyes, I looked outside through the blur and saw Chai sitting alone on the balcony in the morning light. I carefully crawled out of my sleeping net and sat next to her.

"Go back to bed," Chai said softly.

"I'm not tired."

Chai thought for a moment. "Well, instead of watching me, why don't you bring your book and study too?"

I brought out my backpack and read my worn history textbook. We studied until the roosters crowed with the rising sun.

We would study together again in the morning a few days later. We woke up so early that we had to light a candle to see our textbooks. Chai and I made a routine of studying before school, but Kesor was never interested in joining us.

Studying early was necessary during the second semester when our class schedule changed to evenings. Chai was in danger of getting behind in school. She and Kesor now sold bracelets at the beach in the mornings and were often missing class. They were told to be home between eleven thirty and twelve noon, but they rarely returned in time. If they didn't come home by twelve thirty, I had to walk to school alone. Every time they missed school, they would tell Father that there were too many sales. Chai would attend class even if she knew she was late. She was passionate about school and didn't want selling on the beach to prevent her from passing sixth grade. Her determination inspired her to study each morning so she could keep up with her class.

I enjoyed reading in the early morning by candlelight in the misty dawn. The glowing light shone toward wherever the flame was leaning. It almost seemed like the candle was dancing alone in the darkness. Plus, there was no one there to distract us and my brain was able to retain more information. In the end, I was well prepared going into each exam and by providing precise answers, it forced the teacher to give me a higher score. When my teacher asked questions in class during history lessons, I frequently raised my hand and answered correctly. In fact, there were times when I was the only person in class who knew the answer.

On the last day of class, our teacher posted a sheet with grades on the wall near the blackboard. Everyone hustled from their desks to search for their names. I looked up and saw that Chamroeun placed third. Two spots below him, my name was listed in fifth place. We looked at each other with joy, grateful to have passed third grade.

Chamroeun walked home with me and my sisters in the narrow dirt road. Kesor was walking far ahead of us. She was upset because she had failed fourth grade. She would have to repeat it the following year. She had missed many classes while selling bracelets at the beach. I had noticed that ever since Kesor started selling on the beach, she had become disinterested in school.

Meanwhile, Chai was advancing to secondary school, which began with seventh grade. She was excited because she had reached the highest grade of anyone in our family. We talked and laughed along the way until it was time to say goodbye to Chamroeun.

"I'll see you soon," he said, waving goodbye.

"See you," I called back.

We had the same class schedule in fourth grade, which allowed our friendship to continue. We kept working together in class, especially during social studies. We had to discuss Khmer culture, and sometimes the teacher would ask students to draft paragraphs to read in front of class. Geography was added during the history session to help students better understand the regions the Khmer Angkor had conquered. For physical education, one day a week, students had to come before or after class in order to grow plants on school grounds. In math, we solved problems that involved the metric system.

To better understand the subjects, our teacher, Mr. Sovannar, offered one hour of extra teaching every day before class. He called it *Rein Kour*. However, each student had to pay 500 riel per day to attend. I could not. Mother would never give me more than 200 riel at most. I tried to ask Father if I could attend, but he disagreed.

"Extra teaching is for rich kids and bad students. You are not one of them. It is also a way for your teacher to get money from students," Father said. I guess he had a point. The students who attended frequently relied on the session. The teacher would commonly put the exact problems on the board that he had taught during the extra hour.

One time, Chamroeun whispered to me while the teacher was writing a question. "That's the same problem he gave us during the extra hour. You can copy my answer if you want."

Even if I copied Chamroeun's answers, the teacher would never give me full credit. I was not one of the students who attended the extra hour.

Sometimes, he gave me a low score of 5 or 6/10. Some days, I was whipped even if my answers were correct.

One class, I went up to him. "Excuse me, Teacher. Why did I receive such a low score?" I asked. "My answers were correct."

"You have terrible handwriting," said Mr. Sovannar. "I can't give you full credit if I can't read everything." None of my prior teachers had instructed me to improve my handwriting. I knew he was punishing me simply because I didn't attend Rein Kour. There was nothing I could do to improve my score. The only way was to come up with enough money to attend his extra sessions.

From then on, every time I was asked to go buy supplies from the village, I begged for 100 riel. One time, Father was so mad at me when I refused to go buy him cigarettes. He thought I wanted the money to buy marbles. There were times that he did give me money though. When he won the lottery, he was very generous. Father frequently won and received between 50 and 100 dollars.

Gambling became his hobby and many people in the village would follow his bets. Father often asked me to take his numbers to the bookie who was also the owner of our rental house. He would bet 1,000–1,500 riel at a time. I would demand 100 riel every trip to save up for Rein Kour. I also begged Chai and Kesor each day when they returned from selling bracelets on the beach. Chai would give as much as 500 riel on days she had good sales. As I collected more money, I was able to attend the extra teaching hour. Eventually, I started to see higher scores.

During fourth grade, an arrangement was made for Lim to marry a man named Oun, and she moved out to live with her husband near the factory. After she left, Chai and Kesor had to contribute more support for the family. They spent more hours selling fruit and bracelets. One of the days when they were out selling, they met a barang, kind enough to pay for the three of us to attend a school for English instruction.

His name was John. He was an American who had been in Cambodia for many years. He had a great sense of humor and always bought fruit or bracelets from beach kids. We weren't the only ones that John enrolled in English school. There were many more children attending school because of him. From then on, my two sisters and I had to walk to English school five days a week. Classes ran Monday through Friday from seven to eight in the evening. This was separate from Khmer school. Chai and Kesor could attend because Father would not let them sell after five in the evening. The school was located in downtown Sihanoukville, about thirty minutes by foot.

We first learned the English alphabet. Then we progressed to greetings and conversations. The English teacher, Mr. Pha, was much nicer than the ones in Khmer school. He never hit anyone. In fact, he often told us funny jokes. Kesor would make fun of his outfit or his bald head, but he never got mad. He always remained calm, supportive, and persistent.

After attending for three months, I was able to speak a little English. But I was always hungry to learn more. When we got home from class, I frequently practiced speaking English with Chai and Kesor. I would talk to them while they worked on the factory labels in front of the television. Mother cheered us on as she sat nearby. She seemed happy to hear me speak English. I kept asking my sisters to teach me new words. I would repeat them over and over. I realized the more I spoke, the better my pronunciation.

One night as I was practicing, Father suddenly approached and interrupted, "Ruat is coming to live with us in three days!"

"Really?" said Mother in shock.

"Yeah, I just spoke with him on the phone. I told him it's time for him to come live with us." There was a moment of silence. We were happy to hear the news. I sprinted downstairs to tell my elder siblings, who were eating at the table.

On the day Ruat arrived, I was so excited I couldn't wait to get out of Khmer school. After the teacher made his end of class announcement, I shot out of my desk and sprinted home as fast as I could. When I got there, I ran upstairs and saw Ruat sitting next to Father, watching television. He seemed so skinny and dark, wearing a worn t-shirt and trousers.

"Brother! I missed you," I cheered, then hugged him tightly.

"I missed you too," he said with a grin.

This was one of the most memorable moments in my life. I was so thankful to see him again. The family gathered together and ate dinner under the house. Ruat was smiling ear to ear.

# 6

# THE OUTSIDERS

ON THE DAY Ruat arrived, my family and I stayed up late. Nighttime in Cambodia was always full of insects: flying into our house, circling the bright light bulb above us. Sitting in a corner of the room next to Mother, I could hear bugs slamming into the thin bulb and falling on the floor. Then, they crawled and flew back up. Worse, my body was tortured by mosquitoes biting my arms and legs. Yet, I continued to listen to Ruat's story.

"Working for someone else is even more challenging," said Ruat. "The owners only care about their money. They never considered my health or the conditions. There was a time I cut my hand so deeply, the bleeding would not stop. Blood was dripping all over my clothes." He choked up. "No one was there to help me. There was nothing I could do besides cry alone."

After two-and-a-half years of farming, Ruat had been able to save a large amount of money. Now that he was back with us, our financial situation was looking up. This enabled us to raise a few pigs in a cage on the side of the house.

Eventually though, Sokha would leave to live with his new girlfriend in Takeo province, northeast of Kompong Som. Sokha never returned to his wife and child in Prey Veng. My parents tried to remind him, but still he chose to abandon them. It was a heartless decision. But no one in my family could force him.

Ruat assumed Sokha's job as a motodop and helped pay for me to attend Rein Kour, about 20,000 riel (5 dollars) each month. Mr. Sovannar was surprised to see me participating regularly. He knew I was one of the poorest kids in class.

At the primary school level, Rein Kour was a major weakness of Khmer education. Although commonplace in schools throughout Cambodia, it puts truly talented students at a disadvantage and rewards the wealthy, while potentially cheating them of a true education. Father disliked Rein Kour and thought it suppressed the poor and maintained the power of the wealthy. He was right. Most families throughout the country cannot afford to have their kids repeat classes. Education is the only path out of poverty for most. As for me, I was fortunate enough to continue school. All thanks to the support of my siblings.

I finished eighth place in fourth grade and this time, my sisters and I were all able to progress to the next grade level together. Chai had reached eighth grade, the highest level of education ever in our family. Kesor and I advanced to fifth grade.

Two months later, Father bought a property located in Oue Bei (Oh-Bay), meaning, Three Water Streams. To get to the new property, we had to cross a wooden bridge and walk down a narrow path. We built a traditional A-frame house on this land. Ours was the second in a straight line of five other houses.

With most of our money being spent on the new house, Ruat had to search for a job. He was eventually hired as a truck driver for a cloth-ing factory right next to the one where my sisters worked. Ruat was now earning about 100 dollars a month.

That school break, I also started working by selling dried chips on the beach. At eleven years old, Father agreed that I was now old enough to sell. Taking into account my sister's experience, he also thought it was a good way for me to learn English. Every morning at nine, Father dropped me off with Kesor and Chai. He came back to pick us up at five in the evening so we could attend English school. I carried a tray of chips in small bags on my head. I'd walk on the hot sand for hours, searching for buyers. My target market was Western tourists. I wanted to practice speaking English. Plus, white foreigners were more generous. Barangs paid about 4,000 riel per bag versus 1,000 riel from Khmer tourists. Khmer people not only knew the true price of goods but also could not afford more. The majority of Khmer shoppers often negotiated with sellers to get better deals. Selling one bag for 1,000 riel would still gain a profit of 500 riel, however.

Competition on the beach was fierce. Children of all ages carried fruit, chips, bracelets, kroma and sarongs. Most preferred fresh fruit like pineapples, papayas, mangos, bananas and rambutans. But my best customers were parents buying chips for their children. Most people refused to buy, treating me like a pest, and told me to go away. I didn't really know the best or most proper way to sell. Unlike most, I wasn't able to speak English very well.

Sometimes, Chai would buy my chips because she felt bad that I couldn't sell anything. One day, she took the time to teach me how to sell. Together, we approached a Western couple lying on wooden deck chairs tanning in swimsuits.

"Hello, Mister! You want buy fruit?" asked Chai with her broken English. "You want buy bracelet? I can make you bracelet. I can make anything: Cambodia flag, heart, your country flag."

"My country's flag?" said a white man with brown hair wearing sunglasses and a red swimsuit. "I doubt that. Our flag is difficult to craft."

"If you show me, I make it. I make USA bracelet before."

"Wow! That is difficult. But we're from Canada. There's a big leaf in the middle." He proceeded to draw the flag in the sand.

"Yes, I make Canada before. I can do it."

"No. It's okay. It would take you forever to make it. But you can make a colorful bracelet for my girlfriend."

"Okay, what color you want?" Chai pulled out long colorful strings from her black waist bag.

"Surprise me!" said the blonde-haired lady. Chai then picked a few random strings and sat on the sand as she started to create a bracelet.

"What is your name?"

"I'm Chai. And that my brother, Chamroeun."

"Sham-ron? Okay, nice to meet you. I'm Simon and this is Jade."

I noticed his Superman t-shirt. I loved watching Western movies and Superman was one of my favorites.

"You like Superman?" I said pointing at the t-shirt.

The man laughed. "Yes! Superman is my favorite superhero. Do you like Superman?"

"Yes. I like Spiderman too. You Spiderman, I Superman." I giggled.

"No. You are Spiderman and I am Superman." We kept on chatting for a long time. He eventually bought two bags of chips and a bag of fruit and a bracelet from Chai. From then on, when foreigners didn't want to buy my chips, I would just talk to them. This was a technique I had learned from Chai. "Always keep trying to make conversation," she said. "Because at the end of the day, you are practicing to improve your English."

Chai also suggested that I should try asking foreigners to play a game of Tic-tac-toe. If I lost, I would have to walk away. If I won, however, they would have to buy my chips. This was an effective way. I often won the game. Chai taught me a clever strategy to win which allowed me to earn more sales. She told me to always try to be the first mover and pick the middle then a corner spot that could set up a few unstoppable ways of winning. Even if I lost, I often asked them to play best out of three so I could get a chance to redeem myself. Sometimes, barangs would buy my chips because they felt bad or they just wanted me to leave. There were days that I made as much as ten dollars in profit. Father was so proud, he took me to the market and rewarded me with a bowl of white noodles with beef and meatballs.

For the second year in a row, I was in the same grade level as Kesor. Chai wanted to skip eighth grade, thinking that ninth grade was more befitting her age. Despite her desire, she learned that skipping a grade costs money. A friend had told her that she had paid a lot of money to skip a grade. Upon asking her teacher, a price of 100 dollars was demanded, which she was told came from the principal. This was a price that my family couldn't afford. But Chai, with her knack for befriending foreigners, was able to convince a British man, Joe, to pay both for this fee and for a new uniform.

Entering fifth grade reminded me of school in Prey Veng. Rumor had it that this teacher was the meanest in primary education. A student from my previous class told me that this teacher once whipped his brother with a belt strap.

When I arrived at class, I was shocked to see a line of students attempting to get the principal to transfer them to another teacher. Only a few were approved after their parents had paid a small bribe. How aggressive could this teacher be? It surely couldn't be worse than my experience in first grade, could it? His word "stupid" still stuck in my brain. I had learned to hate intentional punishment of the poor and inspiration through cruelty.

I had no option but to attend this class. I sat in the front desk on the far left next to the entrance, sitting with a boy who appeared half Chinese. He had a light complexion and a bowl haircut. He had a fancy white shirt with two front pockets and buttoned shoulder straps. It was an expensive and trendy design. I felt like I needed to make new friends because my best friend, Chamroeun, had moved to a different school.

"Hi, my name is Chamroeun. What's your name?"

"I'm Pheakdei. I'm new to this school. My family just moved from Phnom Penh."

"Why? I heard Phnom Penh is a really fun place to live."

"It was, but Pa got a new job in Sihanoukville, so we had to move here."

"What does he do?"

"He's a high-ranking policeman."

Pheakdei seemed friendly, but I wasn't sure he wanted to be my friend. I thought he was a rich kid, especially after hearing about his father's job. Most rich kids like him don't want to be friends with a poor boy like me. The wealthy students hung out together and spent a lot of money buying snacks.

"I heard that our teacher is mean. Other kids say he hits people a lot. We should work together to not get hit," I said hoping to convince him to work with me.

"Yeah! That's a good idea." Our conversation was cut short when the teacher, Mr. Kosal, entered the classroom. Everyone stood up shouting, "chom-reap-sueh, Teacher." We waited for him to reply.

"Sit down," he said after putting his motorbike key and brown suitcase on the table. "I don't need to explain the class rules. Everyone should know school policy by now." He wrote the date on the whiteboard with a black marker. "One thing I hate is a student missing class without asking for my permission first. I also will not tolerate a student who skips class and then asks stupid questions because they are behind on a lesson. Everyone must come to my class every day on time. If you're late, don't bother coming. Or I will make you kneel in front of the board the whole time."

After taking attendance, the teacher started the lesson. He wrote a few history questions on the board. "Who wants to come up here and answer these questions?" he said, looking for volunteers. No one raised their hand. We sat at our desks in silence, afraid to make eye contact. "You are in fifth grade. You should know the answer for these questions." He looked around. "Fine, if no one volunteers, I will call on you." He pulled out the name sheet. "Choum, Chakra," he called. A student in the fourth row on the far side of the classroom stood up. He nervously walked to the board and stood still while staring at the board for nearly a minute.

"I don't know the answer, Teacher," he said, staring down.

"Okay, stand aside."

"Pen, Chamroeun." I looked up, surprised. I didn't expect him to call on me since my name would be near the bottom of the list. My hands shook. I got out of my desk. There were five questions, all about Angkor Wat and the Bayon Temple. I remembered this topic from fourth grade but couldn't recall the answers.

"Do you know the answer?" the teacher asked.

"No Teacher, sorry."

"Don't be sorry. Just go stand aside. Chan, Champei." A girl from the second desk in the middle row got up and immediately moved over near us without even trying to answer. Everyone laughed.

"Be quiet! Do you think this is funny? Students in fifth grade not knowing anything about two of the most important temples in Cambodia! Let's see how funny it is when you are all up here looking like morons. You should be ashamed of yourselves." He looked at the name sheet. "Chea, Akara." Another girl walked up. This time the questions were answered, one by one, all correctly.

"You are lucky that she could answer the questions," he said looking at the remaining seated students. He turned back to us. "The three of you, open up your hands." He looked at Akara. "Take this. Use this stick to hit each one of them twice, as hard as you can. Do it or I will whip you." He handed the girl a thick wooden stick.

She looked at us with an apologetic face, then raised the stick and hit us one by one.

"You can return to your desk. The three of you need to study more or you will end up here again. Go back to your desks."

I was embarrassed. Most of the class was looking at us. They were probably thinking that we were indeed stupid.

"Now you all know what my expectation is, so be prepared to answer whatever questions I post on the board. Also, I am offering Rein Kour before class. The price will be just like every other teacher, 500 riel a day or 5 dollars a month. But Rein Kour will not help you escape my punishment, unless you study hard. I will keep calling on each one of you until someone gets it right."

Mr. Kosal wasn't joking. The next day, he called on students to solve math problems. There were a variety of equations involving multiplication, addition, division, and subtraction. One problem was so difficult that half of the class, including myself, were standing along the wall waiting to get hit. This time, Pheakdei was the one to provide the correct answer.

I was so mad at myself for not knowing the answers two days in a row. Once again, I pushed myself to try harder. Every morning, I studied for at least one hour before heading to school.

I attended Rein Kour daily, yet I was still posting low scores on assignments. Mr. Kosal persistently assigned unique problems, making it difficult for many of us to receive full credit. When the whole class got a low score on a math assignment, he got so tired of whipping us that he started throwing student notebooks on the floor after grading each one. They slid on the cement floor covered in dirt. Those who received a score lower than 7/10 had to pick up their books and brush off the dust before returning to their seats. He threw mine so hard that a few pages were ripped.

Math was my weakest subject in fifth grade. Economic equations were difficult, and I was never able to solve problems written in a story format. I was concerned that my poor performance would prevent me from passing fifth grade. I had to find a way to get higher scores, so I copied Pheakdei's solutions to study at home. Eventually, I was able to improve from reviewing Pheakdei's notes. In fact, I received one of the highest scores in "Bralang Choumeas Te Muoy" (the midterm exam). At the end of the first semester, the teacher placed me ninth overall. Father was so happy, he bragged about it to everyone at dinner.

"Chamroeun has placed ninth in his class," said Father, patting me on my shoulder.

"Good job," said Lab.

"That's because I am paying for him to attend Rein Kour," said Ruat incredulously.

"You need to stop doing that," Father responded. "He should be able to learn on his own. Teachers nowadays are always trying to find ways to extort money from students. It's terrible."

"It's fine, Father. I am happy to help. Besides, it is helping him get better grades," Ruat added.

"Getting good grades doesn't matter if you don't understand the concepts."

"I do understand the concepts, Father. I study every day," I pleaded.

"I'm not only talking about you. I'm talking about your whole generation. It seems like money, rather than knowledge, is the only way to pass classes."

I didn't reply. Father was right. Many students, including Chai, used money to skip grades without gathering a basic understanding of the necessary concepts.

Ruat listened to Father and stopped paying for me to attend Rein Kour. Even without his support, I still wanted to continue Rein Kour because I was afraid that my placement grade would drop. To fund Rein Kour from day to day, I went around the neighborhood with my next-door friends, Piep and Pon, collecting metal cans and plastic bottles to earn money. One time, we walked all the way to the beach.

"Guys, let's turn around," I said, putting a large plastic bag down as we approached the white sand.

"Why?" Piep asked, "the beach has more cans."

"I don't want my sisters to see me."

"So what?" Pon asked.

"If they see me, they're going to tell my parents." I swallowed. "My parents would hit me if they know I walked this far, picking up cans."

"But there are a lot of cans and bottles on the beach though," said Piep, "that's more money for us."

"No, I can't go. My bag is almost full anyway." I lifted the tip of my bag onto my shoulder and started heading back. I didn't want my family to know I was becoming like a street kid.

"Okay, okay!" Piep said, "we'll go back with you."

Soon the rainy season would arrive. Chai and Kesor stopped selling on the beach because they had minimal sales that time of year. They were hired at a tourist restaurant and bar on Victory Hill, working at night as servers and bartenders to mostly foreign customers. Their shift was six in the evening to two in the morning, every day. They earned roughly fifty dollars a month, plus approximately five dollars a day in tips. This made it extremely difficult for them to attend school. Soon enough, Chai and Kesor decided not to waste the money they made on what was becoming an unnecessary Khmer education. Chai dropped out of ninth grade and Kesor left fifth grade.

I was now the only one in my family pursuing Khmer Education. My schedule was switched to the morning class, while English school continued in the evenings. Not long after Kesor and Chai moved out to Victory Hill, Lim and her husband moved into the cement room downstairs due to financial struggles. A couple of months later, Ruat married a woman who worked with him at the factory. Ruat and his wife also moved in with us.

Meanwhile, Kesor told Father that she had met a man, a barang. She seemed very happy when talking about this new guy. "He is a very nice person," I heard her say excitedly. "He brings me flowers, and he always pays for my food." She smiled. "He also told me that he doesn't smoke, drink or do drugs."

"What's his name?" Father asked.

"Thalen!"

"Sa-len?"

"No, Thalen."

"Thalen. Okay. Where is Thalen from?"

"He told me is he is from America!"

"That's good. America is a good country. You should bring him over. I would like to meet him."

Since Kesor had met Thalen, she frequently came home with bags of flowers, mostly expensive red roses. Thalen always wanted to spend time with her. He took her to the waterfall, Kbal Chhay, which was one of the most popular tourist destinations in Kompong Som. He tried to impress her by buying her a new phone. But the most magnificent gift that Thalen had ever given Kesor was a drawing that looked exactly like her. My family and I had never seen such incredible artwork.

Three days later, Kesor finally brought Thalen to our house. Thalen had blonde hair and white skin with light freckles. He smiled and waved at us. He wore a long sleeve button-down shirt, blue jeans, and a pair of white flip-flops. Thalen's presence had attracted many villagers, including kids, to our house. People were always excited to see a barang. They stood outside of our house, watching Thalen getting off the motorbike.

"Say chom-reap-sueh, like I teach you," said Kesor with her broken English.

Thalen put his hands together in front of his nose and bowed. "Chom-reap-sueh," he said with a thick American accent.

I was surprised to see him attempt the traditional way of greeting in Khmer culture. It was not common to hear a foreigner speak Khmer.

"Chom-reap-sueh, sir," my mother said in Khmer, clasping his hands and bowing her head to show her appreciation. "Are you hungry? I can make something for you to eat."

Thalen looked confused. He turned to Kesor. "She asking you if you hungry," Kesor translated.

"No, thank you. I already ate." Thalen shook his head, patting his stomach.

Kesor spoke to Mother in Khmer. "It's okay, Mother. He's not hungry."

"Well come on in. Take a seat." She led Thalen underneath the stilts and sat at the table.

"Where is Father?" Kesor asked in Khmer, looking over her shoulder to Mother.

"Oh, he went to the market. He'll be back shortly."

"Thalen, sit here," she switched back to English. "I go upstair, comb my hair. I be back."

"Okay." He looked over at me with a wry smile. "Hello!" he said without having any clue who I was.

"Hello," I said.

"What is your name?"

"Chamroeun. Me, Kesor brother."

"You are Kesor's brother? I am Thalen. Nice to meet you."

"Nice meet you!" I approached him then shook his hand. I learned how to do this in English school.

For some reason, I always found Westerners quite amusing and fun to play with. I had the urge to climb on his back, so I wrapped my arms around his neck and gently pulled his shoulders back and forth. He jokingly tried to shake me off.

Minutes later, Father had returned. Thalen, Kesor, and my parents sat on the balcony talking as Kesor introduced Thalen. I positioned myself next to Mother, fascinated to hear more about him. The conversation went through Kesor as she translated Khmer to English and vice versa. Words were often lost due to Kesor's broken English. Yet, Father talked cheerfully, smiling widely while listening to Kesor's interpretation. Mother didn't say much. However, she had a joyful expression as she couldn't keep her eyes off Thalen and Kesor. As for me, I was deeply happy to meet an outsider who came from a "powerful nation" and could potentially be my future brother-in-law.

During *Pchum Ben*, a Buddhist festival, Thalen took Mother, Lab, and me to Wat Otres, (Otres Temple). Thalen wanted to experience Khmer culture. This was a time for Khmer people to remember and present food to their deceased ancestors.

As we entered the temple, many people stared at Thalen. I could hear the elders whispering, "look, there is a barang here." Thalen was taking this in for the first time, and he was totally unaware of the attention he was drawing.

"Chamroeun, what am I supposed to do?" Thalen asked over the noisy crowd.

"You do what I do," I spoke with my limited English.

"Okay, guide me." We got in line behind the other temple-goers. We slowly approached a tall table lined with small pots. One by one, we spooned the rice we had brought into the pots, one for each of the monks in the Wat.

"Tell him to make sure that the spoon doesn't touch the pot. It's forbidden," said Mother.

"Thalen, don't touch pot. It bad," I translated.

He nodded, then carefully dropped the rice high above the pot. People laughed at a Westerner trying to blend in. We then took our gift, a large bowl of food, rice cookies, and bags of dry noodles, to present to the monks who were sitting in a straight line on the carpeted floor.

Each monk wore a bright orange silk robe.

We sat on the floor, legs folded underneath us and to the side. We positioned our hands in prayer in front of our noses. We bowed to the monks as they wished us luck. Thalen had a hard time trying to sit like us. Yet, he smiled while fanning himself, telling me that he was pleased to experience a traditional ceremony. Soon, all four of us climbed on a motorbike and rode off onto the curved dirt road.

Thalen visited frequently. He taught me things like surfcasting at Ordchidea Beach and an improvised form of baseball. For this, he collected a bunch of plastic bags and turned them into a small round ball. He picked up a thick tree branch then walked to an empty space in the neighbor's yard.

"In America, people play baseball. One guy pitches the ball, and another holds a bat and tries to hit the ball as far as he can." He then threw the wrapped plastic ball into the air and swung at it with intensity. The ball flew about thirty yards and landed in the tall grass.

I had no idea what he was talking about. The two most popular sports in Cambodia were soccer and volleyball. Thalen tried to demonstrate baseball for another half an hour, but I still couldn't understand the concept.

"Can you buy football? I no have football," I begged.

"You mean a soccer ball? In my country, we call it soccer. Football is much different."

"Yes. Can you buy? I no have one."

"Okay, first of all, 'no have' is incorrect English. You can say, 'I do not have a soccer ball.' But don't say 'I no have'." To make sure I would understand, he often wrote down the sentence in a notebook in all capital letters, so I could see his corrections.

With him correcting me, I was able to speak a little better every day. During Khmer school, I found myself looking forward to seeing him.

A few weeks later, Kesor and Thalen rented a fancy western-style house in nearby Victory Hill. Chai had also met an American man, Seth, and they started living with each other. Since they were speaking English every day, Chai and Kesor decided that English school was no longer needed. Additionally, John's funds ran out which meant I could no longer attend English school either. The only way for me to improve my speaking skills was to talk with Thalen.

On the bright side, eliminating English School allowed me to focus on Khmer school. This was necessary because not only were the subjects getting harder, but the teaching was getting worse. Mr. Kosal had no mercy and relentlessly punished students for their mistakes. One day, he called on a boy, Pisey, to solve a math story problem. Pisey was one of my friends in fifth grade. He stood speechless without a clue how to answer.

"What is the answer?" Mr. Kosal asked from his chair.

"I don't know, Teacher," said Pisey.

"What do you mean you don't know? I've explained how to solve this type of problem for the last two days."

"I wasn't here the last two classes."

"Yeah, I know. That's why I'm calling on you, to make sure you know how to do it."

"But I don't know how to do it, sir."

"Why didn't you come to class? Where were you?"

"I had a really bad ankle sprain. I wasn't able to walk. My mother wanted me to rest."

"A sprained ankle from doing what?"

Pisey hesitated. I could see his hands were shaking.

"Did you hear me?" Mr. Kosal shouted.

"From playing soccer," Pisey mumbled with fear.

"From playing soccer! Which ankle is it?" Mr. Kosal quickly got up and grabbed a large triangular wooden ruler which he used to draw lines on the board.

"My right ankle, sir."

"Show me!"

Pisey stuck his leg out, and immediately Mr. Kosal used the edge of his ruler to hit Pisey's leg. I could hear the snapping sound as the wood bounced off the bone. Pisey started to cry as he held onto his ankle.

"How dare you move your leg. Show me again!"

"Please sir, please. It hurts really bad," he begged tearfully.

"I don't care! Stick out your leg!"

Pisey had no choice but to slowly reach out with his right foot. And Mr. Kosal smacked him in the exact same spot. It was heartbreaking to hear my friend screaming, begging for mercy. "My leg! My leg!" he shouted over and over. I couldn't believe Mr. Kosal's cruelty.

"You missed two classes because you sprained your ankle playing soccer! Didn't I tell you that I hate students missing class without my permission. Now, you are behind with the lessons. Try kicking a soccer ball now. Get out of my class!"

Pisey's face was covered in tears as he limped past my desk.

"I can't believe it," Mr. Kosal continued. "Nobody looks at him! Open your history textbook and read chapter eight. I will ask questions later."

The class was in shock. Everyone opened their textbooks quickly and read in silence.

Approximately twenty minutes later, a lady burst through the door while her daughter tried to hold her back. The lady was seething.

"Why did you hit my son?" she shouted. "I'm his mother, and I rarely hit him. You are just his teacher, and you beat him on his injured leg? Are you crazy? Do you not have mercy?"

The teacher sat in his chair with a smirk on his face and did not utter a single word in reply.

"My son tries really hard in your class. He studies every night! It is not right for you to hit him like that. You crazy teacher!" She wiped the tears from her cheeks.

"Mother, that's enough!" said the daughter. "Come on. Let's go back home." After a few more minutes of cursing, the daughter was able to calm her down, and they left the school property. The principal then entered our class, narrowing his eyes at Mr. Kosal.

"What is going on? Is everything okay?" the principal asked.

"Yes. She was mad that I hit her son for skipping class."

"We've never had this happen before in our school. Can I talk to you in my office?"

"Sir, there is not much to tell. He didn't know how to solve a math problem, so I hit him. I can talk to you in your office if you prefer."

"Yes, I would like to talk in private."

"That's fine. Everyone, keep reading." The teacher followed the principal out the door. No one knew how to react to what we just had seen. Everyone was whispering to each other. We were trying to guess what might happen to our teacher. There was laughter after someone jokingly repeated the phrase, "crazy teacher."

Pisey didn't come to class for the rest of the school year. If he would ever return to Khmer school, I would never know. However, with only a few exceptions, Mr. Kosal just threw our notebooks on the floor to punish us from then on. Despite his brutal beatings for the majority of the school year, I did learn a lot from his class. He took extra time to explain each lesson. He wanted to make sure everyone understood the concepts. Nonetheless, students were right about him. He was one of the meanest teachers I ever had. At the end of the school year, I placed 13th/40 students. It wasn't my best performance, but I was very relieved that I didn't have to repeat his class.

# 7

# A KHMER WEDDING

THALEN FREQUENTLY VISITED us in the early morning. Mother greeted him with a "sir," one of the few English words she knew. Father would also join him outside for coffee. The sharp aroma of black beans spread through the house. Father loved dipping soft bread into the sweet dark coffee. He often spoke in French with Thalen. Whereas Thalen had taken French in high school, Father was exposed to French because Cambodia was once occupied as part of French Indochina. It was taught in Khmer schools throughout the country before the Khmer Rouge. Yet, they still couldn't understand each other well because of their limited vocabularies.

Thalen called me over to translate. "Tell your father that I have met Chai's boyfriend. We have decided to open a restaurant in Victory Hill."

When the restaurant was completed, they called it, The Khmer Gourmet. It served breakfast, lunch, and tasty desserts, including western cookies and ice-cream. Thalen hired Lab and Lane as servers and dishwashers. It was much easier than working in the factory. Kesor and Chai stopped working in the bar and joined the business. Thalen and Kesor managed the shop from four in the morning until noon, then Chai and her boyfriend, Seth, took charge from noon to evening. The shop provided a little money to pay for supplies, utilities, and rent.

Managing the restaurant required a lot of work. I now had to go to the shop to see Thalen and my sisters on weekends. Thalen was always excited to see me. He would make me a breakfast of eggs, bacon, and hearty bread. It was my first exposure to a true Western meal. The first time he made it for me, I ate only the eggs and bacon. Thalen gave me a strange look.

"Why didn't you eat the bread?" he asked.

"I not hungry."

"No. I mean, you're supposed to put the eggs and bacon in the bread and eat them all together like a sandwich."

"I not hungry, sorry." I was not understanding him.

"Fine." He shook his head. "Hey, I want to show you something." He grabbed my arm and walked me into the kitchen. "This is a photo of my family. You can see my parents, Jeff and Wanda. These are my brothers, Blake and Drew." The photo showed his parents sitting in front and Thalen standing behind them, next to his brothers.

"Why you all have long hair?"

"This picture was taken a long time ago. Drew just shaved his head. I don't know why, but he did it. Come on, I want to show you another thing." He picked up a large map and unfolded it on the shelf of the coffee table. He opened it up with both of his hands. I saw curvy lines and labels all over. I had no idea what I was looking at.

"This is where I am from, Seattle. It is a big city in Washington State. Washington is about the same size as Cambodia."

"Where your house?"

"Just north of the city, here." He pointed on the map. "My parents have a business in Seattle. It takes them twenty minutes to drive from their house to the store."

"They have car?"

"Yes! Everyone in my family has a car. In the US, most people drive cars. There are fewer motorcycles."

"What is motorcycle?"

"Oh, it's like a motorbike, but bigger, faster, and louder."

"Do you ride motorcycle in America?"

He chuckled. "No. It's dangerous to ride a motorcycle in the US. Every-one else is driving a car: you have to be careful so you don't get into a crash.

Life is very different in the US. I can't really explain it well, but maybe one day you can come visit."

"Yes! Okay." I was very excited to hear Thalen talk about visiting the United States. It's a country that many Khmer people, including my father, consider one of the best nations in the world. Visiting an advanced country like the US was a dream for a poor kid like me.

A few months later, when I began sixth grade, Thalen and Kesor got engaged. We were all excited to have him as part of our family. Two days before the engagement, Thalen's parents, Jeff and Wanda, came to visit us. They brought a large cardboard box full of presents. There were t-shirts, Western magazines, and power tools requested by Thalen. I, however, was given a burgundy elongated ball with white laces.

"That is a football," said Thalen. "Let's go downstairs. I'll show you how to throw it." He put his right hand on the laces and threw a spiral right at me. The ball bounced off my arms. "Use your hands to catch it," Thalen continued.

We were soon surrounded by neighborhood kids watching with curiosity. Thalen threw the ball to one of my neighbors standing thirty-five yards away. The boy opened his arms, but the ball bounced off his chest. He threw it back improperly with two hands, the ball traveled in the air without rotation and landed short to Thalen. We had so much fun that we played catch until dark.

Three months later was the wedding. This led Thalen's parents to come back to Cambodia once again. This time they were accompanied by his brothers. Thalen hilariously tried to take Blake and Drew for a ride on the motorbike. It was almost impossible for three large white men to sit on a tiny motorbike. They held on for dear life as Thalen slowly motored forward.

It was wonderful to meet Thalen's family. Although it was difficult to communicate, our lives were changing as we welcomed this family of outsiders into ours.

Khmer weddings last for a day and a half. The ceremony begins in the evening, a tradition for the couple to honor parents and receive blessings from monks before the actual wedding party. Our house was packed with aunts, uncles, neighbors, and more. The ceremony was held in the main room above the stilts. Everyone sat on the floor around the couple. We all bowed while listening to the monks' benediction that continued for roughly three hours.

The room was sweltering. Father turned on multiple fans in an attempt to keep it cool. Drew and Blake had a terrible time trying to sit directly on the wood floor. They were both six foot three. The brothers and their parents kept fidgeting back and forth. Their faces were drenched in sweat. They had no idea what was going on as the blessing persisted. Father handed them each a pillow in an effort to make them more comfortable.

Chai sat next to Jeff and Wanda, translating and instructing them on how to perform their role in the ceremony. They each had to hand a silver wedding bowl containing a candle, rice, cookies, and money to the couple as a symbol of luck. I wanted to explain to Thalen's brothers what was going on, but I was afraid. They were intimidating and constantly used words that I didn't understand.

The ceremony concluded after the parents' blessing. Thalen's family left to rest.

The following day at five in the morning, the officiant began playing Khmer Wedding music, a combination of instruments mixed with high-tone singing, through a large bullhorn speaker. It was tied to the top of a tall pole, situated high above a large party tent. Throughout the day, people ate under this central tent. To prepare for breakfast, chefs cooked porridge in a portable kitchen set up on the backside of our house. The tent canopy spanned the bulk of the lot adjacent to our modest home. Because our property was so small, most of the event was held at the properties of our neighbors. It was overwhelming to see everyone hustling around the house.

The wedding party spent the morning taking pictures. There were at least five different outfit changes for each person, and photos were taken at multiple locations around the city. Thalen had told Blake and Drew that they did not need to bring shoes from home, only to have the photographer tell them they needed shoes now. They spent most of a full day trying to find size fourteen shoes but ended up having to wear flip-flops with their ill-fitting rental suits. The combination of pants and sleeves that were too short for their bodies and improper footwear was quite comical. Thalen's clothes fit well because he had been able to be sized in advance. Unfortunately, he had failed to mention that his brothers were both six inches taller.

As the day progressed, more people arrived. The crowd of guests gathered with the groom and groomsmen for a processional that would span almost a quarter mile. For this portion of the ceremony, every guest had to hold a fancy silver tray laden with a variety of fruits, boxed cookies, and rice donuts. Each tray was nicely wrapped with thin clear plastic.

The Groom's Processional was very colorful, but tedious to those who participate. In Khmer culture, it symbolized the groom bringing gifts to the bride's family. The crowd was positioned in two long lines behind the wedding party. Our neighbor's daughter and I were the ring bearers. We stood in the front of the crowd and led the procession.

An old gentleman rang a large metal bell a few times, and then we walked slowly up the road toward our house. Neighbors stood in front of their houses watching from the side of the road. It was surprising to see a barang groom in a traditional ceremony, and even stranger was the participation of a large barang family. At the entrance to the house, Kesor and my parents received the gifts from Thalen's family. We all followed them into the party tent. Guests sat around the couple and listened to the officiant's instructions.

During lunch, I sat next to Father holding Thalen's puppy, a New Guinea Singing Dog, named "Muoy Pwan," meaning "One Thousand." Thalen and Kesor had bought it for 1,000 riel (25 cents).

"Let go of the dog. It's disgusting to hold it while eating," said one of my father's friends.

"Oh, it's okay. It's my son-in-law's dog. He always takes good care of it," said Father.

"It's strange that barangs like animals. I couldn't care less about dogs."

"You'd be surprised to know how much they care about their dogs. In their culture, they sometimes treat animals just like humans."

Out of the corner of my eye, I saw Jeff and his family all come down together and sit at a separate table.

"What is their nationality?" asked one of Father's friends.

"They are Americans," said Father.

"Wow, you're lucky. America is a really good country. I heard a lot of good things about it. Will you be able to go visit them?"

Father chuckled. "I wish. It is very difficult to get an American visa. Plus, I don't think we can afford to apply. Besides, I can't speak any English. If any one of us had a chance to go, it's my youngest son right here." Father patted me on my shoulder.

"So, you can speak English? Can you understand what they say?" asked one of our neighbors.

"Yes, a little. But I'm not as good as my sisters," I said.

"That's fine. You are still young. You have time to learn. The ability to speak English is very important. Most jobs only look for those who can speak it. Stick with it and you will have a bright future."

Minutes later, the betrothed couple was now positioned next to each other holding a sheathed sword while relatives wrapped layers of red string around their wrists. Everyone then gave the couple gifts of money as a way of wishing them luck.

In the evening, another meal was served to all the guests, most of whom had not participated in the earlier ceremonies. Thalen and Kesor stood at the entrance of the tent greeting the new arrivals. Each guest brought a gift again, most of which was money in the amount of five to ten dollars. The tent was crowded with both Khmers and barangs, who were being served a variety of Khmer foods, including fish soup and fried beef with rice.

Meanwhile, accompanied by Piep and Pon, I walked around the tent, collecting aluminum soda cans and plastic water bottles. The guests often threw the items on the ground, attracting many of the village's kids.

I grabbed a boy's hand and took the can from him.

"What do you need the cans for?" he asked. "Your sister is marrying a barang. Your family is going to be rich."

"My brother-in-law is not that kind of barang."

"Chamroeun!" Lab signaled me. I let him go and ran to her. "Can you tell those kids to not crawl under the tables. They are disturbing our guests!"

I nodded then turned to Piep and Pon. "Okay, we need to stop those people from crawling under the table."

"Do you want me to beat them up?" Piep asked.

"No, this is my sister's wedding. We're not getting into a fight."

"Yeah but how else are we going to get them to leave?" Pon added.

"We'll just tell them," I answered.

"It won't work," said Piep.

We approached a small boy while he was crawling out between the guests' chairs. Luckily, the table had some barangs, they kindly let him out.

"Hey," I said grabbing his arm. "Don't do that! You're scaring the guests."

"Go away! Or we'll beat you up!" Piep added.

"Sorry," the boy looked down in fear. I then noticed his hair was wet with alcohol. Someone had spilled beer on his head. The boy's arms and legs were covered with brown soil. He reminded me of my younger self.

"You can go but don't crawl into the table, okay?"

He ran off.

After dinner, the couple cut the cake while surrounding guests gently threw small flowers at them. They fed the parents first to show respect. Khmer music filled the night, resulting in many people, including Thalen's family and his Western friends, to start dancing in the classical Khmer fashion. They practiced *romvong*, which was dancing in a circle. Men and women alike moved in a slow counterclockwise fashion while folding their palms in front of their chests. Blake jokingly mixed in some American dance moves. It was strange to the locals, but everyone was entertained. Dancing went late into the night beneath the tent, surrounded by moonlight.

A few days later, Father took me to The Khmer Gourmet, needing me to translate. Thalen didn't seem excited to see us. He also brought his Khmer friend, Prak, to interpret, which indicated that this was a serious conversation.

They sat in the front of the shop. "Why did you take our wedding gifts? That money was supposed to be for Kesor and me. Why did you take it?" Thalen let Prak translate.

Father paused after listening to the interpretation. "In Khmer weddings, the parents use that money to pay for the party," Father spoke, hoping that Prak would explain everything he said.

"No! no!" Thalen snapped. "I gave you 2,000 dollars to ask for your permission to marry Kesor. You should've used that money to pay for the party. Not our wedding gifts!"

"The 2,000 dollars was only meant to grant our permission. It is supposed to be an award to the parents for raising the bride. That money is not for the party." Father waited for the man to translate. "Nephew, you know our culture. Please explain this to him." Prak nodded and continued to speak to Thalen. Standing near them, I had no idea what Prak had said. He used many English words that I didn't understand.

Thalen shook his head and went inside.

"He's really mad, Uncle," said Prak in Khmer. "I don't know if you could say anything to calm him down."

"But he needs to understand our culture."

"Uncle, I tried." Prak turned to Father. "Right now, I don't think he cares."

Prak's words worried me. I didn't want Thalen to think that Father was a thief. I went inside, hoping that I could further explain it to him. However, Thalen shut himself away. I saw Jeff sitting in a corner near the kitchen.

He approached me. "Chamroeun, I want you to know that whatever happens between your Father, Thalen, Wanda and I, it doesn't affect the relationship between me and you," he spoke slowly and clearly. "Do you understand?"

"Yes," I said, not fully understanding what he meant.

"We are mad at your father but that won't change what we think of you and your sisters." He smiled. "We thank you for guiding us through the party. We all had a wonderful time."

As much as I wanted to explain the situation to Jeff, I knew he wouldn't understand. My limited vocabulary and broken English could only make matters worse. Part of me thought that if he heard me defending my father, he would think I was betraying Thalen. Nonetheless, I hoped that one day they would understand that Father didn't steal the wedding gift.

Before Thalen's family left the country, I accompanied Lab and Lane to visit them. Wanda was reading articles from a western magazine to my sisters. Meanwhile, Jeff was showing me pictures on his thin silver laptop. It was fascinating to see images of his house and their daily life in America. One of the pictures was taken at a professional baseball game and showed a crowd sitting in a very large stadium. In the picture, I identified a woman who looked Khmer, sitting with Wanda.

"This is Stella. She visited us from California. She is a daughter of a friend we made in the US. Stella is now temporarily living with us. We consider her to be like a daughter," Jeff said.

It was nice to hear that a Khmer woman was living with them. As Jeff continued to click through pictures, images of a city full of large buildings appeared on the screen. One of the structures had a roof that looked like a mushroom.

"This is called the Space Needle. It is the most famous building in Seattle. There is a restaurant at the top and you can see the whole city from there. If you come visit us, maybe I can take you there," he said, looking at me straight in the eyes.

I nodded with a smile and kept looking at the picture. The moment was interrupted when Thalen entered the room looking frustrated.

"There is something wrong with the car. It is making all kinds of weird noises. Dad, would you be willing to take it to the mechanic? I'm not feeling well. The shop is not far from here."

"Okay? How much is it going to cost?"

"It shouldn't be too expensive. Probably five dollars, I would guess."

"All right. Where is it exactly?"

"I know where," I interjected. "I take you there."

"Great," Jeff said with a grin.

I wanted to go with Jeff because I knew Khmer mechanics would over-charge him. Khmer people always try to swindle Westerners.

I sat in the front passenger seat while Jeff drove slowly.

"Your English is pretty good. Have you been practicing with Thalen?" Jeff asked.

"Yes. I talk with him in English all the time."

"How do you like going to school? Thalen told me that he enrolled you in an English school."

"I like it a lot. I have big fun learning English."

"Good. But do you enjoy speaking English? It is a difficult language."

"Yes, I like speaking a lot."

"Well, Wanda and I were actually thinking of sponsoring you to come study in the US. Would you like to come to America?"

I thought he was joking. But when I looked at him just then, I could see a straight face, waiting for me to reply. I could sense he was dead serious.

"Yes!"

"Okay, I will let Wanda know. We will have to find a school that will accept you. Thalen will have to work on the paperwork for you to come. But most importantly, you must practice reading and writing English more."

"Okay, I can do that."

My heart was racing. I visualized myself attending an American school. I pictured seeing those tall buildings and incredible new places. I thought to myself, *what does this mean?* At the time, I didn't fully understand what the value of studying in America would provide. But I was thrilled to hear that Thalen's parents were willing to give me a chance to pursue a superior education. To study in America became my new dream, a dream that I never expected to have.

# 8

# THREE SCHOOLS A DAY

THALEN ENROLLED ME in another English school. The class ran from eight to eleven in the morning, Monday through Friday. Class was taught by Khmer teachers. However, students were not allowed to speak Khmer during class. There were three subjects being taught: grammar, art, and conversational English. The teachers were very talkative, affable, and quick to reward students with western cartoon stickers. This made Western teachers seem much nicer than the ones in Khmer school.

There was also no punishment. If there was confusion during class, they always took the extra time to explain. We frequently watched Disney movies on Fridays. There were also times when the teacher taught us how to sing songs in English. The teacher would sing slowly as she demonstrated the song in a high but gentle voice. We would then repeat after her, line by line. These activities made school seem relaxed and fun.

Every day, I focused on speaking English, determined to improve. Sometimes, Thalen came to pick me up from Khmer school in the evening. He would take me to his house so I could work with Kesor and Chai on learning English. Chai and Seth had moved in with Thalen and Kesor after they closed their coffee shop permanently.

At this time, The Khmer Gourmet started losing money. Most Khmer people were not interested in purchasing western desserts, so they decided to sell to other foreigners.

My family and I felt melancholy knowing that Thalen had to close his shop. I loved eating western cookies especially those freshly baked chocolate chip cookies that Thalen made. The sweetness of the chocolate chips still stuck in my brain. Without it, Lab and Lane found other jobs at a casino. They too, temporarily moved into Thalen's place.

With four of my sisters at Thalen's, I asked to move in too. I still visited my parents every day after Khmer school. Father thought living with Thalen was a good way for me to improve my English.

Plus, Kesor and Chai often cooked delicious Khmer food using expensive meats: pork, beef, and chicken. Furthermore, they often gave me money for school: roughly 2,000 riel each school day. They even threw me my first birthday party when I turned eleven. Most Khmers don't celebrate birthday parties because they can't afford one.

It was a special night. I wore a long button-down shirt and long pants. Chai let me wear Seth's tie so I could look more handsome. She cooked red chicken curry and white rice. We gathered outside on the cement floor and ate dinner together. Like Mother, Chai was a great cook. She always made her meals a little spicy.

After dinner, Chai and Kesor surprised me with a cake covered with lit candles.

"Happy birthday to you!" They sang in a rhythm. Lab, Lane, and Seth joined them and gathered around me. Thalen pulled out his phone and snapped some photos. "Happy birthday dear, Chamroeun! Happy birthday to you!" They clapped and cheered. I smiled then blew out the candles.

"Did you make wish?" Chai asked in broken English.

"No, I suppose to?"

Thalen chuckled. "Yeah," he interjected. "But that's all right."

Chai helped me slice the cake and hand pieces to everyone. We all sat on the floor, enjoying the sweet chocolate cake.

To improve our English, Thalen and Seth bought a small whiteboard and several textbooks for the family. They wanted to teach us proper American English. After a short lesson, we practiced speaking with each other. They corrected us when we said something wrong. Some nights, we watched Hollywood movies instead. It was fun being around them, and there was so much to learn. In the evenings, we would throw around a football or baseball. Thalen and Seth always tried to show off their strength by throwing the football to each other from a long distance.

Thalen also taught me how to design houses on his computer. He found work as a designer with a British man nearby. One time, he allowed me to sketch my own house with his architectural drawing supplies. I just copied his designs because I didn't know what I was doing. Nonetheless, he was proud that I was trying to learn. It was difficult to absorb so many new and valuable things, but just being near them helped improve my English.

In Khmer school, however, my classmates made fun of me. After noticing my connection with Thalen, some students started calling me, barang. During recess, they would shout at me. Some even insulted my sister for marrying a barang. It was a slur, and they used it to talk down to my family while treating me like an outsider. On one particular occasion, I became so frustrated with a boy who was repeatedly yelling "barang! barang!" right in my face that I had to yell back.

"Stop calling me that name!"

"Don't be mad. It's not my fault that your sister married a barang," he said.

"And so what? Do you have a problem with that?"

"Yeah, I do. What are you going to do about it?"

I didn't want to get in a fight, doing so would turn me into a gangster like Mother said. Beating him up could only create problems for me. In sixth grade, many students joined gangs with older kids. They wanted to form an alliance of protection and to gain power over other students. Fights were frequent during recess and after school. One day in recess, I looked a boy right in his eyes after hearing him say he was planning to attack a student after class with three other boys. He saw me staring at him and scowled right back. At the end of class, he snuck up on me and kicked my lower legs.

"Barang, how dare you look at my face? If you do that one more time, I will punch you in the face. You need to watch out," he said, inches from my nose.

My eyes focused on the cement floor. I knew that if I fought back, the consequences would be much worse.

Innocent kids were frequently attacked by large groups of gang members. One day while walking home amidst a group, two motorbikes with a total of six secondary school-aged students quickly approached one of the kids I was walking with. He was a secondary school boy ten yards ahead of me. They laid into him, punching, kicking, and whipping him with their belts. No one stepped in to help. He broke free and sprinted to a stranger's house. His head was bleeding. He stood underneath the house, begging the owner for help. The man grabbed his kitchen knife and headed toward the gang members.

"Who are you boys? Where do you live?" the man shouted at the gang. They quickly mounted their bikes and took off down the dusty road.

Kids from many grades in primary and secondary school joined the gangs. Some students would skip class because they were afraid of getting beat up. If a kid was targeted, there was no way of escaping. Reporting to a teacher meant harsh reprisal. They always found a way to attack that person sooner or later. It was a major problem that many Khmer students, including myself, had to deal with every day.

My classmates kept calling me barang and said terrible things about my sisters. "Be careful, barang!" they warned. "You will be beaten one day. You need to watch your back. It's coming."

I always stared at the dirt to avoid eye contact. My head throbbed with fear, worrying that they could jump me any day on the way home. All of these threats really made me dislike Khmer school and shifted my focus to English school.

Approximately one week later, Thalen enrolled me in a computer school located in downtown Sihanoukville, ten minutes away from my English school. The school instructed students how to type on a keyboard in English and Khmer.

Since I was attending three different schools each day, Thalen bought me a small white motorbike. It was a big deal to not have to ask Thalen or my father to give me a ride. I was independent in a way that I had never been before. Each school day, I rode my bike to Khmer school in the morning from Victory Hill to Oue Pir. After Khmer school, I went to my parents' house for lunch. I changed my uniform for English school. Afterwards, I went straight to computer school.

Three schools a day kept me busy, and I loved riding my motorbike, but on the downside, I hated riding in the dark, especially on rainy nights.

I remember one night on the way to computer school, the headlight was worn, making it hard for me to see potholes. Thunder flashed in the sky without ceasing, the bright lights made a dark night become clear as day. A thunderstorm in Cambodia was always frightening, the loud sound shook the ground, causing me to speed up. Suddenly, heavy raindrops came out of nowhere. Water splashed into the bike's engine, killing it instantly. I tried frantically to restart it, slamming my foot on the kick-start pedal over and over, but the motor refused to start. The only option was to walk the motorbike along the side of the flooded street soaked by the torrential rain.

After pushing for half of a mile, I was chilled to the core. My mind told me to abandon the bike and ask a motodop to take me to school. Yet, I couldn't leave my bike behind. It could easily be stolen. After all, it was the most expensive gift I had ever received. I continued to push the bike in the flooded road full of garbage. Luckily, there was a gas station nearby that allowed me to park. I stood underneath the roof by the pumps waiting for the rain to stop. After thirty minutes, the bike finally started up again, but the rain kept on falling. I had no choice but to ride in the wetness and hope it wouldn't die again.

Each night, I stayed up late so I could keep up with the lessons in both Khmer and English. Studying all the new concepts made me feel like my brain would explode.

Lab sat on a futon couch to practice dealing cards. She looked at me with an apologetic face after seeing me struggle to keep my eyes open.

"Go to bed if you're tired," she said.

"I'm fine. I have to finish my homework."

"Well then focus and do it properly. Don't just do it so you can get it over with. Pay attention to your assignment so you can learn something." She gathered all the cards.

I nodded.

"You are lucky to be going to a computer school. That's something that our family couldn't provide. You need to understand that."

"I know. I'm trying to as hard as I can every day."

"Pretty soon, you'll become the most educated person in this family."

If it were not for our financial struggle, I was certain that she would have finished Khmer school. Lab's comments were a well-needed reminder of how lucky I was to be attending not only one, but three different schools. If Thalen had not come along, my family was unlikely to have ever been able to pay for me to attend English, computer, or even Khmer school in the long term. In fact, there was no guarantee that my family would have been able to keep me in school even in the short term. Our income had been declining after Ruat and Lim were married. My parents didn't have any income. We didn't have extra land to farm nor the money to invest in domestic animals that could've allowed us to generate money for food and to pay for electricity. This could easily have forced me to drop out of school to become a motodop.

At a young age, I wanted to have a successful life. Hard work, and the luck of having Thalen as a brother-in-law, could ultimately lead me to accomplishing my dream of becoming the first person in my family to pursue higher education.

Two months later, we sold our house because Thalen had purchased a larger property in a village called Oue Bram (Five Water Stream). It was a quiet area surrounded by tall trees. But I thought it was creepy because the land was only a quarter mile from a graveyard. Normally, one would not want to live near a burial ground. But there were already a few families living in small houses nearby. Thalen's plan was to build a house so he wouldn't have to keep paying rent. It was also a chance for him to live with us and get to know our family better.

There was a lot of work to be done constructing a house. We began the project by digging a deep well to have ready access to water. Then we poured a cement foundation and built a small square wood house on short stilts to avoid flooding. Whenever I was in between school, I rode my motorbike to Oue Bram to help out as much as I could. Father, Ruat, and Thalen were building the walls. Thalen brought many advanced Western tools like screws, saws, and drills. Sometimes, Father refused to use Thalen's equipment and continued to use his handsaw, nails, and hammer instead. He wanted to demonstrate proper Khmer construction to Thalen. Meanwhile, I stood nearby to hand them whatever they needed. I wasn't much assistance, but they appreciated the contribution.

One Saturday when I did not have English or computer school, I arrived at Oue Bram after Khmer school to see Thalen sitting on top of the developing roof. He was wearing a straw hat as he hammered long chunks of thatched grass. He had developed such a terrible sunburn that his back and shoulders turned bright red. I could see him peeling part of his skin off. In this condition, he wasn't able to continue the project. He sat on the table underneath the house, resting in the little room that Father had built as a temporary living space. I wanted to help, so I climbed up to the roof and started attaching the thatched grass.

"Be careful. You can seriously get hurt from that height," said Father.

"Don't worry. I won't fall."

"Okay, well, try to do a good job. Make sure you don't leave any gaps or it will leak when there is rain."

"Chamroeun, wear my hat," said Thalen, tossing it up.

Progress was slow, but after a few hours, I was able to cover most of the front. I nailed as much as I could before nightfall.

"That's enough for today, Chamroeun. We should go home. It's gonna get dark soon," said Thalen as he collected his tools from around the house.

"Okay, I coming down." I wiped the sweat from my cheeks. While climbing down, my shirt was soaked through with perspiration. My whole body smelled like a wet dog. Nonetheless, I was glad that I had been able to contribute.

"Good job, Chamroeun!" said Thalen, patting me on the back. "To reward your hard work, I'm gonna take you to dinner tonight."

"Okay, thank you." I smiled then scooped a cup of ice water from a small red cooler.

Over the next few months, Father built a second cement house right next to the main house. His was directly on the ground with a galvanized metal roof. This was needed because all of us could not fit in one small wooden home.

Meanwhile, Chai and Seth rented their own house near Victory Hill. Thalen and Seth were not getting along after The Khmer Gourmet was sold, and Chai thought it was best if they lived separately. Truth was, Seth and Thalen's relationship had changed since the time Thalen's parents had first visited. I was told by Chai that Seth had read an email sent by Jeff, reporting to his family back in America about his experience in Cambodia. In the email, Jeff had said that Seth was a video game addict and a lazy person who was always watching TV instead of looking for a job. Jeff thought that Seth was taking advantage of Thalen because Seth wasn't helping to pay for food and often ate what was provided by Thalen. In reality, Seth had attempted to find a job but there wasn't much opportunity. He wanted to help pay for food, but he didn't have money. His family in America rarely helped him out.

Seth was crushed after reading Jeff's letter. He assumed Thalen agreed with what Jeff had written. It was one of the main reasons why Seth hated Thalen and his family.

After the houses were completed, Ruat got hired as a truck driver and went with his wife to live on a mountain in Oue Pir. However, Lim and her husband continued to live with us after having a son named Hou.

To decorate our property, Thalen and Kesor bought a variety of flowers and plants, including banana trees. Mother even raised chickens and ducks. Our property started to look like a garden peppered with poultry. Thalen also brought his dog, Muoy Puan, for security. In Cambodia, people raise dogs as guard dogs.

Living in Oue Bram was one of the most peaceful times I remember for my family. For the first time, we didn't have to worry about having enough money to buy food. Every morning, Kesor would give Mother five dollars to buy groceries from the market, and Thalen would drop her off at the market.

At night, Thalen would watch Hollywood movies with us on his silver computer. Sometimes, he even let me pick my own movie from the DVD store. Even after turning twelve, I still chose Disney movies. I just couldn't get enough of cartoons.

As a sixth grader, I felt like English and computer school offered more valuable lessons about countries around the world. Learning about different cultures, foods, and music was fascinating. Around this time, in an effort to learn more about Western daily life, I attempted to read one of the magazines that Wanda had brought from America. Seeing images of a person climb a mountain sculpted in the likeness of a human face was incredible. The more I looked, the more I felt how little I knew about the rest of the world.

My curiosity inspired me to keep working hard. I was able to pass all of my classes. I received As and Bs in English school. Additionally, I passed the final exams in computer school. I received two certificates, one for "Basics of Computer Typing Skill, Microsoft Word, and Excel," the other for, "Computer Concepts and Microsoft PowerPoint." As for Khmer school, however, I placed 17th/40 students. I was now advancing to secondary school.

Father was so proud that he bought fancy glass frames to hang my certificates on the wall in his house and show my siblings.

"This is a big deal. You are now the only person in this family to receive certificates from a school," he said, smiling ear to ear. "Did Thalen see this?"

"Yes. I showed them to him earlier, and my English grades."

Minutes later, Thalen arrived on his motorbike, holding a few soda cans. He approached me while I was playing with Hou in the garden.

"Jeff and Wanda have found a school that is willing to accept you. We need to start getting the paperwork together, and schedule an interview so you can go," he said with excitement.

"Really! Thank you," I said with elation. I couldn't believe what I had just heard. What did this mean? What were the chances of me studying in one of the most powerful nations on Earth?

# 9

# THE FORGOTTEN ONES

"WANDA AND I have found a private school called St. Luke that would like to have you come study," said Jeff, speaking on Thalen's phone. Private schools were the only institutions that would accept international students to study for more than one year. "We are really excited, and we are hoping that the embassy will let you come study here," Jeff continued.

"Yes, me too!"

"Great. Our intention is to have you come study for two years: seventh grade and eighth grade. Thalen told us that he will start applying for your visa, and I wanted to let you know that we will do whatever we can to support you."

"Okay, thank you."

It really cheered me up hearing from Jeff. I rarely got to talk to him on the phone. The most common way for me to communicate with him was by email. Thalen had created an account for me.

Jeff frequently sent me images of places in America and many incredible photos of street art. One of the most striking black-and-white pictures that he sent me were of battleships being bombed by airplanes near an island. I did not understand anything about this particular event, but it was oddly upsetting to see the thick dark smoke spreading across the sea. These photos were very intriguing. Thalen always sent appreciative messages back to Jeff for taking the time to send me pictures.

From that point forward, Thalen and I spent time on paperwork almost every day. He would take me to the internet café where we searched for the proper way to apply for an F-1 student visa. It's a nonimmigrant visa for international students attending school in America. Students must return home when they are done with their academic journey, however long it may be. To learn how to apply, Thalen spent a long time on the US Embassy and other websites. He copied and printed the instructions step by step. In my eyes, Thalen was incredibly efficient at finding accurate information online.

"Okay, so first we need to make you a Cambodian passport. Then, we need official transcripts from all three of your schools. We also need a copy of your birth certificate and a copy of your family book with all the birth dates and photos of your family members. Your family should have one, right?" asked Thalen while jotting down the steps.

"I don't know. I think my father have it."

"We need to ask him when we get home. For now, let's focus on figuring out how to get you a passport. I have the address of the place that makes them. It's in Phnom Penh. Maybe your father can take you there since he has more experience traveling than me."

A few days later, Father took me to Phnom Penh to make my passport. Thalen came too. He wanted to make sure everything would go according to plan. After taking my ID photos, Father, Thalen and I remained in Phnom Penh for the rest of the afternoon.

"Is there anything you want to do here?" Thalen asked.

"I don't know," I said.

Thalen bit his fingernails, thinking. "I know what we can do, we can go see the Killing Fields."

"What is that?"

"You don't know what the Killing Fields are?" He lowered his eyebrows. "It's about the Khmer Rouge, man. Did you not learn about it in school?"

I shook my head. At age thirteen, I had never heard of the Killing Fields. The teachers in Khmer school almost never mentioned it. I occasionally heard some teachers tell short stories about living during the evil era, but not a single lesson in class covered the terrifying event. I once heard my fifth grade teacher joke about lazy students not finishing their homework. "Being lazy won't get you anywhere," he said. "You all are lucky. If you were born in the Khmer Rouge era, you would be killed for your laziness." At the time, I had no idea what he meant nor why the Khmer Rouge would murder lazy people. Mother occasionally told me that the Khmer Rouge soldiers forced her and many Khmers to work in rice fields every day from early morning until evening. People were exhausted and overworked. Yet, they had to continue working to survive. If a person disobeyed the soldiers' orders, he or she would be taken to a jungle and would never be seen again.

"You have to go see it," Thalen added. "I mean, it's brutal. You're not gonna like it. But since you're Khmer, you have to go see it. It's an important chapter in your country's history."

I told Father about the place Thalen wanted to take me. However, he wasn't interested in going with us.

"You guys go ahead," he said in Khmer. "I'll wait for you at the hotel."

"But don't you want to see it?" I asked. "Thalen said this place is really important to our history."

Father's voice changed to sorrow. "I lived through that time. I am aware of the event. I know what the *Khmer Kraham* did. That's not something I want to see again."

Khmer Kraham was another name given to the Khmer Rouge because they wore a red krama as a part of their otherwise all black uniform.

Father's words shocked me. I couldn't imagine what he had gone through. I knew he survived the genocide, but I rarely heard him talk about the Khmer Kraham.

Father sat still. He looked into the streets of Phnom Penh with a frown on his face. I wished I knew what was going through his head.

I remember Mother told me her academic journey ended when the Khmer Rouge took over the country. The regime forced my mother and many other students to quit school and work in the fields. It was one of the reasons why many Khmer people, like my own mother, were illiterate.

I once saw Mother attempting to read a news magazine. "At?" she tried, "wait, that's in," she paused, taking a long look at the word. Seeing Mother's struggle broke my heart. I sat by her side.

"Chamroeun, can you read this sentence for me?" she asked.

"Sure, Mother." I held the magazine. "On Tuesday, at two thirty in the afternoon, there was an attempted robbery at the market in downtown Phnom Penh. Two robbers were caught by the policemen and will be serving prison time." I paused to notice Mother was listening closely.

"Is that all?"

"No, there's more of the article. Would you like me to continue?"

"That would be great."

I kept reading. Mother was always intrigued listening to stories and didn't go anywhere until I finished.

Thalen and I left the hotel later that afternoon on a motodop. Sitting in the middle, I barely had enough room to breathe. Thalen was much bigger than the driver and me, forcing us to squeeze together. Worse, the ride was long, and streets were flooded with vehicles, causing the driver to stop frequently. Sweat dripped down my forehead and I almost felt like I was being cooked alive. Fortunately, the traffic died off as we went further out of downtown. About half an hour later, we got to our destination.

There, I saw a big sign on the entry gate, saying, "Choeung Ek Genocidal Center." I followed Thalen inside.

"Be respectful, okay?" Thalen turned to me. "This is a serious place. Whatever you think, just keep it to yourself."

I continued to follow Thalen and soon enough, we were surrounded by a number of pits in the ground, a few feet deep. Being young, I was clueless of what I was looking at.

"What is this?" I asked. Thalen rubbed his face and looked at me with a straight face.

"This is where a lot of people were killed. I read about it. The executioners brought the victims here and beat them to death. They didn't even use bullets because it was too expensive." He shook his head, feeling disgusted. "So instead, they used tools like machetes and axes to cut peoples' heads off. It's pretty messed up, man."

At the moment, I couldn't fully understand what Thalen meant. My English was still limited. As we kept walking, we came across a big tree covered with bracelets. A sign at the bottom was written in Khmer and English, saying, "killing tree against which executioners beat children."

I was in complete shock after reading such a dark message. But this wasn't the only sign there. As our tour went on, I saw an empty shelter with writing that said "mass grave of 166 victims without heads." There were many more shelters like this across this field, some even had items that belonged to the victims. I remember seeing a glass box full of worn clothes. A variety of outfits in different sizes lay in a pile. I wished I knew who they belonged to. Many signs indicated how people were killed, but I didn't see one mentioning a victim's name.

"Let's keep moving," Thalen said, "it's almost evening."

Thalen and I then went inside a building known as the "Memorial Stupa." There was a big written note on the entry door. "WOULD YOU PLEASE KINDLY SHOW YOUR RESPECT TO MANY MILLION PEOPLE WHO WERE KILLED UNDER THE GENOCIDAL POL POT REGIME".

I remember entering the room: in front of me were hundreds of human skulls stacked on top of one another in a huge glass box. My jaw dropped. My skin crawled. I was frightened to see so many skulls in one place. I looked up and noticed that there were more levels of glass boxes stacked high above me. I scanned and scanned but couldn't spot a person's name. I wished I knew who they were so their names would not be forgotten.

Staring at the skulls brought tears to my eyes. My heart sunk to my stomach as I realized I didn't know why this terrible event had happened to my country. I closed my fists while holding back anger. I asked myself, *how could someone commit such an evil act?*

Pol Pot was the leader of the Khmer Rouge and was responsible for killing over two million people. I may not know the victims' names, but I would never forget what Pol Pot had done to my country.

"So, what do you think?" Thalen asked as we walked toward the exit gate.

"It sad . . ." I looked up to him. "But I don't know much . . ."

"Yeah, it's pretty messed up. It seems like they were trying to kill as many people as they could while they were in power." He paused. "But do you know what Pol Pot's main intention was?"

I shook my head.

"Based on what I read, he wanted to convert Cambodia into the world's largest rice producer." He glanced at me. "And he didn't want smart people on the farms because they didn't belong. Smart people could slow their plan down by resisting work. That's why Pol Pot chose to eliminate many of the educated people. And that led to a genocide."

Thalen's comment hit me. I was terrified to learn that education was a threat to the Khmer Rouge. Father often told me, "education was the key for success," but I would never have imagined that so many innocent lives were lost because of it. But despite Cambodia's darkest chapter, even after visiting the Killing Fields and witnessing thousands of skulls, I wasn't scared of pursuing knowledge.

Day by day, we started collecting the necessary documents for the visa. It was a tedious process, and we were spending a huge amount of money procuring each official paper. Thalen's parents funded the whole process. They sent Thalen money frequently so we could continue assembling everything. He needed to print countless pages of paper at the internet shop. The passport itself cost about 160 dollars.

Two months later, we had received my passport, family book, and official transcripts from the Khmer, English, and computer school. Furthermore, we had to translate the Khmer transcripts into English so the interviewer could read them.

"All right, now we need an original copy of the acceptance letter from St. Luke, the I-20, and the SEVIS forms which will be provided by the school," Thalen said.

The I-20 form is known as the *certificate of eligibility for nonimmigrant student status for academic and language students.* It is an important document provided by a designated school to prove to the US government that I was qualified to study in America.

"As soon as we get those forms, we can schedule an appointment date for the interview. But as for now, we need to be patient and wait for my parents to complete the steps on their end," Thalen continued.

"How long we have to wait?"

"I don't know, my parents have a lot of stuff to do. Right now, they are working on the sponsorship process. They have been talking to a few lawyers in Seattle. This whole thing is a lot more difficult than I'd expected."

"Why so difficult?"

"The US government wants to see a bank statement from your parents. They want to make sure that your family can afford to send you to study in America. We both know that your family is poor, and there is no way that your parents can actually pay anything. People have been telling my parents to lie by transferring money into an account under your parents' name. But we can't do that. We won't lie. We need to be honest and do this the right way."

Preparing the application was extremely stressful. After three months, it was still not ready. It was irritating that we had worked so hard, yet we still felt so far from completing the task.

While we waited, I continued attending Khmer and English school. In seventh grade at Khmer school, there were a number of subjects being taught: mathematics, human anatomy, literature, history, sports, and English. Sports were taught on an empty soccer field nearby, every Tuesday and Thursday. We paired up with another student and raced each other down the length of the field.

Secondary school was expensive. Students were required to wear new uniforms with full names stitched on the front of the shirts. Additionally, students had to buy quizzes and exams from the teachers almost every day. Teachers sold each test for 500 riel in almost every subject. Students would automatically receive a zero if they did not buy the exam. On the second week of school, three quizzes appeared on the same day. Father would only give me 700 riel for school each day. Most teachers would not allow students to owe them money. Some students started skipping class because of their debts, and others simply could never come up with enough money to pay the teachers. Whenever I could not afford the exams, I had to sit in my desk quietly while watching my classmates writing down answers. This is what prevented many students, including Chai, from advancing to higher levels of education.

Day after day, I got whipped as Khmer school became harder. Worse, my interest in it was declining, and yet my English proficiency was increasing. In fact, I was the only person in my class that was able to read English words precisely. However, this made me a target.

Other students thought it was an unfair advantage that I had an American brother-in-law. I could hear them talking about how unusual it was for a Khmer woman to marry a barang. I just sat in my desk quietly ignoring them.

In seventh grade, fights broke out all the time. Students got beat up just for talking to a girl that a gang member liked. I remember talking to a girl sitting in front of me. She was prettier than most girls in our class. We only exchanged answers on our homework once, but this prompted a boy to come up to me during recess.

"I saw you talking to my girl!" he said, gripping the collar of my shirt. "Stop it! Or I will beat you!" I didn't bother replying. I knew the boy had connections with other gang members. I often saw him hanging out with multiple people from different grade levels. Innocent students frequently got jumped by gangsters in secondary school.

One day toward the end of class, I looked out the window and saw five students carrying large tree branches, belts, and even short rusty machetes. They were standing underneath a tree in front of my classroom. When everyone was exiting school, these gangsters chased after one of my classmates. The boy sprinted toward a ninth grade teacher, who was sitting in his wife's shop. The teacher approached the gang members, then started calling the principal on his phone, forcing the gangsters to run away.

Unfortunately, the boy only delayed his beating. The following day, as he sat at his desk, a gang member approached him with a belt wrapped around his right hand with the buckle hanging down. He viciously whipped the boy repeatedly in the face, then quickly sprinted out the door. Everyone was shocked to see this in the classroom. Some girls screamed. Blood dripped down the boy's face. Part of his forehead was cut wide open. He tried to keep the blood away from his eyes. His white shirt turned red almost instantly. The boy was rushed to the hospital by a teacher from the class next door. Blood remained smeared all over his desk. No one was safe in secondary education.

Male students were constantly trying to prove they were the toughest in school. Most of them didn't come to learn. I was sick and tired of seeing students beaten up. I was afraid that I would be the next victim. I felt that I had to do whatever was necessary to get the F-1 visa. It was the only chance to get away from this brutality.

A few months later, Jeff and Wanda were able to send us all the required documents. They emailed us original copies of the I-20, SEVIS Identification, sponsorship information, and recommendation letters from St. Luke

School and Stella—the Khmer woman living with Jeff and Wanda. The last step was to complete the Nonimmigrant Visa Application known as "Form DS-160," and create a confirmation page. We finally were able to schedule an appointment for an interview at the US Embassy in Phnom Penh.

"Nicely done!" Thalen said with a big smile. "Now all we need to do is pay for the appointment. Then you can start preparing for the interview."

"Is the interview difficult?" I asked.

"It could be. Based on the information listed on the website, the hardest part is to get an approval on the 214B."

"What is that?"

"It's a statement where you need to prove to the US Embassy that without reasonable doubt, you will return to your home country when you are done with school. The embassy can reject you if you can't provide enough evidence to show them that you will come back. They are afraid that people will want to live in the US forever, especially a kid from a third-world country like you."

"That is hard. How I get them to believe me?"

"There are some samples posted on the internet. I'll write them down so you can practice later."

It was becoming clear that the chances of a Khmer student obtaining an American Student Visa were slim, especially with my family's financial state. I had often heard that students who received an F-1 student visa were rich. Their parents were wealthy enough to sponsor them to study overseas. Despite coming from a poor family, I still had hope. I believed in myself and was convinced that as long as I answered the questions precisely, there was a chance. I had to find a way to overcome this challenge.

One week before the interview, Thalen quizzed me every day after school. He wrote questions on three-by-five-inch flashcards. "Why do you want to study in the US?" Thalen asked, portraying the interviewer.

"I want to study in a better school, so I can achieve a better education," I followed the answer he had written.

"Remember, speak slowly so they can understand you. You should also talk about your experience in Khmer school and why you need to pursue a better education."

"Okay, I try say that."

"Are you going to come back to Cambodia after you are done with school?"

"Yes! I will come back when I am done. My intention is to learn as much as I can, and then I will come back home to live with my family."

"Good. Keep practicing these notecards. I'm sure you will be fine. You should start packing soon. We will be leaving to Phnom Penh in five days."

# 10

# THE INTERVIEW

ON THE MORNING before the interview, the sun was shining brightly, and the air was hot and humid. Our village was quiet. I could hear birds twittering all around us, singing among themselves. Thalen, my father, and I left Kompong Som that day. The three of us rode in a large bus with many other passengers along the narrow busy highway from the coast to the capital. It was a harrowing trip, with the traffic steadily increasing, and cars, motorbikes, and trucks barely able to pass one another along the two-lane road. The scariest elements in this mix were the defenseless pedestrians and speeding bicycles also traveling along the side of the highway. Over the first hour, we had already seen two bizarre accidents, at least one of which was a fatality.

I remember looking out the window and seeing a man lying facedown near his motorbike on the asphalt, surrounded by a large crowd of people. His shirt was covered with blood. I looked away. My skin crawled. Every time the bus driver attempted to pass a slow vehicle, I gripped my seat and leaned out the window to see if the road was clear. I was worried that we would be part of accident number three.

"Relax, the driver knows what he is doing," Father said.

"The road is really small. I'm worried he will hit someone, or they'll hit him."

"Everything is going to be fine. I can assure you the driver has plenty of experience driving on this road. Besides, we're in a very large bus; we're the ones most likely to survive if anything happens."

After four hours on the road, we reached Phnom Penh. Thalen rented a room in a hotel near Wat Phnom, where the US Embassy is located. We then headed to the market, where Thalen bought me a brand-new button-down shirt. He wanted to make sure that I looked sharp for the interview. He also bought me a tie and a belt so I would look a little more formal. This was important, and we thought I should dress like it was.

When night arrived, the three of us sat in the room with two full beds, and a small black TV mounted to the wall in the corner. My father watched a soccer match, while Thalen and I reviewed the paperwork one last time. Every document had its place in the folder. Thalen checked each file, then he quizzed me until he was convinced I was ready. It was my final practice before the actual interview. I spoke comfortably, clearly, and with confidence. Father lay in silence, appraising my responses.

"Lab say I should talk about coming back to visit important place like Angkor Wat, to show them I really will return," I said to Thalen. "Should I say it?"

"That's good, but I don't know if it's good enough. I think you should mostly talk about how much your family means to you, and how much you want to see them when you're done."

"Okay, but I never see Angkor Wat before. I think it important. I want see it."

"I'll tell you what, if you pass the interview, I'll take you to see Angkor Wat."

"All right, I try my best." After two hours of prepping, we wrapped up all the documents and went to bed. I could barely sleep that night. I thought about failing, and what a shame it would be if I was rejected. Worse than that, I didn't want to let Thalen and his parents down. They were spending a tremendous amount of time and money on my application. I had to find a way to convince the US Embassy that I deserved the F-1 student visa.

We were up early preparing for a six thirty in the morning departure. Father and Thalen dressed in trousers and button-down shirts. I wore black pants, the grey shirt we had bought the day before, and black shoes. Thalen tied a blue tie around my neck to complete the outfit. This was my first time wearing proper western clothes. We soon left the room and headed toward the embassy. After fifteen minutes of walking the bustling, diverse streets of Phnom Penh, full of street vendors and businesses, we decided to take a *tuk-tuk* to be on time for my eight thirty in the morning appointment.

While riding there, Thalen had a nervous look on his face. He finally broke his silence and spoke loudly over the clamor of traffic. "I talked to my parents this morning, and they wanted me to wish you luck."

"Thank you." I tried to calm myself by staring at the shops passing by. I couldn't stop thinking about the questions I might be asked.

"You're going to be fine. Just be friendly. Tell them that you're a little nervous but you're mostly excited for the opportunity."

"Okay, I will."

"The interview should only take around fifteen minutes, so you'll be done in no time." Thalen patted me on my leg. I was still apprehensive. My heart was beating so fast, I thought it would burst out of my chest. If I didn't stay calm, there was no chance I would perform well.

The tuk-tuk driver pulled over near the entry to Wat Phnom. Across the street was the enormous US Embassy building, surrounded by a tall black metal fence. A crowd of people were standing on the median in the middle of the road waiting for the embassy to open. Meanwhile, I sat on a bench, alone, at the bottom of the hill. Thalen paced nervously, biting his fingernails. My father went up to the temple at the top of Wat Phnom. He wanted to pray so I might receive good luck. People continued to arrive as the appointment time approached. Some came in fancy cars wearing casual attire. Eventually, I saw a security guard come out and set up two signs, one for immigrant applicants and the other for non-immigrants.

"Chamroeun! It's almost time. Get ready," Thalen called from a distance.

"Okay." I grabbed the paperwork folder and headed his way.

"Where is your father?"

"I think he went up there to pray. He'll be back soon." Thalen grinned but didn't say anything. He didn't want to disrespect Khmer culture. Father was a believer and regularly prayed for our family to have a better life. Soon enough, Father was walking down the steep hill toward us.

"What took you so long?" I asked.

"There were a lot of people in the temple, and I wanted to have a good prayer so Buddha will help you."

"I don't think praying is going to help, Father. I still have to answer their questions."

"Yes, but it is better to ask for a blessing."

We crossed the street and headed toward the triangular median. People were walking from there toward the gate and forming a line.

"Good luck!" Thalen said and patted me on the shoulder. My nerves were on the rise. Yet, I gave them a smile as a show of confidence, then took a deep breath and walked toward the line. Protocol dictated that they couldn't go with me. Security only let five people in at a time. Within ten minutes, I was entering the checkpoint at the front gate.

The security guard handed each applicant a red visitor card. Another guard searched for weapons before letting anyone pass. I clipped the card to my shirt and exited the checkpoint. It was a short walk to the main building from the gate.

When I walked into the interview hall, I had to take a number and wait for the announcer to call my name. The waiting room was spacious and full of chairs lined up in rows. People were anxiously sitting holding their folders of paperwork, no one fully knowing what to expect. On one side of the room, I saw large photos hanging on the plain white walls. Eagles and people with many skin colors hung in place. One of the most fascinating images was a large crowd of soldiers standing around a gigantic American flag. It was a powerful message of patriotism.

On the opposite side, there were a dozen counters, each with a person standing behind protected glass. They were the interviewers. Each counter had a speaker installed in the glass to allow people to communicate back and forth. Most of the windows were filled with applicants in a standing position. I was intimidated. I watched an interviewer ask a question, then stare directly at an applicant's face while listening to the reply. A few appeared to be struggling to answer. I saw them request a Khmer translator because they were unable to speak English.

It wasn't long before my number was called on the speakers. I looked up and saw E145 was flashing in green on a small digital screen attached beneath the white ceiling. This was not for the interview, but for identity purposes. I had to go to a small room near the counters and place all of my fingers on a print-scanning machine. I was then given another number. This one was for the interview. While sitting on a metal chair waiting for my turn, I noticed that a number of people did not pass. Frequently, the interviewer handed the passport along with their paperwork back to the interviewee, and they would amble off with disappointed faces. Over the course of an hour, I only saw a few people receive visas. It looked like my odds were worse than I had imagined.

My number was finally announced, guiding me to the eighth window. The interviewer was a Caucasian lady with blonde hair, thick cheeks, and a kind face. She wore a light blue button-down shirt. I approached the window with a smile, trying to follow Thalen's advice. I handed her my folder through a small gap at the bottom of the thick glass.

"Hi! Sorry, I am a little nervous but I am happy for the opportunity," I said slowly, trying to make sure she would understand.

"That's okay, I get that a lot," she said through the high-pitched speaker. "How do you pronounce your name?"

"Chom-ron."

"Got it. How old are old?"

"I am thirteen years old."

"So, it says here that you are applying for an F-1 Student Visa. Is this correct?"

"Yes, I am."

The interviewer browsed through my paperwork. I stood still, trying to remain calm, yet, my heart was pounding like I had been running for a thousand miles. The sound of the speakers kept on announcing the next numbers. I glanced to my right and saw a few people, in their mid-forties, answering questions in Khmer. To my left, a lady in her mid-twenties was speaking broken English as she was explaining her reason for visiting America.

"Why you are applying for a student visa? What is your reason for going to study in America?" she asked, then proceeded to open my folder and inspect the paperwork.

"I want to increase my knowledge. America have better schools and I want to learn more about the world."

"What's wrong with the schools here?"

"It's not good. I don't learn much from my teacher. They give me small knowledge which is why I want study in America so I learn more."

"Okay, but why America specifically? I mean there are many other nations that have great schools. Why did you pick the US?"

"I pick the US because I have a American brother-in-law. His parent give me a chance to study there. And a school in America is kind enough to let me come study. This is great opportunity for me to continue my education."

"What is the name of the school?"

"Saint Luke Middle School."

"Who are you going to stay with if I let you go?"

"My brother-in-law parent, Jeff and Wanda Griffin."

"Where do they live?"

"Seattle, Washington State."

"How well do you know them?"

"I know them very well. They come visit my family few time. They gave my family many presents. They very friendly."

"What about your brother-in-law? How long have you known him?"

"Two to three years, he is very nice guy. He teach me English, throw football, fishing, and many more."

"What is his name?"

"Thalen McCain Griffin."

"How long has he been married to your sister?"

"One to two years."

"What is your sister's name?"

"Kesor Pen." The interviewer looked at one of the documents written in Khmer. She arose from her seat and went to the back of the room to have a Khmer translator read the document. My hands shook while watching the Khmer lady look over the document. I feared that I had provided inaccurate information. Five minutes later, she came back to the window and continued the process.

"What does your brother-in-law do for a living?"

"He use to open coffee shop. Now, he draw house for people."

"How long has he been living in Cambodia?"

"About four years . . ." I guessed without knowing the correct number.

"When was the last time your brother-in-law's family visited you?"

"About one year ago. Jeff and Wanda come to Thalen wedding with two other son, Blake and Drew. They are Thalen's younger brother. I talk to them at the wedding, they are friendly. I also talk to Jeff and Wanda on the phone a lot after they leave."

"Got it. So how many years will you be studying in America?"

"My brother-in-law tell me that I study for two years, seventh grade and eighth grade."

"What happens after that?"

"I can continue studying if my guardian continue sponsor me. If not, I come back home and live with my family here in Cambodia. I want to come back when I am done, I want to be with my family."

"How many siblings do you have?"

"I have two brothers and five sisters. I am the youngest." She picked up another document written in Khmer and went back to the translator. I saw the Khmer lady nod to specify that the document was accurate.

The interviewer returned to the window. "Are your brothers and sisters working? What kind of jobs do they have?"

"My brothers are motodop. Three of my sister work at factory and my other two sister just stay home for now."

"What about your parents?"

"My father use to be a farmer, now he stay home with my mother to look after the house."

"I see." She looked at me then at my paperwork with a short pause. "I'm going to tell you the truth, it is not common for an American family to sponsor a Cambodian kid to go study in the US. Most of the time, a student is being supported by their own family. I am afraid that if I let you go, you will enjoy living in the US so much that you won't want to come back." She had a stern expression and started gathering all of my paperwork, including my passport. I interpreted this as a sign that she was going to deny me.

I quickly spoke up. "If you let me go, I learn as much as I can about the world I know nothing about. And I come back and help teach other students what I learn. I do as much as I can to help. I promise." I looked at her straight in the eyes, my whole body trembling inside.

I had to be brave and do what was necessary to convince her. Seeing firsthand how many people suffered from a lack of education had inspired me to want to make a difference. My intention was to do whatever I could to help my country. Especially the poor kids just like me, who were desperate for an opportunity to gain knowledge. After living in Cambodia for thirteen years, I knew that my country had tremendous needs. This had inspired my wanting to help ever since I was young.

The interviewer gently smiled, then looked at her computer for a few minutes. Then she reviewed my paperwork again.

"Is that your intention? Going to study over there and come back to help other students when you're done?"

"Yes. Many Khmer student include myself don't learn much about the world. So, if you let me go, I come back and help teach them to increase their knowledge."

"I see. It's great that you intend to help others. Cambodia definitely needs someone to make a difference. But are you sure that you will come back and do what you said?"

"Yes, I will."

"When does school start?"

"September the second."

"What grade will you be in again?"

"I start in seventh grade."

"Is your sister planning on going to live with you in Seattle?"

"Maybe. I want to live with my sister and my brother-in-law, but I don't know yet."

"All right. Well, congratulations. You are one lucky kid."

She stamped my passport and put it in a blue basket with a few others. She handed back my paperwork folder along with a purple piece of paper.

"Am I good to go?"

"Yes! Come back tomorrow at four thirty to pick up your visa. Don't forget to bring that purple slip with you."

"Okay, I will. Thank you so much!" I said with excitement then quickly grabbed my folder and practically skipped toward the exit door. The people in the room looked at me in disbelief. I did not waste time. I went out of the interview room as fast as I could without running. I was so happy I could not wait to share the news with Thalen and Father.

Immediately after I exited the gate, I saw Thalen raised his palms up and shrugged his shoulders, giving me a questioning look. I pumped my fist in the air multiple times with a big smile and crossed the street to meet them.

"I pass! I'm going to America!" I said joyously. Right away, I saw tears falling straight down from Thalen's eyes behind his dark sunglasses. He was in total shock, but I knew he was grateful to hear the news. I had achieved a task considered impossible for someone in my position.

"Very good! Very good! My son is going to America," Father said.

"I can tell based on his reaction. Good for you, Nephew," said a gentleman nearby. Thalen took off his sunglasses and wiped off his tears.

"Good job! You did it. I'm proud of you." He patted me on the shoulders.

"Thank you. The lady tell me I need to return to the embassy tomorrow evening at four thirty."

"All right, no problem. But first, let's call my parents and share the good news. They have been waiting all night." Cambodia is fourteen hours ahead of Seattle. Thalen dialed the number, then handed me the black Nokia phone. It rang for a few seconds, and then I heard Wanda's voice answering.

"Hello," she said in a groggy voice.

"Hi Wanda! It's me, Chamroeun."

"Oh, hi Chamroeun. Are you done with the interview?"

"Yes, I finish. I pass!"

"Really, yay! Good job!" she exclaimed. "Jeff! Chamroeun passed his interview," she said to Jeff over the phone. "Jeff said congratulations. We are so happy for you, Chamroeun. We can't wait to get you over here."

"Thank you! Me too."

"You must be so relieved. Thalen told us that you were really worried, and you were right to be. This was a difficult process, and we are so glad that the embassy let you come."

"Thank you, thank you for all of your help."

"You're welcome. It wasn't all us you know. Your brother-in-law did a lot. You should thank him as well."

"I know. I will."

"Great, well, we're gonna go back to sleep. It's night over here, but congratulations once again."

"Thank you." I handed the phone back, then the three of us got in a tuk-tuk and headed back to the hotel.

"Hey," I said to Thalen over the noisy engine with a big smile, "thank you for your help."

"No problem. I'm glad that you passed." He tapped me on my leg with a big smile. "Your life is going to change."

"What you mean? I'm still going to be the same. I'm still going to be Chamroeun."

"Just trust me. Your life will change when you get to Seattle."

# 11

# THE JOURNEY

I HAD NEVER been on an airplane before, and the thought of being so high up in the sky was terrifying. The travel time from Phnom Penh to Seattle was scheduled to be twenty hours and fifty minutes with a six-hour layover in Taipei. Unfortunately, Thalen and Kesor were not able to travel at the same time. Kesor and Thalen passed their interview two weeks after mine, but Kesor's visa delay was longer than anticipated. Jeff and Wanda wanted me to arrive in Seattle one month before school would start. They felt that it was important that I be settled in and familiar with the new environment.

An inexperienced boy with limited English and no Chinese language skills could easily get lost along the way. My fear caused me to lobby Thalen to change the date.

"Can I wait for you guys buy your ticket, so we all go together?" I asked Thalen.

"No. My parents already bought the ticket for you. Besides, it's really hard to find available seats. You need to go."

"But I never been on airplane before. I'm scared."

"You are going to be fine. Flying is pretty safe. I've flown all over the world without any problem. Don't worry. I'll write down a plan for you, so you'll know exactly what to do."

"Okay, but I'm still worry I get lost."

"Jeff and Wanda told me that they have requested a person to look after you during your trip. That person will help guide you through the entire process."

I was still anxious no matter what he said. There was no changing this. The only thing I could do was pack and spend as much time as possible with my family before leaving.

One evening, I went over to the cement house to see my parents. I sat at the table near Mother, watching Father smoke cigarettes on his bed as he listened to news on the radio. "Two years is a really long time. I'm worried for you," Mother said, swinging a kroma to keep mosquitoes out.

"I'll be okay, Mother. Jeff and Wanda will take good care of me."

"Why can't you stay and keep going to school here? Why do you have to go?"

"I have to go because American schools are better. It was really difficult for me to get the visa. I have to take advantage of this opportunity." Mother looked at me but did not say a word. Maybe she didn't fully understand what it meant to study in the US, or perhaps she didn't believe there was much difference. Mother had received very little education. She'd reached seventh grade, but she had frequently failed classes. Occasionally, teachers let her pass because they were tired of her repeating the same class over and over.

Despite being illiterate, she still pushed me to attend class because she did not want me to end up like her. She knew that I was the only person in the family that might get the chance to finish school. Allowing me to study away from home was a burden that my parents were reluctant, but willing to bear.

The final evening in Oue Bram had arrived. Mother made one of my favorite dishes: sweet and sour fried pork. Despite everyone's enjoyment, it was difficult knowing I would be leaving my family behind.

After dinner, everyone found their own entertainment. Kesor and Thalen went to buy movies at the market. Lab was exercising with her hula hoop near the well while the rest of my family was watching television. Meanwhile, I sat alone in the garden, staring at the stars in the evening blur. It was a clear, peaceful night. A light wind blew through the tree branches surrounding the house. It was almost orchestral.

"What are you doing?" Lab asked, putting her hula hoop down.

"I'm just thinking. Mother is not happy about me going. I don't want her to worry."

"Mother has always been like that. She's always worried whenever someone is away."

"I'm going to miss you guys. I don't want to be away," I cried.

Lab rubbed my back. "Everything is going to be fine, Brother. Don't worry too much."

"Promise me that you will take care of our parents, especially Mother."

"Okay, I promise. But I need you to promise me that you won't disappoint our family. You are the only one left that has the chance to finish school. I don't want you to end up like Ruat and Sokha, messing around with girls, smoking, gambling, and lying. Just don't do stupid things, okay? You need to be smart and do what's right. That is all I want."

"I will do my best."

Lab was always passionate about education, even after dropping out. Growing up, she constantly pushed me, Chai, and Kesor. She ensured that each one of us would be punished if we did not attend school.

I remember one night back in Oue Bei, Chai and Kesor skipped English school so they could go to a friend's birthday party. Lab was so mad, she brought them to a dark alley near the house, away from my parents' sight, and whipped them repeatedly.

While laying on a green hammock underneath the tall stilts, I could hear Chai and Kesor sobbing. "Sister, please . . . I didn't want to miss my friend's birthday," Chai mumbled.

I got up and peeked my head over the cement wall. I saw Kesor and Chai standing in the dark, wiping tears away. Lab stood in front of them, holding a stick.

"Do you think that going to your friend's birthday will benefit you? Do you think that going to parties will help you find a job in the future?" Lab asked.

"It's just one class. Why is it such a big deal?"

Lab stepped closer to Chai and slapped her. I could hear the striking sound of Lab's palm hitting Chai's cheek. Chai covered her face, crying louder. My heart dropped.

"How dare you? Do you know how lucky you are to attend an English school? Why don't you look around and think how many of our neighbor's kids get a chance like you?"

Chai continued to cry.

"I'm sorry, Sister. We won't skip a class again," said Kesor.

This was a cruel beating, but Lab's intention was to help guide us. Lab believed in the value of education just as much as Father. To her, attending an English school could prevent us from working in a Chinese-owned sweatshop. Despite the harshness, I appreciated Lab's passion for school.

The next day, I began my departure for Phnom Penh, I gathered all of my luggage. Thalen suggested I bring a few books to read during the long flight. In addition, he gave me a notebook of instructions for when I entered the airport. He sketched out maps of the airports in Phnom Penh, Taipei, and Seattle. He drew step-by-step instructions for my passage through each airport so I wouldn't get lost.

"Follow my instruction and you'll be fine. I'll go over it with you on the bus." Thalen put the notebook in my luggage.

"Okay," I said. "Who going to Phnom Penh with me?"

"Just your father and I. Kesor doesn't want to go. I asked your mother, but she told me that she wants to look after the house."

"I make sure I say goodbye to her before we leave."

A few minutes later, Ruat rode in to say goodbye and to help take us to the bus station. He was not alone. Chai and Seth arrived shortly after him.

"I'll miss you," said Chai in Khmer, hugging me. "Father tells me that you going for two years. Come visit us when we get to the US."

"Okay, sounds good."

"Chamroeun!" Thalen shouted from a distance. "It's time to go."

I walked inside and gave Mother a warm hug. "Goodbye, Mother. I have to go. I'll be back," I said, eyes watering. I felt sadness well up, but I tried to push it down. The expression on her face made me want to stay. Yet, I was committed to leaving because it was the only opportunity for me to pursue an adequate education.

"Okay, Son. Take care of yourself. Don't forget to call us."

We rented two rooms in a hotel near Riverside in Phnom Penh. We had to spend one night in the city so we could get to the airport on time for my flight in the morning. Thalen wanted Father to taste an American meal so he took us to a restaurant near the Riverside. The area was laden with many Khmer and Western shops. People from all around the city went there to exercise or simply relax and enjoy the great view of Tonle Sap.

After dinner, Father and I stayed in our room. I lay on a wooden bed next to Father as we watched a soccer match on television. Like many Khmer people, my father was a big fan of soccer. He loved watching international teams compete against one another. It was his belief that soccer creates unity and entertainment for all people, regardless of their nationality.

"Does Cambodia have a national soccer team?" I asked.

"We do, but it's not as good as other countries. We only compete against neighboring nations."

"Which country has the best team in the world?"

"I don't know, but I heard people say Brazil is really good. They have a lot of talented players. I also heard that France has a good team as well. But I think there are many better teams out there."

"Does America have a good soccer team?"

"I don't often hear people talk about the American team, so I can't say if they are good. But I can assure you, their team is better than ours."

"But if America doesn't have a very good soccer team, then why did you say America is the best country?"

"That has nothing to do with sports. What makes America great is the freedom their people have. When I listen to the radio podcast, the news often says that America has a law that allows their people to do and say whatever they want no matter who you are. They have more human rights than us. In our country, if you say something bad about the government, you could get arrested and put in jail for a long time." Father looked at me with a serious face. "But America is not perfect. They dropped bombs inside of the northeastern border during the Khmer civil war."

"I never learned about that in school. What happened during the civil war?"

"It was a war fought between two groups. One was the communist party called Khmer Kraham led by Pol Pot. They were fighting against the Khmer Republic led by Lon Nol. The Americans bombed most of the Khmer Republic's army, allowing Khmer Kraham to take over the country."

"But Americans are good people. Why did they do that?"

"People said America was fighting the Youn [Vietnamese], but the war spilled into parts of eastern Cambodia. The bombs killed many Khmers. Despite all of that, I do think America is a good country. They always try to help poor countries like ours. Khmer people like them because they have done many good things. But I'm sure that you will learn more about this when you get there."

"I'm afraid, Father. My English isn't very good. I'm going to have a hard time understanding the teachers. I'm worried that I might not be smart enough to pass the classes. I don't want the teachers to beat me for speaking broken English."

"That's why you need to practice reading and speaking more. The harder you try, the better you'll become. Besides, people will only speak English over there, so your speaking ability will improve."

"Even if I can speak better, reading English is really difficult. There are many new words to learn."

"That's okay. That's why you are going to school, so you can learn more. You are very lucky to have this opportunity. During the Pol Pot era, people would be punished or even killed if they were caught reading a book."

"Then, how did you learn how to read and write?"

"I was in seventh grade before the Khmer Kraham arrived. Back then, schools were better because teachers were more educated. But most schools were destroyed. The Khmer Kraham banned education and forced students to work in the rice fields. Sometimes, I would stay up late, light a candle, and read a book that I had hidden from the soldiers."

"Did you ever get caught?"

"Yes, one time a soldier yelled at me for it. I thought he was going to kill me. Fortunately, he only ripped my book and hit me a few times."

"You never told me much about the Khmer Kraham. Why?"

"Because it is a horrifying story that I don't want to talk about. It was a dark time. It still hurts when I think about it." Father had a distant and sad tone. His face was full of mournfulness. I could not imagine what he had been through. Father was dangerous to a group like theirs, not only because he believed in education, but because of his awareness of what was going on around the world.

We took a tuk-tuk in the morning toward Pochentong Airport, the biggest in the country, also known as Phnom Penh International Airport. It was magical to watch the airplanes accelerate and take off into the blue skies.

The driver parked his vehicle at the lot in front of the main building. I grabbed my luggage and headed for the entrance. There was a crowd of people waiting to say goodbye to their relatives. As we were walking, Thalen handed me his phone.

"Hi Chamroeun!" Wanda spoke. "Are you excited for your trip?"

"Yes, I am very happy come to Seattle."

"Oh good. I wanted to tell you that we are so happy to have you come live with us. I also wanted you to tell your father that we will take good care of you, and we are so glad that they allowed you to come study here."

I told Father what Wanda had said. He smiled.

"When you get there, tell her that I am so thankful for her family giving you an opportunity to study in America. It means a lot to me and our family." I nodded.

"It's almost time. You should head in," said Thalen. "Don't forget to follow the instructions in the notebook I gave you. It is really important to not get lost. Remember, you can always ask an airline employee for help."

I nervously looked at my father, struggling to find proper words to say goodbye. "This is it. I have to go."

"Take care of yourself and be useful. Try to help Jeff and Wanda as much as you can."

"I will Father." I gave him a big hug. Letting me go was a sacrifice that he had to make, so I could gain what he never could. I hugged Thalen too.

"Have a safe trip. I'll see you soon. Don't forget, there will be a person to help guide you along the way."

"Okay, thanks. See you." I walked away.

I went inside the airport to check-in. I received the tickets, one from Phnom Penh to Taipei, and one from Taipei to Seattle. After going through the security process, I didn't see anyone come to help me find the gate. I pulled out Thalen's instructions and tried to follow his sketch of Pochentong Airport. On the first page, he wrote, "step 1: find your gate. Read the signs, they will lead you there."

As I scanned my surroundings, I saw lots of signs. Some were beneath the ceiling with symbols for bathrooms and stairs along with arrows pointing in all directions. Near the bathrooms, I spotted a large rectangular poster showing gate numbers. The arrow was pointing up ahead. About five minutes later, I was able to find my gate. Once there, I saw a large airplane standing tall behind the glass windows. Its wings were spread wide away from the long round body. It was amazing to see an airplane up close.

I sat on a metal chair among a crowd of people of all ages for a half hour until the passenger service agents started the boarding process.

"Hi," I said, then handed my ticket to an agent lady, who had straight black hair and wore a dark green uniform.

"We are boarding first-class passengers, your seat is in the economy section, so you have to wait for a little bit," she said politely in Khmer, then handed me back my ticket.

"Oh, I'm sorry. I didn't know." I stood aside and let the others pass. The lady scanned passenger tickets and kept glancing at me. I tried not to make eye contact. I was embarrassed. Not long after, she announced the economy class, and I slowly got in line once again.

"Is this your first time flying?" she asked while scanning the ticket.

"Yes."

"Are you here with relatives?"

"No, I'm flying alone."

"Wow, you must be brave. Well, good luck."

"Thank you." I grabbed my ticket and went into the skybridge. I could hear the loud jet engines. It felt like the entire structure was shaking as I approached the plane.

When I entered the airplane, a flight attendant guided me toward my seat in the back. Each row had six seats, with a narrow aisle splitting three seats on each side. I found mine right next to the window. Two older men were in my row. I sat down with elevated nerves. I noticed that the two gentlemen had gray seatbelts strapped around their waists. I grabbed my own seatbelt, strapped it together, and bounced nervously in my seat.

Approximately fifteen minutes later, the plane moved away from the gate. As it sped up, the harsh bouncing made it seem like I was in a car. The pilot taxied for a long time before we reached our runway. It stopped for a few seconds, then suddenly the engines roared to life as the plane jolted forward. Within seconds, it had lifted off the ground and headed into the sky.

The plane gently oscillated up and down. I was terrified. My body shook as I grabbed tightly onto the armrests. Looking out the window, I saw the ground far below, with small vehicles moving along the roads. The higher we flew, the more I wanted to scream. My heart raced. My head sweat. It was an overwhelming experience. I was shocked to see how relaxed everyone else seemed. Some people had even shut their eyes and were trying to fall asleep. I tried closing my eyes too, but it didn't help. When the plane leveled off, I peeked through my window out into the vast blue atmosphere. The sun was glowing brightly above thin white clouds, which spread in every direction far beyond what my eyes could see.

It was therapeutic to see such a spectacular view. Even though my mind was still racing, I rested my head against the wall and observed the world below. I saw square green rice fields spreading for miles.

I pulled out Thalen's notebook and tried looking over his plan again, in hopes of being prepared for my arrival in Taipei Airport. Six hours for a layover was a long time. I did not know what I would do while waiting for the next flight.

When we landed in Taiwan International Airport, the plane quickly taxied to the gate. Everyone grabbed their bags from the overhead compartments and stood in line preparing to deplane. Meanwhile, I was stuck in my seat, struggling to pull the seat belt apart. For a moment, I thought it was broken, prompting me to bounce up and down to escape.

"You have to pull the top of the belt to release it," said a Khmer gentleman next to me.

I lifted and it released.

"Thank you." I grinned, feeling embarrassed.

I got up, grabbed my backpack, and scooted toward him and into a tight aisle with all the other passengers waiting for their turn to get out. When our turn came, we exited the skybridge and went our separate ways.

"Good luck the rest of the way," he said, waving at me.

"Thank you. You too." I waved back. The man walked away cutting through a large crowd of people, dragging their luggage in all different directions. I stayed where I was, hoping that the person Thalen's parents requested would show up. I stood near the wall next to the gate for roughly thirty minutes, yet no one came. I eventually realized I had to find the gate on my own.

Taiwan International Airport was gigantic. There were so many shops: Starbucks, Gucci, and more. I was awestruck by everything around me. An incredible number of television screens were mounted to the walls, showing all kinds of commercial products. I was completely distracted by how modern the Taipei Airport was. Seeing so many new items made me want to keep exploring the whole complex. Nevertheless, I had to stick to Thalen's notes and not go too far. I knew in this size airport, getting lost could result in missing my flight.

I looked at the instructions. By now, I was no longer able to find any posters showing directions toward the gates. I was worried that I was already lost. I made the choice to start following people walking with luggage even without knowing their destinations. I spotted a lady I had noticed on my previous flight heading in the opposite direction. I turned around and tracked her from a distance. I felt weird following a random person, but getting to the gate was more important. The lady glanced back a few times glaring at me, but didn't say anything. She might have thought I looked suspicious because of my light orange hair that Thalen had highlighted. He wanted me to try something new.

I walked slower, keeping my distance. The worst part was waiting for her outside of a women's restroom. It was an awkward and dubious plan, but I was convinced that she could lead me to the gate. However, after the lady came out, she went back in the same direction we came from. I laughed at myself after realizing that she was just going to the bathroom. Not wanting to take anymore risks, I went up to a lady who looked like an airline employee. She was wearing a tight blue skirt and jacket and holding a walkie-talkie.

"Excuse me," I said in English with my hand waving to get her attention. "I don't know my gate. Can you help me?"

"Sure. Do you have your ticket with you?"

"Yes, I do." I unzipped my backpack then handed her the ticket.

"Oh, your flight won't leave for another four hours. You have a lot of time. Are you hungry? I can take you to the food area so you can eat before you get on your flight."

"Yes, I'm hungry."

"Good. Follow me. I will take you there." The lady took me to an escalator leading to a second floor. Since it was my first time riding one, I held on tightly to the handrail hoping that I wouldn't fall backwards. "So, where are you from?"

"I'm from Cambodia."

"Nice. I heard a lot of good things. I have friends who've visited Angkor Wat."

"Oh, cool. Have you go there?"

"No, I don't travel that much. But I do want to visit one day. Right now, I'm just too busy." Upon reaching the second floor, we were surrounded by many restaurants. "I'll leave you here for now. I'll come back to get you soon."

"Okay, thank you."

I went into a restaurant with a food buffet. Coming from a third-world country, I had never seen anything like this. I was fascinated that anyone could grab whatever food they wanted around the room. This strange setup convinced me that the food was free. I picked up a paper plate and loaded it with white rice and roasted chicken. I then walked out to a seating area. To my left, I saw the cashier looking in shock after noticing I didn't pay. Yet, he didn't say anything and let me walk away. It was not my intention to steal food. In fact, Thalen had given me money for snacks.

At thirteen years old, and in an airport for the first time, I simply had no idea of what was going on. It was only in reflecting years later that I came to realize I had stolen my lunch.

About an hour later, the lady had not shown up. I was super nervous about missing my flight and thought she had forgotten about me. After being in the airport for three and a half hours, I was still nowhere near my gate. My worrisome nature forced me to leave the food court and continue to walk around, searching for signs. Soon, I was able to spot a middle-aged man, wearing an airline uniform standing behind a counter. Fortunately, he was available to take me to my gate.

There, I sat on the metal chair in the waiting area, trying to relax before getting on an airplane once again. I looked around the room and saw many people were falling asleep during the late-night layover. Our boarding time was almost midnight.

I was exhausted but there was no way I was going to fall asleep and miss my flight. I opened a magazine and tried to look at images to keep myself entertained. It didn't work. I gently slapped my own face multiple times to prevent myself from falling asleep. A woman was laughing at me a short distance away, probably thinking I was crazy. I continued to sit there and gently shook my head from side to side. Soon enough, people got up, collected their bags, and prepared to board. This was it. I really was heading to the US. I stood in line with happy thoughts racing through my head. I could not wait to see Seattle.

The flight from Taipei to Seattle was much longer, almost twelve hours. The airline used an even larger plane with many more passengers than the previous one. There were two aisles, dividing three sections of seats. The sides had three seats, whereas the middle had five. My seat was much more comfortable due to a thicker cushion. In addition, there was a small square touch screen television attached in the back of each seat. I was amazed to see something so technologically advanced. I pressed random buttons trying to figure out how it operated. After a short period, I was able to stream movies for free. I put on a set of headphones and watched movie after movie alone in the dark, while the people around me slept.

The most intriguing element of the seat-back TV was a satellite image of the airplane flying over the vastness of the Pacific Ocean. The plane was in the middle of nowhere. I zoomed out to see nations all around the globe. The massive landscapes of countries I had hardly even heard of were sprawled across the screen. Some were covered with lights, others shown in pitch black. I looked at Cambodia and saw it was mostly covered in darkness. I was not surprised. I knew Cambodia was a poor country. But it was sad to see the number of lights glowing in our neighboring countries. I knew that Cambodia could be like those nations if the Khmer Rouge had not existed.

Hours later, the pilot made a landing announcement. Everyone buckled their seat belts as the plane began its decent. Outside the windows, I now saw houses and roads full of cars. The pilot flew low above the highway; soon enough, the plane touched down on the runway. I saw tall trees across a green landscape. I was relieved that I had made it safely. It was an even better feeling to realize that I had landed in the "most powerful nation on earth."

After getting off the plane, I continued to follow other passengers that had passed security. I knew those people were going to the same place I was; the place where Thalen told me to pick up the luggage and meet Jeff and Wanda. I got on an underground rail-tram along with many other passengers. About five minutes later, there we were in the baggage area. Bags came out onto a slide and fell onto a large oval track that went around in circles. I waited there for ten minutes, but I didn't see Jeff or Wanda. I picked up my bag and went searching for them. Thalen's notes ended with "meet Jeff and Wanda at the luggage area." I kept on walking and hoping I would see them. Suddenly, I heard a female voice calling my name from a distance.

"Chamroeun! Chamroeun!" I turned around and saw Stella waving as she raced over to me. She pulled out her phone to call Jeff and Wanda. "I found him! I found him!" I then saw Jeff and Wanda walking briskly from a distance.

"Hey sweetie pie! How are you?" Wanda said as she gave me a hug. Jeff gently tapped me on my shoulder, smiling. He wore glasses and his hair was turning gray. He seemed older than the last time we met.

I looked at them with elation. "I'm fine. I'm happy to be here." This was one of the happiest moments in my life.

# 12

# A NEW WORLD

THE FIRST THING I noticed were the many ethnicities together in one place. Caucasians, Asians, Africans, Hispanics, and Arabs were walking through the airport. I was blown away to see such diversity. I remembered that Thalen had told me there were all kinds of people living in the US. "American" did not refer only to white people, but to people with all different skin colors. Anyone could be American if born in the US. Or, as long as they passed the test to become a citizen.

We walked through the busy baggage claim area toward the exit door and crossed a short skybridge with glass walls which led from the terminal to a large parking structure. When we stepped off of the skybridge, I immediately felt the cold air hit me and started shivering. It was summer in Seattle, but it felt much cooler than a rainy day in Cambodia.

Jeff's car was a large white Cadillac Sport Utility Vehicle. He helped me open the passenger door carefully to make sure it didn't hit the vehicle next to it. I climbed in and sat next to Stella in the middle row. Jeff slowly drove through the parking garage toward the exit. The exit ramp spiraled downhill, looping round and round. Meanwhile, I was sliding all over the place. I had forgotten to put on my seat belt. Most cars in Cambodia did not even have them. I partially fell from my seat, sliding toward Stella.

"Put your seat belt on!" said Stella taking my arm.

"Stella, can you help him with that?" Wanda asked, turning to me. I quickly pulled the seatbelt strap, then buckled it across my body. "Chamroeun, everyone has to wear a seatbelt in Washington State. It's required by law."

The freeway turned, and we had an astonishing view of downtown Seattle. I leaned to my right and through the windshield I saw curving overpasses intertwined with exit and on-ramps. Ahead, there were tall towers reaching to the sky. Bright lights were glowing from each building. Large stadiums dotted the southern skyline, each covered in blue and green lights. It was an overwhelming scene. I was astounded by my first look at a truly advanced city. To my left, I could see the port as a ferry slowly moved away from its terminal. I was in a new world.

"Welcome to Seattle, Chamroeun!" said Wanda with a big smile. "Look at those buildings! They are huge!"

I was enthralled with the incredible view. Although I had seen pictures on Jeff's laptop, I was still in disbelief. I ducked down to try to get a better angle of the top of the buildings. One of them was so tall, I only saw the bottom half. Within minutes, we had passed the skyscrapers and continued north. We passed the Space Needle. My jaw dropped. What was once a small image was now reality. Its pointed roof stood high in the air, accented by colorful lights shining against the early evening sky. It was magical. It looked exactly like the picture Jeff had shown me, like a giant white mushroom growing at the edge of the city. I could not wait to visit it. I stared at it until we drove out of sight.

Ten minutes later, Jeff exited the freeway. We had reached a suburb with wooden houses built directly on the ground. Some homes were surrounded by fences along the side of the roads. Stop lights were installed at almost every intersection. Drivers stopped when the lights turned red. People were obeying the law. Later, we reached streets that had red octagonal stop signs on white metal posts. Soon, we entered an area with many trees lining the sides of the road.

"Are we almost there?" I asked Stella in Khmer.

"We are about five minutes away. They live in an area surrounded by trees. It's like a jungle." Soon, Jeff slowly turned down a long gravel driveway. The area was surrounded by tall pine trees. We went around a curve and I saw Drew and Blake standing near a white Subaru sedan, waiting to greet us. They were wearing gym outfits: shorts and t-shirts.

"Hi Chamroeun!" said Drew, smiling after seeing me getting out.

"Hi Drew! Hi Blake!" They each gave me a hug.

"Good to see you. How was your flight?" Blake asked, grinning.

"It fine."

"Nice. Glad to hear it."

"Let's go inside and check out your room," said Drew with my large suitcase in tow.

We walked up the path toward a very large craftsman home built out of wood and stone. Flowers and short green grass grew in a half circle drive near the front door. Next to that, there was a small pond with lily pads floating on a surface of clear water. In addition, there was a gray swing and a silver barbecue grill on the opposite side of the house. We went through the side door, entering into a laundry room with a white tile floor. There was a refrigerator, a washer and dryer, and exercise equipment. We then entered a TV room with a brown leather couch and a black flat-screen television mounted to the wall. A strong smell of wood polish and leather kicked in, making me nauseous. The interior of the room had wood paneling and there was plenty of furniture. To the right was a kitchen with a white countertop and cabinets, another refrigerator, and a sink in front of a window overlooking the front of the house.

Jeff and Wanda's house was huge. It contained five bedrooms, three bathrooms, an office, two dining rooms, and a spacious living room with a blue leather couch and a piano. It also had a massive recreation room in the basement. Every room was painted white and accented with family photos and artwork. The wood often creaked as we walked through. We ascended a staircase that curved around a chandelier hanging from the ceiling.

"Here's your room!" said Drew after opening the door at the top of the stairs. I went inside and was astounded to see how big it was, almost the same size as the wooden house in Oue Bram. The smell of wood polish was getting stronger, making it a little difficult to breathe. I was overwhelmed as I took in my new living space. A full-size bed was made up with a few pillows. Behind it, light shone through a window with shades slightly drawn. To the left, there was a black television sitting on an oak dresser in front of a small closet. To the right, there was a computer resting on a matching desk with a black office chair. There was also a red lounge chair near the door.

I had never had my own room before. Growing up, I had to sleep near my siblings. We even had to share blankets while lying on a grass mat.

As I absorbed my new accommodations, Drew tapped me on my shoulder. "How do you like your room?" he asked.

"It really nice. I like it."

"This used to be Thalen's room. Jeff and I tried our best to prepare it for you," said Wanda.

"Thank you so much."

"Sure. The upstairs bathroom is not ready yet. Jeff and I still need to work on it. You can use our bathroom downstairs for the time being."

"Okay, I do that."

"Great. Well, I'm glad you like it," said Drew. "Blake and I are gonna take off now. It's getting late. But good to see you, Chamroeun. I'll come by again tomorrow."

I wished I could talk to Drew and Blake more. I remember being around them at Kesor's wedding. Drew had a great sense of humor. I often saw him laughing as he was speaking with his family. I even saw him trying to blend in with the Khmer culture as he practiced the Romvong dance with villagers. Blake was more serious, however. He was quiet and intimidating; I never saw him talk to any Khmer at the wedding. Nonetheless, it was really nice of them to come see me, especially on my first evening in Seattle.

"Are you hungry?" asked Wanda. "There's some leftover curry that Stella's boyfriend, Bob, made earlier."

"Sure. Can I take shower first?"

"Yes, of course. I'll get you a towel."

In America, houses have water pipelines connected in a sophisticated system that makes it much easier to access consistently clean water. Back home, I had to use well water with a ladle and a bucket. I would crouch and wash myself with a rag and soap.

After the shower, I put on a pair of shorts and a t-shirt. I went downstairs where Wanda helped me microwave a bowl of curry and white rice.

She put it on a placemat atop a rectangular coffee table in the living room. I sat on the comfortable brown leather couch. Stella was sitting nearby watching a Hollywood movie on the large flat screen TV.

While eating, she kept changing the TV channel and eventually found an action film, *Ironman*, and left it on a short while.

"Okay, I think I'm gonna go to bed. You can change the channel and watch whatever you want."

"How can I turn off?"

"Oh, just press the top red button on the controller." Stella pointed to the button on the remote. "Just turn it off when you're done watching. Good night!"

"Okay, good night!"

It was eleven thirty at night, but I was wide awake. Nighttime in Seattle meant daytime in Kompong Som. I continued to watch the movie until early morning. Then, I washed my dish and headed to bed. I lay underneath a warm blanket on a soft latex mattress with a comfortable pillow. My body was exhausted from the long trip, but jet lag kept me awake until at least four in the morning. I lay there replaying the spectacular sights of the city. Finally, my eyes grew heavy and I fell asleep.

A few hours later, Jeff woke me up, telling me that we were going to an island, Decatur, located far away. I packed my warm clothes: jeans, shorts, t-shirts, and my only sweatshirt, and squeezed them all into my backpack. I went downstairs and asked Wanda if there was time to explore the surrounding area before we left. She gave me Drew's old jacket. It was a winter coat that had a front zipper and side pockets. It fit perfectly. It was the nicest coat I had ever put on.

I walked down a set of cement stairs near the garage and stepped out into a wide-open lawn surrounded by large pine, cedar, and poplar trees. Jeff and Wanda's property was massive: about four acres in total. Their house was built in the middle of the lot on a hill. I could barely see any of the neighboring homes. Down below the house, the vast empty land was covered with short recently mowed grass. While walking, I saw squirrels climbing on tree branches near the garage. Birds flew around under the clear blue sky. I saw one land on top of a neighbor's roof. My nose tingled as I inhaled the cold morning air. It was so nice to see and experience a clean, natural environment. Not long after exploring the lower yard, I saw Drew's white car heading down the driveway. He came by and asked if he could take me for a drive in Wanda's car.

Drew opened the garage door and right away, I saw a small white sports car with a black canopy roof parked next to another small red car. Drew climbed inside the white one and started the engine. The throaty rumble of the exhaust was powerful even as Drew was backing up. Suddenly, the roof opened then folded itself in the back behind the two black leather seats. I stood nearby, a little giddy with excitement.

"Get in!" he said. I quickly opened the door and sat down.

"What car is this?"

"It's a Porsche Boxster!" He put it in first gear and accelerated up the gravel driveway. Drew drove fast as soon as we hit the smooth asphalt road. The engine roared whenever he pressed on the gas.

"I like this car! It's really fast!" he said over the noise of the breeze. Drew, at six foot three inches tall, had his head sticking up over the top of the windshield. The wind had his hair blowing in all directions as he drove.

Later, we arrived at an empty parking lot in front of a sprawling building complex. "Come on, let's go inside."

"Where are we?" I asked.

"We're at your school, St. Luke. Let's go check it out."

I had not even seen a picture of St. Luke. The buildings looked like a home, with flowers growing near the entrance doors. Drew and I went inside and down a hallway decorated with posters. We turned down another hallway and walked by a classroom with an open door. I saw a thin, middle-aged teacher decorating her room.

"Hello! I'm Drew. This is Chamroeun. He's from Cambodia. He will be attending this school in the fall," Drew spoke politely as we entered the classroom.

"Oh hi! I'm Ms. Sherman. Nice to meet you!" She had a big pleasant smile and shook our hands. She seemed relaxed and spoke with a soft voice. Her hair was tied back, and she wore small earrings. "What grade will he be in?"

"Seventh grade. My parents considered putting him in eighth grade, but they thought it might be a little too difficult for him to handle."

"Oh good! I'm actually an English teacher for seventh graders. So, I will have him in my class. How long has he been here?"

"He just arrived yesterday, actually."

"Oh, wow! Welcome to America!" She smiled. "How do you like it so far?"

"It's great. I really like it, but it's cold." I said slowly, trying to make sure she would understand.

"Cold? It's summer. It's hot out there!" Her eyes narrowed in confusion.

Drew chuckled. "It's much hotter in Cambodia. He's not used to the cooler temperature here. That's why he's wearing a jacket."

"I can see that. I was gonna ask about the coat. So, how do you know each other?"

"Chamroeun is my brother's brother-in-law. He's a good student, so my parents sponsored him to come here to study." Ms. Sherman looked at me with a genuine dimpled smile after hearing Drew's compliment. I remained silent.

"That's great. So, he will be here for seventh and eighth grade then?"

"Yes. That's the plan."

"Super! That's so nice of your parents."

"Thank you! Well, we just wanted to come by and look around so he would be more familiar with the school. It's nice to meet you, and sorry if we distracted you from your work."

"Yeah, likewise! Don't even worry about it. I was just putting a few posters on the wall."

"Okay, thanks for your time, Ms. Sherman!"

"No problem. Take care." She turned to me. "And I'll see you when school starts."

I had never seen a teacher as friendly as Ms. Sherman. She had a positive attitude and talked in a charming tone. Most importantly, she made me feel comfortable in this new school, despite knowing nothing about it. I was glad to know that she was going to be one of my teachers.

When we got home, Jeff was still loading supplies. I saw tennis rackets, coolers, and luggage in the back of his SUV.

"Do you need help?" I asked while getting out of the Porsche.

"No, but you should go get ready though. We're leaving shortly."

I went up to my room and grabbed my backpack. I came downstairs and sat on the couch to wait for Jeff and Wanda. I saw Jeff in the dining room, trying to catch his cat named Truman, who had brown fur. It was laying underneath the piano. He kept calling the cat's name until it came out.

I was amazed to see how gently Jeff treated his cat. Some people in Cambodia even ate dogs and cats. Dog meat was expensive. A normal size dog could cost between five and ten dollars. The demand for dog meat was high and dogs were sometimes stolen from peoples' homes at night.

Soon, it was time for departure. We all climbed in the car, and I quickly buckled my seat belt. Jeff drove carefully up the driveway and onto the main road with the boat in tow. Meanwhile, I was fading. It was now past midnight in Kompong Som. I rested my head against the car door and my mind drifted off as I fell asleep.

I heard a knock on the glass window. I opened my eyes.

"Sorry to wake you, but I need your help moving everything from the cart and into the back," Jeff said after opening the car door.

"Yes, sure." I got out and started moving groceries from a cart into the back of the car. They had bought plenty of food: fruit, vegetables, cereal, meat, and even muffins.

"That's lot of food," I said.

"Yeah, we got a lot," said Jeff. "People don't go to the market every day here in the States. Everyone has fridges to store their food, so it lasts for a long time."

There was so much food that we ended up putting some on the back seat.

After we'd gotten to Washington Park, and the boat was in the water, Jeff started up the engine, and we pulled away from the dock. The loud engine screamed, and the small boat blasted a long jet of water behind us, creating a rooster tail of white bubbles.

There were many islands around us and it was difficult to distinguish one island from another because they were all rocky and covered with tall evergreen trees. The entire region had been carved out of bedrock by glaciers in the last ice age. The San Juan Islands are the areas that the glaciers spared, which did not end up as gravel in the Southern Puget Sound.

Roughly fifteen minutes after leaving Washington Park, we came into view of Decatur Island. We pulled into a bay where cabins were built near the water's edge. Jeff pulled the boat up to a long dock with a tall flagpole. A light breeze caused the American flag to gently flutter. Seagulls squealed as they grazed near the shallow beach. Up above the island, a Bald Eagle soared across the bright sunny sky.

Jeff tied the boat, and I helped them unload. We were staying in a wooden cabin near the shore.

"This place is one of the San Juan Islands, Chamroeun," said Jeff, pointing at a map hanging on the wall. The map was peppered with islands and stylized with buildings, sailboats, cargo ships, and whales. "There are many islands in the area. I can show you around tomorrow."

The San Juan Islands are about halfway between Vancouver, Canada, and Seattle. The map made it look like a fabulous place, so I was excited to see more.

The next day, we got on the boat and cruised around the San Juan Islands. Jeff directed the boat into an area near an island so Wanda could lower her fishing line into the deep sea.

"Wow! Did you guys hear that?" Wanda asked.

"No, did you catch something? What is it?" said Jeff.

"Over there!" She pointed to an open sea. Within seconds, another splash appeared. This one was much louder, and we all heard it.

"Jeff, I think it's a whale!" she shouted. "Look, I can see its tail."

I looked in the direction she pointed. Water was shooting up, but I didn't understand what was happening. Jeff started the engine and headed closer to the location of the last splash. I saw several black and white whales swimming together. They dove up and down and sprayed water in the air. I was in disbelief. I had never seen anything like this. Growing up, I had occasionally seen marine life on television. Mother often asked me to put on programs about animals. She loved watching wildlife. This, however, was much more entertaining. I was not alone in my awe. Jeff was moving around the back of the boat trying to take pictures. He snapped multiple shots as the whales moved farther and farther away.

"Those are called Orcas, Chamroeun," Wanda said in an excited tone. "They are huge. Even bigger than this boat."

I didn't know that there were names given for certain types of whales. "Trei Balen," meaning whale, was the only name that I heard Khmer people use.

"Can you get us closer to them?" Wanda continued.

"I can, but I don't think we should get too close." Jeff followed the whales staying at what he deemed a reasonable distance. He knew it could be dangerous to harass them. A whale could easily sink our boat.

A crowd of boats soon appeared as people got word that a pod of Orcas was playing nearby. Some were cautious, accelerating away if the whales looked to be getting near them. Others were driving their boats awfully close and, eventually, following them all the way to the shipping lanes. Coming in close contact with Orca whales was a pleasant surprise not just for me, but for Jeff and Wanda, and apparently a ton of other boaters.

This was not, however, the only fascinating thing I was to see in the San Juan Islands. When we returned to Decatur, Jeff spotted a strange looking ship anchored in the bay. It was painted white and gold and sported massive sails. It almost looked like a pirate ship from the movies.

"This ship is called Lady Washington. It's a really famous ship," said Jeff while guiding the boat closer.

"I think I see it in movie before," I replied.

"Yeah, I think you're right. It looks like it's from Pirates of the Caribbean," said Wanda from the passenger seat.

Two days later, Drew and Blake arrived. We went fishing as a group. Drew and Blake stood in the back casting and reeling the fishing line. After one hour, they didn't catch anything besides seaweed and small dogfish (little sharks) that they didn't want to keep. Even worse, their lures frequently got stuck on the bottom of the sea floor. Drew was so frustrated. He kept on pulling the line, yet never seemed able to get it free.

The current brought in a lot of seaweed as we continued to fish. The boat's impeller clogged, but Drew used a small rake to clear the intake. He lowered most of his upper body into the freezing water to do so, dragging the debris from below the boat. Blake and I held his feet to make sure he wouldn't fall. He successfully removed all the seaweed, after which Jeff restarted the engine.

"I'm cold, Mom," Drew said with his hair and shoulders dripping wet. Wanda wrapped a blanket around his body and snuggled next to him to warm him. Looking at them made me homesick. It brought up the memory of my mother hugging me as we were leaving Prey Veng. I felt pained being away from her. This was going to be a tough commitment, but I had to make it through to search for a brighter future.

Later that evening, I stood on the beach alone. Using a wooden stick, I tried to hit small rocks. I kept hitting until dark. It was a quiet evening, and the water was calm. I could see the clear reflection of a crescent moon on the nearly imperceptible ripples. The temperature dropped quickly as the sun faded away.

"Chamroeun!" Wanda shouted from inside the cabin. "Thalen is on the phone. He wants to talk to you."

"Okay, I'm coming." I ran straight toward her. "Hello?" I said, breathing heavily into the phone.

"Hey, what's up? How are you?"

"I'm fine. How about you?" I sat on a chair outside.

"I'm okay, just getting ready to leave Cambodia. How do you like Decatur?"

"It's really nice. I like it a lot." Wanda brought out a chair and a blanket and handed them to me. "Thank you." I wrapped the blanket around my body.

"Decatur is a pretty place. My family goes there every summer. Wanda told me that you caught a fish. Was it big?"

"Yes, it's really big. Bigger than fish at the market."

He laughed. "I don't know about that. There are a lot of big fish sold at the market. But good. Sounds like you're having fun."

"How is everyone at home?"

"Everybody is doing well. Kesor and I took your family out to dinner last night. They had a good time."

"Okay, how my parents?"

"They're doing fine. Your father is actually right next to me. Do you want to talk to him?"

"Yes, sure." I then heard Thalen speaking Khmer to my father while handing him the phone.

"Hello?" said Father with a joyful tone.

"Hi, Father. How are you?" I said in Khmer.

"I'm good. How do you like America?"

"It's great. There are many cars on the road. I don't see any motorbikes. I saw tall buildings that are so high in the sky. Everything here is incredible."

"Really? Wow, that is really something. I wish I could get to see all of those things too. So, how are Jeff and Wanda doing?"

"They are doing well. We came to an island a couple days ago. Blake and Drew are here as well."

"Nice. Well tell them I say hi."

"Okay, I will."

"Great. Well good to hear from you. Take care of yourself and work hard in school."

"Yes, I will, Father. Tell Mother I say hi, too."

"All right, I will. Here's Thalen."

"Hey, so Kesor and I will be there in a couple of days, so I'll see you soon."

"Good. I'm happy you are coming. I want to live with you and Kesor."

"Do you not enjoy living with my parents?"

"I do, but I know you better than them. I don't even know they like me."

Thalen chuckled. "Of course, they do. They just sponsored you to study there. Don't worry too much. My parents are happy to have you living with them. Anyway, I have to go, but let me talk to Wanda real quick."

I went inside and handed her the phone. I heard them talking about me. Suddenly, I heard Wanda look up with a smile.

"Yes, of course, we love Chamroeun!" she said then approached me and gave me a warm hug.

It was a comforting feeling. Jeff and Wanda had been friendly, but I didn't know what to expect living with an unrelated family. I was relieved to know that she enjoyed having me around. Nonetheless, I was really looking forward to seeing Thalen and Kesor. I could not wait to continue this wonderful journey with them.

# 13

# THE UGLY TRUTH

THALEN AND KESOR arrived in Seattle just one week after me. We talked the entire drive home from the airport. Just like me, Kesor was astonished as she absorbed our new environment. She kept on staring out the window, looking at the vehicles on the freeway and the amazing architecture around us.

"Welcome to Seattle!" I said to Kesor, trying to copy what Wanda had said to me one week earlier. Kesor looked at me with a genuine smile.

"Are you guys hungry?" Wanda asked. "Do you want us to stop anywhere on the way?"

"Yes! I was going to ask if you could stop at Dick's so I can get some burgers. I haven't eaten real hamburgers in forever." Thalen looked at me and Kesor with a small laugh. "Sorry but the food over here is just better."

For the first time, I found myself in complete disagreement with Thalen. I did not feel that American food was tastier than Khmer food. Most of the meals I had eaten in Seattle had a strange flavor. They made it hard for me to swallow and didn't sit well in my stomach.

Jeff exited the freeway and drove to Dick's Drive-In. The place was packed full of cars that Jeff had to wait for a big enough spot to park his SUV.

Thalen got one white bag filled with several burgers. He hastily devoured them, taking large bites and chewing quickly. His joy was palpable. It looked like he had never eaten something so delicious before.

When we were in Kompong Som, Thalen often went to gas stations or western restaurants and ordered western meals: pizza, hamburgers, and hotdogs. He always complained about the quality of the food, especially the hamburgers. He said Cambodian beef was too chewy. He was right. Back in Cambodia, Mother often sliced beef in thin layers for salad, making it easier to chew. Whenever she made beef soup, she cooked for a really long time to soften the meat. Trying to grind my teeth on it made my jaw tired. Occasionally, I just swallowed the meat instead. Although Cambodian beef was tough, my family was always excited to eat it.

Since we were new to America, there were many places to explore. Thalen and his parents took me and Kesor to downtown Seattle the following morning. We went inside a gray tower called the "Jackson Federal Building." Jeff hoped to meet with a person named Maria, who had helped Kesor with her visa application.

Listening to their conversation, I began to realize how significant Maria was to Kesor's journey. Her visa application had been more difficult than everyone expected. Processing of the paperwork was repeatedly delayed. Fortunately, Maria was able to help by providing alternative solutions regarding how to complete the paperwork. She was an assistant to the Washington State senator Patty Murray and had plenty of experience with immigrant visa problems. Maria contacted the immigration agency in California to help speed up Kesor's application. This ultimately allowed Thalen and Kesor to arrange an interview.

We later learned that if Kesor had received her visa before me, it would have been more difficult, or even impossible, for me to pass my interview. Furthermore, if Chai had gotten her visa too, it would've eliminated the possibility of overcoming section 214(b) of the Immigration and Nationality Act, which states that nonimmigrant visa applicants must show that they were not intending to immigrate. Having two siblings already applying for immigrant visas would look suspicious. The US Embassy would assume my intention was to stay if I had two sisters living in the US, both of whom would likely become American citizens. Denying my visa would have been an easy decision at that point, regardless of what I had to say. Luckily, my appointment was scheduled before Kesor and Chai. Otherwise, I would likely never have received this opportunity.

Apparently, unbeknownst to me at the time, no one had thought I would pass my interview anyway. The most optimistic immigration attorney, who had experience helping Khmer immigrants to America, suggested I might have a "slim chance." All other professionals and lawyers that Jeff and Wanda had contacted said I could not possibly pass for two main reasons. First, they said I could not overcome the 214(b). Specifically, it would be "impossible" for me to convince the US Embassy that I would return home, and it would be assumed that my intention was to stay in America forever. The promise of returning home to help others was in my eyes the only hope to earn this opportunity. Second, my family was poor and thus unable to pay for my tuition. Despite the risky path, Jeff and Wanda's actions demonstrated that the truth can prevail. I really was "one lucky kid."

The next morning, we went to Jeff and Wanda's store in Seattle. When we arrived, I saw a large building with red writing, "Bedrooms & More" on two sides. Jeff and Wanda were entrepreneurs and had started their business in 1972. Since then, their company had grown.

Wanda took us in for a tour. The place was well decorated. There was artwork on the walls including above many of the beds. One room had pictures of Thalen and Kesor in a rubber tree plantation in Cambodia.

Wanda kept showing us more of the store. She even offered Thalen and Kesor jobs. "Do you want to work here, Oun?" Thalen asked. "Oun" meant babe.

"Sure, I work here!" said Kesor.

"Great." Wanda turned to me. "And you mister, your job is to do well in school."

"Yes, I know."

Thalen and Kesor began working at Bedrooms & More. In addition, they bought a new white Toyota Corolla for transportation. I went to visit Drew at the warehouse. Being at the store was boring because there was not much for me to do besides getting out of the way of customers. It was much more enjoyable at the warehouse. We watched funny videos on his computer. We even played basketball with some of the warehouse crew.

Jeff and Wanda left town on a Sunday morning for Wanda's tennis tournament. They were going to be gone for two days. Thalen had to work that day. Kesor and I decided to stay home to do laundry and organize our rooms. Kesor also wanted to make Khmer food for dinner so we could all enjoy it together. It was a special day because according to Thalen, Seattle's football team, the Seahawks, were playing their first preseason game. While cleaning my room, I even wore an old Seahawks jersey that Jeff had found for me.

When evening arrived, Kesor made red curry with white rice. We sat in the television room waiting for Thalen to get home. The food looked perfect, and the smell of the spices made me so hungry. I could not wait to eat.

"Can I eat it? I'm hungry," I said in English, always trying to improve my speaking ability.

"No Chamroeun. Thalen be home soon."

"When he be home? It's already six o'clock."

"Let me call him." Kesor got up and grabbed her phone. Jeff had given all of us new iPhones a few days ago so we could reach each other. "He's not answering." She attempted several times, but the call went straight to his voicemail. "He probably busy at work. He call me back."

"He told me he return for the game. But they already playing and he's not even here."

"I don't care!" She snapped. "We have to wait for him."

I was frustrated, yet I had no choice but to obey Kesor's order. My stomach rumbled as we continued to sit on the couch quietly watching the football game. I saw players running around while carrying the ball. Each athlete was wearing all manner of equipment: helmet, shoulder pads, and padded pants. In spite of all the protection, some players were still injured. I was entertained, but wished that Thalen were there to explain the rules. We waited for another hour, but there was no sign of him.

"It's seven o'clock now and he not calling you back. Can I eat? I'm hungry."

"Go ahead. Eat. I save some for him." Kesor rolled her eyes.

I scooped some lukewarm curry onto my rice plate and started shoveling down the food. Kesor picked up her spoon and ate slowly with me. I felt terrible for her. She kept checking her phone.

"Don't worry. Maybe he at Drew and Blake house watching the game with them."

"Maybe. I can call Drew." She picked up her phone. "Hey Drew. What's up?" She walked away from the loud sound of the television. She talked to him for a long time. Kesor then sat down on the couch, staring at the plate in silence.

"Is Thalen there?"

"No, he's not there. I don't know where he is." She grabbed her phone. "Make sure you put food away when you done."

Kesor stared at the carpet in silence for a few minutes then got up and headed to her room. At that moment, I was getting nervous. After putting the food away, I went upstairs to my room. I sat on my bed looking at the driveway through the window. I visualized Thalen parking his car in front of the garage. I imagined asking him questions. *Are you okay? Where have you been? Why did you not come home and watch the game with us? Why did you lie to me?* The more I thought about it, the more concerned I became. I continued to sit in my room waiting for Thalen to show up. By eight thirty in the evening, there was still no sign of him. I decided to call Jeff. The phone rang for a long time, but I kept calm. I knew that Jeff normally went to bed early. After a few more seconds, Jeff finally picked up.

"Hi Chamroeun. What's going on?" Jeff asked, groggily.

"Hi Jeff. I'm sorry to call late but you know where Thalen is?"

"No. What's wrong?"

"He went to work in the morning but never come home. Kesor talk to Drew but he's not at Drew house. I'm worried about him. Is he at work?"

"I don't know. I doubt he's at work. The store is normally closed at this hour. Have you called him?"

"Yes. Kesor call him many time, but he not answer the phone."

"Okay." Jeff had a short pause. "Let me talk to Drew and I'll call you right back." I hung up and sat quietly. My hands shook gently. About five minutes later, Jeff called back.

"Hi Chamroeun. I talked to Drew, and he is going to spend the night at our house. But for the time being, make sure all the doors are locked, and stay in your room."

"Jeff, is Thalen okay?"

"I don't know. I tried to call him, but he did not answer me either."

I took a deep breath. My heart was pounding like it was about to jump out of my chest.

"How are you doing?" Jeff continued.

"I'm worry about Thalen. I want to know he okay."

"Don't worry, Chamroeun. I'm sure he's fine. Thalen is an adult, and he can take care of himself. I'm sure he will return home eventually. But you should go to bed. It's getting late. Drew will be there soon."

"But why Thalen not coming home? Is he staying somewhere for tonight?"

"I don't know. I'll come back tomorrow. Everything is going to be fine."

I lay on my bed and tried to calm myself down. I knew that Thalen was a smart man and could overcome any obstacle. He had plenty of experience traveling, and wherever he was, I knew he would find a way to come home.

A couple of hours later, I heard car tires on the gravel driveway. I quickly got out of bed hoping that it was Thalen. I looked out of the window and saw Drew and Blake getting out of the car. I went back to bed with disappointment. I closed my eyes and kept telling myself that Thalen would return soon.

Early in the morning, I woke up, quickly got out of bed, and went straight to Thalen and Kesor's room across the hall. The door was not fully shut. I could hear voices chatting from behind. I entered the room and saw Thalen lying in bed talking to Kesor. I was relieved to see that he was okay, but was also angry at him for making us worry.

"Where you go last night?" I asked firmly.

"I don't know, man. Can I talk to you about it later?" He stared at the ceiling.

"Why not tell me now? I want to know. You said you come watch the Seahawks with me. Where were you? Why didn't you come home?"

He looked at me with shame on his face. His eyes were bright red as if he had not slept all night.

"Chamroeun, let him rest. We can talk about it later," said Kesor.

I walked away, frustrated. I was hoping to get an explanation from Thalen. I knew he had done something terribly wrong, and he was trying to hide it from me. Whatever it was, I felt I deserved the truth. The situation had forced Jeff to come back earlier than expected. He arrived later in the afternoon without Wanda because she was still playing in the tennis tournament.

Jeff sat on the couch in the dining room talking to Thalen quietly. I heard their voices muttering, but I was not able to sense what they were saying. They spoke for a long time, but Jeff was doing most of the talking. Thalen sat on a chair staring down at the floor, listening to his father. About half an hour later, Thalen walked through the kitchen. He saw me sitting on the couch.

"Chamroeun, do you want a burger? I'm making some," he asked. I knew he was trying to make up for his mistake, but I was still irritated that he had not yet told me what happened. "Chamroeun, did you hear me?"

"I don't know. I'm not hungry."

"I'll just make you one. You can eat it later." Thalen went outside and cleaned the barbecue grill. Suddenly, Jeff entered the kitchen, glancing at me as he approached the counter. He crossed his arms.

"Can you go check with Thalen and see if he needs any help?" Jeff asked.

I went out the laundry room door and sat on the gray swing a few feet from the grill. Thalen saw me but did not comment. He continued to flip the patties and tried not to make eye contact. For the first time, I felt awkward being around him. I wanted to talk as usual, but was too angry to engage in conversation. Jeff came outside with a curious look on his face.

"Did you talk to him?" he asked Thalen.

"No. Do I really have to do this right now?"

"Thalen, you told me you would." Thalen put his hands on his hips, then looked up to the sky and exhaled. He sat next to me.

"Chamroeun, I'm sorry for not returning home last night. I know you guys were worried about me."

"Where you go?"

"I was out doing stupid things that I should not have done."

"Doing what?"

He hesitated, then stared directly at me. "I went out last night, and umm . . . I used drugs. This is something that I'm not proud of, but I'll never let it happen again."

I was confused. I remember Kesor once told me, "Thalen doesn't smoke, drink or do drugs." I had been around Thalen for several years and had never seen him smoke or drink. After hearing Thalen's answer, I felt like I had been given a false impression.

Thalen got up and walked away. I continued to sit on the swing by the grill in complete shock. I stared at the ground heartbroken.

"I talked to Thalen earlier, and he told us that he will do his best to stop," said Jeff in a low tone. "He was addicted to drugs long before he met you and Kesor. Addiction is really difficult to handle, and we need to support him so he can quit for good." He flipped the patties. "No one is flawless you know. Everyone has problems. Thalen is a really smart person, but he's made some bad decisions. He has to deal with it. He loves you and Kesor very much, and he says he will work to be better."

"Jeff, I love Thalen like my brother. He done a lot for me and my family. If not for him, I would not come study here."

"Yes, I know."

"I hope he can change."

Jeff looked at me with a gentle smile. "Me too . . ."

# 14

# AMERICAN SCHOOL

A FEW DAYS before school started, Wanda took me to get my uniform. St. Luke was a private school with an established dress code. Boys wore navy-blue or khaki pants and white polo shirts. Gray or navy-blue sweaters were allowed if the weather was cooler. Girls wore plaid skirts or the same uniform as the boys.

Wanda ended up taking me to a suburban shop thirty minutes away.

"Okay Chamroeun, we need to get you a few pairs of pants and shorts," she said. "Which color do you like?" She picked up a pair of khaki pants and checked the size.

"I have the blue one," I said. Navy-blue pants were also a part of the Khmer uniform.

"I'll just take both colors so you have a couple. Now, we also need to get you a few shirts, a pair of shorts, and a sweater." She went through each pile and picked out two white shirts and a sweater. Then she spotted a blue vest. "This is a cute vest. I'll get you this one too. Just remember to keep them clean. It's a part of your school policy. Besides, these uniforms are expensive, so you need to take good care of them. Okay?"

"Yes, I take care of them."

Wanda's comments reminded me of my mother, who regularly told me to keep my uniform clean because we could not afford another one.

Mother always negotiated prices with vendors before buying. She wanted to get as many discounts as she could. But things were different in the US. Customers didn't negotiate the price since every product was labelled with a price tag and shoppers had to pay that exact amount. I was stunned to see the total price was over 200 dollars. It would take my elder sisters several months to generate this kind of money. Luckily, Wanda was able to afford these clothes without complaint. Nonetheless, I would take good care of them so she wouldn't have to spend more.

The evening before school began, Thalen and Kesor took me to St. Luke for the Open House night. We explored the classrooms and buildings. On the first floor was Ms. Sherman's classroom, a large kitchen, and an assembly room. We walked up a short staircase to the second floor where we saw a narrow hallway with many more classrooms. The light gray tile floor was smooth and shiny. I saw a reflection of myself in the tiles. Posters and banners were hanging along the hallway. Long bright lights hung from the ceiling.

Ahead of me, I spotted a girl who looked to be about my age. She was in front of a classroom next to her mother, examining the signs hung on the door. She even smiled at me when we were in view. Kesor kept glancing at the girl, she nudged me to talk to her. I stayed quiet because I had no idea who she was or what grade she was in. We soon exited the building and headed to the car to return home. Along the way, Kesor and Thalen were talking.

"Why didn't you talk to her? She was cute," said Thalen while driving.

"I don't know her. I don't speak to someone I don't know."

"Well, that's how you make friends. You talk to people."

"Maybe she can be Chamroeun's girlfriend," said Kesor jokingly.

"Yeah . . . in the US, white girls love brown guys. So, you're in luck."

I had never talked to them about girls before. Mother specifically told me to do well in school and not to think of them until I was much older. Father also mentioned that girls only like smart guys who were "successful."

When morning arrived, I dressed for school. Wanda had bought a bunch of groceries for me to pack. In America, teachers did not sell snacks. School ran from eight thirty in the morning to two thirty in the afternoon, Monday through Friday. I made a peanut butter and jelly sandwich and put it in a plastic bag. I grabbed an apple, a few snack bars, grapes, and an applesauce cup. I zipped up my lunchbox then sat in the television room waiting for Jeff to get ready.

Since this was my first day attending an American school, I did not know whether my teachers were going to be nice or cruel. Nobody had mentioned anything about the type of punishment given by American teachers. The more I thought about it, the more nervous I became. I knew I would be an easy target since I could barely speak, read, or write English. Jeff entered the room holding his briefcase.

"First day of school! It should be exciting. Are you ready?" he asked cheerfully.

"Yes, I'm ready." I knew Jeff was trying to encourage me, but I felt scared and wished I could stay home. My jitters reminded me of the first day attending Khmer school. Except this time, I did not have Mother to push me. I had to be brave and overcome any obstacle that I might face. I picked up my backpack and lunchbox and followed Jeff out to his SUV. I sat in the front passenger seat anxiously picking my fingernails.

"Will teacher hit me if I do something wrong?" I asked.

"No! The teachers here are very friendly. They would never hurt you."

I was relieved. I leaned my head back against the leather car seat, trying to convince myself that everything was going to be fine. "You're going to have so much fun at this school. I bet you'll make a lot of new friends," Jeff continued.

"I'm not here to make friend. I'm here to learn." Jeff smiled but didn't reply. We soon entered the school grounds. He drove slowly behind a line of vehicles. There were students wearing traffic safety vests and holding red stop signs to warn the drivers as students climbed out of the cars. Jeff stopped near the front of the line and let me out.

"Okay. Have a good day at school. I'll probably be the one to pick you up this afternoon, so just wait here when you're done."

"Okay, I wait for you."

Ahead of me, students stood next to the entrance to the school building. They appraised me with curious faces as I entered the front door.

Once inside, I noticed the building was quiet. I thought the reason that everyone stood outside was because they didn't want to come in early.

I opened the door and saw Ms. Sherman sitting behind her desk. She was reading a piece of paper. Upon hearing the sound of the door shutting, she looked up in surprise.

"You're not supposed to be here yet, sweetie," she said. "Students normally come in when the bell rings. But don't worry, you can come in for today. It's almost eight thirty anyway."

"Okay, thank you." I walked to my desk, feeling embarrassed.

The classroom was well organized. Individual desks were lined up six across and three deep. Each desk had a natural wood top. The rest was painted black. They were all labelled with students' names. My desk was located in the far-right corner of the back row next to large picture windows adorned with gray curtains. The wall behind Ms. Sherman was decorated with small posters of educational quotes, placed around a large whiteboard. My favorite was an image of an apple used as a reference to education. High on the wall, there was an American flag hanging from a short metal pole.

When I sat down, I noticed that the desk could be opened. Under the wooden table top, there was a metal tray where I discovered two stacks of textbooks. I unzipped my backpack and started putting my notebooks in the remaining space. When the bell rang, students entered the room in small groups. I could hear noisy voices chattering in the hallway. Some were even laughing as they entered the room. After everyone was settled, Ms. Sherman introduced herself to the class.

"Good morning everyone. I'm Ms. Sherman and I am your homeroom teacher." Her face lit up. "I'm excited to start this amazing school year and I can see that you all are excited as well." Ms. Sherman glanced around the room. "Before we get started, let's all stand up and pray to the lord. I'll lead the prayer since this is our first day." She lowered her head, shut her eyes and began saying the prayer in a soft voice. "Hail Mary full of Grace . . ." Everyone joined her and continued praying together in a rhythm. "The Lord is with thee. Blessed are thou among women and blessed is the fruit of thy womb Jesus. Holy Mary Mother of God, Pray for us sinners now and at the hour of our death, Amen."

While growing up, I had learned very little about Christianity or Catholicism. I attended the church in Oue Bram a few times, and I heard fascinating stories about Jesus Christ and his apostles. But I was never interested in becoming a Christian. My intention was only to receive the gifts that were given by the missionaries. Father would get mad at me if he suspected that I had attended church. He thought missionaries were ruining Buddhism by converting children into Christians. To him, using presents to attract poor people, then persuading them to believe in another religion, was wrong.

Christianity was not a popular topic in Thalen's family either. They were non-believers and never mentioned much about any religion. Jeff had told me that I had the right to make my own decision on whatever I wanted to believe. The family would support me, regardless. Yet, Drew and Blake occasionally gave me a hard time for attending a Catholic school, saying that some teachings might not be accurate. To them, believing in God was like believing in Harry Potter.

Despite my family's criticism, I did have respect for Christianity and other religions around the world. Every religion contains valuable lessons that can inspire individuals to become better people. Living in a Buddhist family, I was taught to respect my elders and be kind to peers, in hopes of receiving good karma. In spite of differences, we all deserve peace, love, and happiness. This is a basic principle that should bind all of us, regardless of our faith, nationality, or skin color. I was not a believer, but was still thankful that a Catholic school had given an opportunity to a Buddhist boy like me.

After finishing the prayer, Ms. Sherman looked at me with a smile. "Class, we have a couple of new students joining us. Could you please stand up and introduce yourselves?" I slowly stood up, nervously looking around the room to see everyone staring at me. My heart was racing.

"Hi, my name is Chamroeun. I'm from Cambodia. I'm happy to be here and to study with you all." I smiled.

"Thank you, Chamroeun. We are happy to have you here as well. Welcome to our school." I sat down quickly. "Everyone, Chamroeun is new to the area. He arrived in the US about a month ago. Please introduce yourself when you get a chance."

I was taken aback by her kindness. I'd never had such a heartwarming welcome before. I looked around the room and saw several students still looking at me with compassion. I avoided eye contact, not wanting to be anyone's enemy. It also turned out that I was not the only international student in my class. There was another new student, sitting in the front row. Ms. Sherman also asked her to stand up and introduce herself to the class. Her name was Sunny. She was from South Korea. She was shy, staring down the whole time. After her introduction, she sat down abruptly and continued to stare at her desk. I couldn't help but feel a little eased to see that I was not the only international student at St. Luke.

Ms. Sherman opened a handbook that was given to everyone, then listed the class rules. I was surprised by the rule about not using cellphones during class. Most Khmer students didn't own a phone. I didn't hear anything about punishment either. Ms. Sherman mentioned that a student would receive "detention" for misconduct, but she did not say anything about whipping students for violating class policy. Still, I was not convinced that other teachers were as nice. Ms. Sherman went on about other school activities, including assembly shows and dances from week to week. It sounded like this American school would be enjoyable. St. Luke offered a number of subjects in seventh grade: math, science, reading, social studies, physical education, English, spelling, and religion. In addition, students were allowed to select an elective class: music, art, or computer programing. My experience at computer school in Cambodia inspired me to pick computer programing. Most of these subjects covered important lessons that I had hardly learned in Khmer schools.

The only class that was related to a subject in Khmer school was math. Yet, the teacher taught using a completely different strategy. Students could use calculators in class and even on exams.

In Khmer school, teachers would consider this to be cheating. Students needed to learn how to solve math equations by using their brains only. Teachers made fun of those who relied on calculators, calling them, "idiot," "lazy," or "calculator brain." I was called a "calculator brain" many times by different teachers throughout primary school. At St. Luke, students were required to bring a calculator every day because some geometry problems needed one.

In social studies, I had a pleasant teacher named Ms. Carter. She was very energetic and frequently smiled while talking to students. She surprised me when trying to pronounce my name. She had a seating chart and each student was assigned a seat for each class.

"Cham-ro-eun, Pen," she called.

"Here," I said, raising my hand.

"Did I say it right?"

"Yes, you say it right."

"Your name seems familiar. Are you Cambodian?"

"Yes, I am."

"Chom-reab-sueh!" She put both of her palms together and raised them up in front of her nose and bowed. I was surprised that she knew the Khmer greeting. Students looked at her wide-eyed.

"Cham-reab-sueh! How you know?"

"I've been to Cambodia several times. In fact, I know a family living there. They are Khmer but I consider them as my own. I'll bring some pictures to show you sometime."

"Okay, sounds good."

"Everyone, chom-reab-sueh, means hello. It's a polite way of greeting, and it is said with the hands held together in front of your face, just like this." She demonstrated to the class one more time. Some students attempted to practice the greeting with each other, while those standing near the wall waited for their names to be called. They could hardly say the word with their thick American accents. Nonetheless, I was thrilled to see they wanted to learn Khmer culture and could not be any happier to have a teacher who had not only been to Cambodia, but could speak a little Khmer.

In science class, Ms. Kennedy used a projector hanging from the ceiling. She spoke in a genial tone while explaining a lesson about the environment and ecosystems. Pictures of animals, lakes, mountains, and jungles were part of the slideshow. Then, an image of her with her family popped up on the screen.

"This is a picture of me in South Korea. I visited my son over the summer. It's pretty there. Does anyone know where South Korea is?" she asked, looking around the room for an answer. No one raised their hand. The teacher pulled down a large map from the top of the whiteboard. "Can someone come up here and show us where South Korea is?"

I raised my hand at the same time as another boy a few tables to my right, near the back of the room. Ms. Kennedy chose me. "Yes, you, come on up." I got up and walked around the table to the map.

"South Korea is here," I said pointing at the location.

"Very good. What is your name?"

"Chamroeun."

"Cham-ro-eun? That's an interesting name. Where are you from?"

"I'm from Cambodia."

"Can you show us where that is?"

"Sure, it's right here." I pointed at the map.

"Very good. Thank you for showing us. You can go back to your seat."

I sat down, delighted to show my knowledge to the teacher. While living with Thalen, he often showed me maps of countries in Asia and around the globe. He loved geography and frequently hung maps on the walls. Thalen also attempted to teach me about populations and major cities. He always wanted me to know more about the world.

While sitting on my stool, I felt multiple students gazing at me. They seemed amazed at my knowledge. A blonde girl sitting to my right looked at me with a smile on her face and said, "good job."

"Thank you," I said, continuing to sit quietly. But I was happy that a white American girl was willing to talk to a brown boy like me.

During recess, I stood outside watching everyone play on a large cement playground. Students from the lower grades were playing jump rope and hopscotch. Farther to my right, I saw my classmates playing basketball and throwing a rubber football from a short distance. Some were screaming with pure joy, making the place noisy. Watching them play put a smile on my face, and I wished I could participate. Before long, I saw two girls from my class approaching.

"Hi, I'm Megan."

"And I'm Seren," said the girl on the right. They had blonde hair and were wearing plaid skirts and gray sweaters.

"Anyways, we just wanted to come say hi," Megan continued.

"Okay, I'm Chamroeun. I'm from Cambodia."

"Yeah, we know. We're in the same class." The girls giggled. "We should hangout. We can go to the mall or other fun places."

"I'm new here. I don't know any place, sorry."

"No problem. Well, nice to meet you."

"Yes, nice to meet you, too."

The girls walked away quickly, but it was brave of them to come introduce themselves. In fact, there were many more students who came to talk to me as recess progressed. Some even asked me to play basketball with them. I refused because I did not know how to dribble a basketball. I stood nearby and watched instead. One boy seemed talented. He could even bounce the ball between his legs. He drove past several defenders and easily put it in the basket. His next shot was blocked by a taller boy. The ball flew from his hands, rolling near me. I picked it up and handed it back to him.

"Thanks. I'm Gary, by the way," he said in a rushed tone.

"I'm Chamroeun."

"Chamron? Can I call you Cham?"

"Sure, fine."

"You should come play with us."

"No, I'm okay. I don't know how to play."

"All right, no problem." He dribbled back to the basket and kept on playing for the rest of recess. Despite my lack of familiarity with basketball, I was able to throw the football with a few of my classmates. We stood about twenty-five feet away from each other, then threw the ball back and forth. I threw the ball with a spiral.

"Dude! Where did you learn how to throw a football like that?" asked a boy, Parker, who had long blonde hair covering the sides of his face.

"My brother-in-law teach me."

"Does he play football?"

"Yes, he play quarterback when he in high school. Now, he coach at Lakeside."

"That's cool. Are you gonna play football?"

"I hope so. I like football. But I don't know yet. I ask my guardian."

There were many sports played in America, but football was by far the most popular. Thalen, Blake, and Drew all played quarterback when they were in high school. I wanted to be a quarterback, too. Sometimes, I practiced throwing a football outside of Jeff and Wanda's house alone. Since this was my first year attending an American school, Jeff and Wanda did not want me to play football yet. They were worried that it might prevent me from focusing on school. Football was a difficult sport that can take a significant physical toll on anyone, let alone a small Cambodian boy.

On a Tuesday night in November, I sat in the television room doing homework. Jeff, Wanda, and Thalen sat on the couch nearby watching the news. It was election night in America. Everyone was up late, paying close attention to the results. Later that night, the news media announced the African-American candidate, "Barack Obama," was elected as the next American president. Everyone in the room was elated, giving each other high-fives. They seemed so happy that Barack Obama had won. The television showed footage of massive crowds from around the country cheering. Some people were in tears. Others were hugging each other with huge smiles on their faces.

"Chamroeun, this is a big deal. Obama is going to be our first African-American president," said Jeff with joy.

"He's also very smart. I hope that he will do great things for our country," Wanda added. Jeff's statement surprised me. I didn't know there were no candidates of color elected as the US president before Obama. To me, America was a country full of diversity. Anyone could be an American regardless of skin color. Knowing that Obama was the first African-American president shocked me. Why hadn't there been people of color elected as president before? What had taken America so long to elect an African-American candidate? Nonetheless, I was excited to be present for this historic event.

Approximately one week later, I found out that Chai had arrived in America. She would be living with her, now, fiancé Seth in North Carolina. They were planning to get married within a few months. Since leaving Cambodia, I had not talked to my sister. I had been in America for over four months, but my life was completely dominated by school. Every school day, I woke up, made lunch, and wouldn't be done with homework until late at night. I barely had time to call Father. One thing was certain, attending one American school was not any easier than going to three schools a day in Cambodia.

On a quiet night around nine thirty, I sat alone in the television room doing my homework. Out of the blue, I received a phone call from another area code–919. It was strange. Who could be trying to reach me at this hour?

"Hello?" I answered.

"Hi Chamroeun. How are you?" said Chai in English, sounding low.

"I'm fine. What's going on?"

"Nothing much. I just feel lonely." There was audible sobbing coming through.

"Chai, you okay?"

"I miss you. Why you never call? I'm all alone."

"I'm sorry. I been busy with school."

"Is school more important than family?"

"Chai, I have homework every day. I don't even have time to call Father. I'm here for school. You need to understand."

"I get it, Chamroeun. School is important. But it don't kill you to call me once a week." I sighed, but didn't say a word. "You have to come to my wedding. I pay for your plane ticket if I have to."

"I'll ask Jeff and Wanda."

"Are you serious? Why ask them? I'm your sister. I tell you to come."

"I live with them! I ask them first!"

"All I want is you be here on my wedding. It mean a lot to me if you come."

"I'll let you know."

It broke my heart to hear Chai so lonely on the other side of the country. I really wanted to visit her, but school was hard, and I had no free time.

I remember asking Wanda while riding with her on the way to school. Kesor was also in the car, sitting shotgun, eating a cup of noodles.

"Chai getting married soon. Can I go?" I spoke politely.

"Where is the wedding taking place?"

"Chai live in North Carolina right now," said Kesor. "But they move to Florida soon and get married there. I think they want to move there because Seth dad live there."

"When is the wedding?" Wanda glanced at Kesor.

"About a month away, I think."

"Well Chamroeun, you have school." Wanda continued. "You can't leave and fall behind your class."

"But Chai say I only go for a few day."

"It doesn't matter, Chamroeun. You are in the middle of your semester. You can't leave." Wanda looked at me through the rearview mirror. Kesor turned her head to me, but she knew there was nothing she could do to change Wanda's mind.

I bit my tongue. In my heart, I knew that school wasn't the main reason. Chai mentioned that her event was on a Saturday. I would have to leave on Friday and return on Sunday. This meant that I would miss only one day of school.

In my heart, I knew Thalen and his parents didn't want me to be near Chai's fiancé, Seth. When I asked Thalen, he got mad from simply hearing his name. He glared at me, saying, "if Wanda says you can't go, then you can't go. And stop asking me about it, okay?"

Despite his comment, I still had hope that Thalen and his family would change their minds.

# 15

# MY COMMITMENT

AS THE SCHOOL year went on, I became closer with some of my classmates. We met up for sleepovers and played video games. Stella helped me set up a Facebook account so I could chat with them online. With so many devices at Jeff and Wanda's house, practically every room offered a distraction from school. If there wasn't someone to watch movies with in the TV room, I'd be in the office scrolling through funny YouTube videos.

For a while, the family didn't seem to notice my laziness. They offered to help, but they didn't push me. And neither did my teachers. Even when I got a 60 or even a 70/100, my teachers didn't whip me.

Some days, I went to class without finishing my homework. I remember one night, lying on the couch watching a TV show, *Knight Rider*. Everyone else was at the grocery store. I had homework and a quiz in spelling class the next day. However, I had forgotten to bring my textbook home. I asked Thalen over the phone to take me to St. Luke, but school was closed at that hour. I didn't know what to do besides watch television. Minutes later, everyone arrived home. Wanda walked into the kitchen and rinsed out the sink.

"Did you finish all of your homework?" she asked.

"Yes, I had most of my homework done," I lied.

"Thalen told me that you have a spelling quiz tomorrow. Why aren't you studying?"

"I forget my book at school. I don't have anything to study."

"Well, could you call your friends and see if you can borrow one of their books?"

"Okay, I call them." I continued to lay on the couch.

Wanda then took a few steps closer and spoke sternly. "Chamroeun, I did not pay for you to come here so you can watch TV. Get up and start calling your friends." I turned off the television and called my friend, Jayden.

"What's up, Chamroeun!" he answered.

"Hey, I forget my spelling book at school. Can I borrow your book for tonight?"

"Yeah, let me check." I heard the sound of his footsteps walking on the wooden floor and what sounded like shuffling through his backpack. "Do we have anything due?"

"Yeah, the spelling homework is due tomorrow. We also have spelling quiz in class."

"I'm not too worried about the quiz. The words are pretty easy. But I still have to finish the homework, so I don't think I can let you borrow it. Sorry, dude."

"That's fine. I figure out."

"All right, see you tomorrow."

I called a few more friends, but they didn't have the textbook with them either. They were in a different class, and their assignment was not due for a few more days. I started to get nervous. I heard Wanda talking loudly about me to Thalen in her bedroom. I called Jayden again.

"Hey, can you tell me the words from the chapter?" I asked.

"Okay, but why?"

"I want to learn so I can be ready for quiz."

"But I thought you also need the book to do your homework? You can ask Ms. Sherman tomorrow for an extended date. I'm sure she will let you turn it in later."

"Yeah, but I want to study for the quiz. Just tell me some word."

"All right, here they are, written, spoken, taken."

"Wait. Can you spell them?"

"You don't know how to spell these words? They are really easy. But yeah, I guess. Written. W-r-i-t-t-e-n. Spoken. S-p-o-k-e-n," he paused,

"Chamroeun, there are like thirty words. It's gonna take me a long time to spell them all. I also have to do my homework. Can you just ask Ms. Sherman tomorrow?"

I exhaled. "Okay, I try."

When I got to school, I attempted to complete the assignment during other classes. Luckily, spelling class did not begin until after lunch, allowing me enough time to finish. During recess, I brought out the textbook and practiced spelling the words. I tried my best to remember as many words as possible with the limited time remaining before class. Despite my effort, I received such a low score that Ms. Sherman allowed me to retake the quiz the following day. Even then, I only got 65/100.

It kept getting worse.

One morning, Wanda was supposed to take me to school. I hadn't finished my essay for English class. I was typing away at the last paragraph when I heard Wanda's footsteps in the hallway.

"Chamroeun! We have to go or I'm gonna be late for my tennis practice!" she shouted from downstairs.

"I'm coming! I have a few more sentence to write then I'm done."

I heard footsteps walking away. Then I heard the front door slam shut and the car engine start. I looked out the window and saw her drive away. Luckily, Thalen was still at the house that morning. I sat back down in my chair and kept writing. The house phone rang. I hustled to the office and answered the phone, but Thalen had picked up a moment before me. I kept quiet.

"Can you take Chamroeun to school? We had to leave because he wasn't ready. I think he was doing his homework," said Wanda in a nasty tone.

"Okay, I'll take him," said Thalen.

"Can you make sure that he gets his stuff done before you guys leave?"

"Yeah okay, I'll check."

"I'm really disappointed. I mean, he's not trying at all. He had all night to do his homework, but he chose to do it right before leaving the house. You need to talk to him about this. It's unacceptable."

Tears fell as I printed my paper. I was embarrassed. How had I allowed myself to be in this position? I knew that I could do much better.

A few days before Chai's wedding, I was told again that I could not attend. Kesor was the only person that went. Wanda did not want me to leave school. She said I would fall even further behind if she let me go. I was extremely upset and did not have the guts to tell Chai myself. I asked Kesor to tell her instead.

I felt like a traitor letting Chai down. I did not know how to explain it to her. The truth was that even if I did not have school, I knew Wanda would not allow me to go, anyway. To Jeff, Wanda, and Thalen, Seth was a lazy video-game addict. They never wanted me to be near him.

A week later, I received my first report card from St. Luke. The school was based on a trimester, and thus, would release a progress report and report card three times during the school year. All the reports were accumulated at the end of the year, and the official grades would be released at that time. Everyone sat at their desks, nervously waiting for Ms. Sherman to hand them out. She called last names alphabetically. One by one, students got out of their seat and went to get their marks. Some people were happy, others seemed sad. No one shared their grades, but quickly sealed the reports back in the manila folder and put them in their backpacks.

Watching their reactions made me worry. I sat in my desk anxiously waiting to check my grades. I hoped that somehow, I would get better results than I deserved.

I opened my report and saw B's in English and religion and an A in physical education. All the rest were C's except a C minus in science and an incomplete in reading. I was not shocked to see how terrible my grades were, but I did not expect them to be this low. I sat at my desk quietly ashamed of myself. I didn't know how to explain this to Thalen and his family.

These grades might not seem terrible to some, but I knew I could have done better. Since failing first grade, I had always strived for the best and placed top ten in almost every grade in Khmer school. I never received any C's in the English school in Cambodia either. I often thought I was one of the smartest in my class. I didn't think Thalen and his family would have given me the opportunity if I had gotten C's.

"Guys, this is just a progress report. It's showing you what the grades are right now," said Ms. Sherman, going back to her desk. "So, don't worry too much. You will all get a chance to improve your grades moving forward. Also, tonight is parent-teacher conference night. If you have any questions, feel free to come in for an appointment."

On the way home, I sat quietly listening to Jeff talk.

"Are you doing all right?" he asked after I had been silent for a while.

"Yes. I'm just tired," I lied.

"I got an email from your school about the parent-teacher conference night. Did you get your progress report earlier today?"

I had butterflies in my stomach. Yet, I knew I had to come clean or I would be in worse trouble.

"Yes, I get it today."

"How did you do?"

"Not good, but I work harder. I can do better."

"Have you been asking your teachers for help?"

"No, but I ask them when I go to school."

Jeff did not seem mad, but his expression showed that I had let him down. His tone had changed from joyful to serious. Nonetheless, I knew he expected more from me.

Later that evening, Thalen and Wanda took me for a meeting with Ms. Sherman. However, Thalen was the only person that went inside. Wanda was mad and refused to go in. I was too embarrassed to talk to Ms. Sherman. Together, we waited for Thalen inside the car. It was an awkward silence. I had never seen Wanda this upset before. I could hear her breathing heavily, seeming like she was about to beat me.

"Chamroeun, what is going on? Is it because you've been watching too much TV?" she asked in a rage.

"I don't know. I work harder."

"Well, yeah! You have to if you want to keep going to school here. I am disappointed. I thought you were better than this."

Even if she didn't beat me, her words cut through my chest. I was reminded of when I had failed first grade. For the second time in my life, I felt so dumb. I couldn't be more ashamed for wasting their money. I cried quietly. I was afraid she was going to send me back to Cambodia. Jeff and Wanda had to pay 18,000 dollars for just one year. Wanda's words weren't cruel, but they served as a wake-up call.

Fifteen minutes later, Thalen returned to the car. He saw the tears on my cheeks but said nothing.

"What did the teacher say?" Wanda asked.

"She seems to like Chamroeun and says that he is a good student. She said that he needs to start asking the other teachers for help." Thalen turned around and tapped me on my leg. "You need to do better, man. That's the only way for you to keep going to school here."

I nodded. "I work harder," I mumbled.

Thalen started the car and drove us home.

From that moment on, I committed myself to becoming a better student. I asked my teachers for help when I didn't understand a certain topic. When I got home, I worked on my homework. I attempted to read the chapters by myself to improve my reading. When I didn't understand the words, I asked Jeff, Wanda, or Thalen for an explanation. No matter how hard I tried, I was still struggling in social studies, science, and reading. I continued to receive low scores on the quizzes and exams. However, I didn't let the results affect my resolve. In fact, I used it as a motivation to study even harder.

After receiving a 56/100 on a social studies test, I breathed heavily while staring at the score. At the end of class, I waited for every student to leave before approaching Ms. Carter.

"Hi Chamroeun, how can I help you?" she asked after seeing me getting closer.

"Hi, I want to ask about my exam score."

"Yeah, actually, I was going to talk to you about that. Have you been studying before you take the tests?"

"Yes, I study a lot but I still do bad. How can I do better?"

"Let's see," she brought up my test and went over some questions I got wrong. "Is reading English difficult for you?"

"Yes, I think the hardest thing is understanding the questions. Some question have difficult words I don't know."

"Yeah, I know what you mean. I would be devastated if I had to take a test written in Khmer. I tell you what, if you want to come in tomorrow morning around seven o'clock, I can go over the test with you. Is that okay?"

"Okay, I'll be here."

The next day, Thalen took me to school early. It was six thirty and still pitch-black outside. The temperature felt freezing at this hour. I wore my gray hoodie sweater every day to keep warm. Upon arrival, I went straight to Ms. Carter's classroom. We sat at one of the desks and went over the exam. She read each question slowly, explaining what it meant. Then, she let me pick the answers on my own. Thanks to her interpretation, the questions seemed much easier for me to understand. When we finished, Ms. Carter bumped my score up to an 82/100. She was convinced that most mistakes were caused by the language barrier.

"I noticed that you seem to know the answers to most of the questions. Is the way these questions are written too hard for you to understand?"

"A little bit. My reading is not good. Sometime I don't understand the questions."

"I'll tell you what. From now on, you can come in and take your exam early in the morning. I will go through the questions with you, okay?"

"Yes, that is great. Thank you."

"Arkoun." In Khmer, *arkoun* meant thank you. "Did I say it right?"

"Yes, you did. Your Khmer is really good."

Ms. Carter only knew a few words, but frequently attempted to speak Khmer with me in class. She always made me feel welcome.

My performance began to improve in other subjects as well. English, religion, and computer studies were easier because students only had to complete small projects and write short essays. On one assignment, Ms. Sherman asked us to write two paragraphs about the scariest thing we had done in our lives. I decided to write about my journey to America. Ms. Sherman was intrigued by my story. I received full credit for that particular assignment.

In science, I had to present a daily report based on a topic related to the environment. My topic was rubber plantations in Southeast Asia. Thalen brought a fake rubber tree from work to help me present my report. On the due date, Thalen, Kesor, and Stella took me to school early and helped set up the tree in the classroom. The artificial tree was seven feet tall and fairly realistic.

When the time for my presentation came, I stood next to the tree and read my report out loud to the class. I picked up a sponge and gently brushed downward along the line of white sap to a small bucket attached to the base of the tree. "The white sap known as latex is used to create important everyday items like tires, shoes, and even mattresses." I read off my notes. "Rubber wood is made into furniture. Rubber trees and their plantations are an integral part of the regional economy and throughout the world." I had practiced reading these words at home to ensure that I would pronounce them correctly. When I finished, everyone clapped. Ms. Kennedy got up and walked over to me.

"Good job!" she said. "Guys, this morning, his whole family came to help set up this rubber tree, just to show you what it looks like. It was not required, but he chose to bring it, anyway. I am really impressed."

Looking back at my project, I realized I didn't cover the ugly truth of rubber plantations. In Cambodia, most children in rural areas worked agricultural jobs. Rubber plantation, tobacco field, or cassava cultivation work was very common. In the more urban regions, poor kids found work in hazardous occupations like brick making. These jobs required long hours of labor in the hot weather to receive extremely low wages; five dollars or less per day. Agriculture and manufacturing required cheap labor regardless of age. Children from ten to fifteen years of age were often forced to quit school. Ruat had to work in a rubber plantation for two years after we left Prey Veng. These challenging jobs were the only route to sustain most impoverished families.

Despite this accomplishment in science, I kept receiving low scores on Ms. Kennedy's exams. Science was my worst subject. I had never learned much about the environment in Khmer schools. Being unfamiliar with the subject made it seem like I was learning a new language within an already new language. Every day, I put more time toward science than any other subject. Still, I kept failing the exams. I was frustrated and went to talk to Ms. Kennedy at the end of class. She offered to let me retake her test. However, I had to create the exam on my own. I had one week to make it look like an actual exam by creating multiple choice, true or false, and short-answer questions. I then had to answer those problems without looking at the textbook.

The retake exam boosted my previous score up to 72/100. More importantly, this proved a brilliant way for me to learn. Creating and answering my own questions helped me become more familiar with the material. After that, I raised my hand and answered questions in class with confidence. She saw how effective her retake method had been and offered this option to everyone who had scored below 70. Some students thought this was too much work. For me, I had to do everything necessary to improve my grades.

During the Christmas break, I was frequently asked to help straighten up the house and decorate. Jeff would also ask for help to unload the groceries from his car. They had done a tremendous amount of shopping for Christmas. On some days, the moment I stepped out of the house to help him, my face would sting and my eyes would burn from the cold. It made me think that it was going to snow soon.

On Christmas Day, Drew, Blake, and his fiancé, Krystal, came to the house early to celebrate, while Stella and her boyfriend had their own plans. We gathered around the large table in the dining room for breakfast. Wanda made Eggs Benedict which were fantastic. Everyone was practically licking their plates.

After doing the dishes, we sat on the couch and started on the presents. Wanda pranced around the tree, pretending to be Santa, picking out gifts and handing them out. Most of the gifts had Thalen, Kesor, Drew, Krystal, or Blake's name on them. Toward the end, Wanda and Jeff surprised me with a new black bicycle that had been hidden in another room.

I got so excited. I went to sit on my new bike, gripping the handlebars, pretending I was riding. The bike was tall. My feet barely touched the ground. I slowly navigated the living room and entry hall. Looking through the solarium windows, I noticed small snowflakes falling.

"It's snowing!" I said with joy, immediately dismounting the bike. Everyone came over.

"Wow, it's beautiful. I don't remember the last time it snowed on Christmas," said Jeff. "Not bad for your first Christmas, huh?"

I smiled at Jeff, then kept staring out the window.

When school began again, my hard work paid off. I received better grades heading into the middle of the school year. I earned A minuses, B's, and B minuses. Though, I still received a C plus in science. Thalen was quite pleased with my improvement. He hung the report on the fridge to show everyone.

My recent "success" had boosted my confidence. Whenever I had an upcoming test, I stayed up late reading the text and making flash cards. Literature, social studies, and science lessons required hours of studying.

I sat in the television room alone and quietly read the answers to myself. Sometimes, I read the flashcards out loud and woke Wanda by mistake. She would enter the room wearing her bathrobe, her face weary and eyes barely open. She stood under the bright kitchen lights, "don't forget to turn off the light when you're done."

"Yes, I will."

I kept reading my notes silently. If I did not finish, I would wake up early to review my flashcards again. Occasionally, I asked Wanda to quiz me. Even better, Wanda's reading tone was almost identical to my teachers, especially in spelling. Wanda pronounced the words slowly and clearly. With her help, I consistently received higher scores, often in the mid-90s. Wanda was pleased to hear the results.

Later in the semester, I received an award. I was named "Most Confident" for giving a speech in English class. My topic was, "How to build a Cambodian House." I showed pictures of me helping Father and Thalen construct our wooden house in Oue Bram. I also included other pictures of me and my family. The whole class seemed fascinated by my speech. Many classmates had asked questions about life in Cambodia, and the interest in learning about my country felt great. Even better, the teacher told me that my speech was one of the best.

One day in the spring, Kesor told me that Chai was coming to visit us. It had been nearly a year since I'd seen my sister. Chai arrived on an afternoon toward the end of the spring. I was in class and could not go with Thalen and Kesor to pick her up from the airport. I was struggling to concentrate in class. I was imagining how angry she must be that I had missed her wedding. Nonetheless, I was extremely excited to see my sister.

When I made it home, I saw Thalen sitting on the couch near Kesor in the television room. There was no sign of Chai.

"Where is Chai?" I asked.

"She's upstairs in the guest room," said Thalen. I dropped my backpack on the floor and raced up to see her. For a moment, Chai was unaware of my presence, silently and gently unpacking her luggage. She looked different. Her hair had dark orange highlights, and her skin was much lighter.

"Hi Chai," I said nervously. She turned around, her face laden with sorrow.

"Hi Chamroeun. What up?" she spoke in broken English.

"Nothing. I'm here to see you."

"That's new. I don't know you care about me." I could see her eyes getting watery.

"Chai, I'm sorry. I want go to your wedding but I have school."

"Whatever. I'm over it."

"I'm glad you come visit."

"Yeah, I guess this only way for me to see you."

I stood quietly staring at the carpet.

Chai came over and gave me a big hug. "I'm not mad at you, Chamroeun. I understand you have school. It's okay. I'm over it." Despite her comments, I was disheartened.

Chai's visit was going to be short. She could only stay for a week and a half. Every day, Thalen and Kesor took her to see fun places around Seattle. On the weekend, we all went to see the Tulip fields near Mount Vernon, an hour north.

On Chai's last day, she took me to the Space Needle. We went to the top and walked around the observation deck. We had a gorgeous view of the Puget Sound along with Seattle's skyline. It was a clear day. I could see Mount Rainier far behind the city. It was an incredible sight. I was delighted to experience it with my sister. But I was sad knowing that she would be leaving the next day. I tried to joke around to hide my sorrow. I just wished she could stay longer.

On the last day of school, Ms. Sherman handed out the final report cards. I sat at my desk, nervously tapping my feet. I knew my grades had improved, but I still didn't know what to expect. What explanation could I have for Jeff, Wanda, and Thalen if I ultimately received substandard grades? I truly believed that I had put in my best effort.

Ms. Sherman announced my name. I went to grab the manila folder and returned to my desk. My hands were sweaty as I slowly opened the report. I looked at each subject and saw A's and B's and not a single C. My lowest grade was a B minus in science. Not perfect grades, but I was ecstatic. All of my hard work did make a difference. I sat at my desk smiling, telling myself, *I did it. I did it. I passed all of my classes.*

# 16

# HARDSHIPS OF FOOTBALL

EIGHTH GRADE WAS proving to be more difficult than the previous year. Teachers assigned more homework to better prepare students for high school. Reading proved tiring, especially in the later hours of the day. My body felt fatigued, making it harder for me to concentrate or even stay awake.

One evening, it took until twelve forty-five in the morning to finish my last assignment. I stacked my school books on the cement shelf in front of the fireplace and headed upstairs to bed.

I was about to enter my room when I heard sobbing that sounded like Chai, coming from the bathroom. Chai had come back to visit us once again, arriving a few weeks earlier. She had even stayed for Blake and Krystal's wedding. I looked into the dark hallway and saw that the door was shut and a sliver of light was shining from the gap at the bottom. I moved closer to the door as I heard a voice on speakerphone.

"It's my fault. I should never have let you go. I knew you were going to stay," said the person on the phone. The high-pitched tone sounded like Chai's husband.

"I'm sorry," said Chai. "I have to stay. I don't want to be away from my family."

"After what we've gone through, you chose them over me? That is so unfair. How could you do this to me?"

"I'm so sorry, but I have no choice," Chai sobbed. "I have to go." I heard the sound of a phone being placed on top of the sink. She continued to cry quietly.

"Chai? Are you okay?" I asked in a low voice. She continued to cry. I opened the door and saw her in front of the mirror wiping tears from her cheeks. Her eyes were red. "What's wrong?"

"Nothing, you should go to bed. It's late." She grabbed her phone and went to her room. I was torn that she was unwilling to open up to me. But no matter how hard she tried to hide her problems, I always found out.

Both Chai and Seth had agreed to file for a divorce. Chai had decided to stay in Seattle permanently. I was not surprised. I knew she was suffering while being away from us. Chai always wanted to live with us, but her husband was not willing to consider moving west. His dislike of Thalen meant he was never interested in coming to see Kesor and me. But Chai still loved us dearly and did not want to continue living so far away. It was a heartbreaking choice, but to her, nothing mattered more than family.

Growing up, Chai once told me, "you can always find a better friend, a better husband, or wife. But you can't find a better family than what you already have. I would never choose anyone over our family." This had always been a part of her, ever since she was young. Nonetheless, it was saddening to know that she had chosen to end her marriage just to be with us.

Chai enrolled in design school. Classes were in the evening three days a week. Additionally, she started helping part time at Jeff and Wanda's store to pay for her tuition. She received roughly 200 dollars per week after paying for rent at Jeff and Wanda's. Chai also chose to send some money to our family in Cambodia for food every month, which left her barely enough money to pay for school.

While working at Bedrooms & More, Chai reconnected with Thalen's best friend, Ryan. Thalen and Ryan had taken the original trip to Cambodia together, and it was then that Thalen had met Kesor. Back then, Ryan had been interested in Chai, but he had to fulfill his duty as a doctor in the US Navy. Ryan had always been there to support Thalen, ever since they were young. Most importantly, he was the person who had persuaded

Thalen to visit Cambodia in the first place. When studying anthropology at Pomona College, he had developed an interest in the incredible temples built by our Khmer ancestors. If not for Ryan, Thalen would have visited Africa instead. He wanted to explore an East African country like Ethiopia. Ryan, however, wanted to see Angkor Wat and was committed to traveling to Cambodia with or without Thalen. Fortunately, Thalen capitulated and travelled with his best friend, ultimately leading him to my family. Who knows how the story would have unfolded if Thalen had gone to Africa.

Ryan was in town after his first tour in Iraq. He frequently came over and took Chai out for dinner and fun places around Seattle. Ryan and Chai would eventually start dating. Chai even brought Ryan to one of my football games. They sat on the bleachers with Thalen and Kesor, watching me play on a rainy day. After seeing my progress in seventh grade, Jeff and Wanda were finally letting me play football during my second year in America. This was my fourth game of the season.

It was a hard-fought game. We were competing against an equally matched team. The wet conditions were negatively affecting the game. Quarterbacks struggled with passing, and receivers were dropping the wet ball. Coach Foster frequently called run plays, meaning that I, because I played running back, had more carries than usual. Yet, I did not perform well that day. I lost yardage on many of my carries. Their defense was tough. Players consistently beat our blockers to hit me behind the line of scrimmage. My body ached. The defenders were huge and had spectacular tackling skills.

On one play, a few defensive players burst through the linemen and took me down immediately after the quarterback handed off the ball. Their face masks cut into my arm causing me to bleed. I lay on the turf in pain while my body shivered in the freezing rain. I looked to my left and saw my opponents celebrating. The tackler was pumped up, flexing his muscles toward his teammates. I was intimidated. Football really was a tough sport that pushed me to the limit. Every game was a new test that challenged my will to either keep on trying or just quit right there.

In many ways, football was like school. My experience from St. Luke taught me to not give up and keep pushing until the school year was over. When I had failed a test, I did not quit. I just learned to try harder until I could get a better result. Playing running back, I had to be committed and put my body on the line to help my team win. When I was knocked down, I got back up because my team was counting on me.

By the end of the third quarter, I was still struggling and my team was trailing by seven points. In hopes of tying the game, Coach Foster called a trick play that involved me throwing the ball. He called me to the sideline to tell me what I needed to do.

After listening, I jogged onto the field nervously, knowing that I had to convert this trick play so we could tie the game. I approached the huddle.

"Okay, I snap the ball, you all have to block. James, you run a straight go, I pass you the ball." I looked around and saw confusion on their faces.

"Dude, what are you saying?" asked Nate. "I can't understand you!"

"I snap the ball then pass it to James."

"What the hell kind of play is that?"

"I don't know, that's what Coach Foster said. You all have to block like a run play. Except for James. I'm taking shotgun snap. On one, ready . . . Break!" We broke out of the huddle and quickly aligned in our positions. Some were cursing at me while jogging toward their spots.

"Down!" I said from roughly four yards behind the snapper. "Red 80! Red 80! set . . . hut." I grabbed the ball then sprinted five yards to the right, my eyes were staring at James as he was bursting downfield along with a defender. I stood still, waiting for him to get open. Within seconds, a big defensive lineman approached, forcing me to get rid of the ball. I took one step forward then threw it as hard as I could. I released the ball just in time before the defender took me down. My face mask was buried in the turf, causing rubber pieces to cover my face. Suddenly, I heard the loud sound of people screaming. I looked up toward the sideline and saw Coach Foster grabbing his head with disappointment. Many people on the bleachers were standing with their palms raised up. I saw James jogging back toward the huddle with shame on his face. The play ended up as an incompletion, but seeing his expression indicated that I had made a terrible throw. Our offense did not score as the game went on and ultimately led to our first loss of the season.

The next day, I went to visit Drew at his place. I had to help Drew and his friend, Paul, organize their messy garage so they could have more space to park their cars.

"How do you like playing football?" Drew asked.

"It's okay. Some people are rude to me."

"What did they say?"

"Some of them make fun of my accent. They say they don't understand me." Drew and Paul looked at me with concern.

"Did you say anything back to them?" Paul asked.

"No. I don't want to get in fight. I don't want to get kick off the team."

"Chamroeun, you have to defend yourself," said Paul with rising anger in his voice. "You can't let those people bully you. If they make fun of you next time, tell them that you might not speak perfect English, but at least you're going to school. You're here to learn, to improve your English. You have to defend yourself, or they will continue to make fun of you."

On a cloudy afternoon, I arrived to practice early. I saw a few of my teammates near the blackberry bushes chatting.

"What's up guys?" I asked.

"Not much, we're just talking about how we lost the game," said Nate, glaring at me. "Why did coach put you in as quarterback? That was such a stupid play."

"I don't know. I do what coach say."

"I don't know. I do what coach say." He spoke with a mumbling voice trying to mock my accent. "No one could understand you in the huddle. If you can't even speak English, why do you even want to play quarterback?"

My hands were shaking. Yet, I didn't want to be a gangster like Mother said. "What you saying?"

The boy looked at his friends then laughed. "I'm saying that you suck. You shouldn't be calling plays because no one could understand you."

"Why you say mean things to me like that? What's your problem?" Nate's eyes widened. "I don't speak good English but at least I go to school. What about you? You can't speak another language like me." I glared at him and the people near him. "You not better me. I'm faster than you. I can play your position if I want to. You can't tell me what to do. So, shut up. I'm tired of it."

Everyone was stunned. They didn't say a word. They looked at me with shame, and some even walked away.

From then on, people didn't pick on me as often, which allowed me to focus on improving my game. In one game, I broke off some fantastic runs and scored two touchdowns in the first quarter alone. On defense, I was making precise tackles and even had an interception. The coaches and my teammates were impressed. Coach Foster used me more on special teams: kickoff, kickoff return, punt, punt return, and field goal block. My teammates celebrated with me whenever I made big plays. People were tapping me on my helmet saying, "good job" or "atta boy."

Our final playoff game started on a Saturday night at seven thirty. Jeff even brought his camera. It was a way for my family back in Cambodia to see me play. Father was fascinated to learn more about American football after hearing I was playing. He often asked me questions about it on the phone. Father often thought I was talking about soccer unless I called it *coconut ball* because of its shape. Nonetheless, he was proud to hear that I was playing the most popular sport in America.

When we arrived at the stadium, I was surprised to see a large crowd in the bleachers. The team started off by practicing plays on offense and defense near the end zone. Just like us, our opponents were practicing drills on the other side of the field. Their players were making loud noises trying to intimidate us.

"Let them talk. We'll respond when the game starts," an assistant coach said.

I looked toward them and saw white and red uniforms performing hitting drills. Their pads crashing together made a loud crunch which echoed throughout the field. I could visualize how painful it would be to be tackled by them. Fear entered my mind.

A coach's assistant approached me. "Stop staring at them and pay attention to the play!"

"Yes, Coach."

Soon enough, it was time to start the game. My teammates and I lined up on the field to return the kickoff. I stood on the 20 yard-line, nervously waiting to catch the ball. The crowd cheered loudly. Players jumped up and down feeding off the energy. I glanced at the bleacher and saw Jeff sitting near the top row, holding a camera aimed toward me. I told myself that *I must play well so Father could be proud of me.*

The kicker booted the ball high in the night air, and it came spinning toward me. I caught it against my chest, then burst straight downfield following my blockers. I heard loud contact all around me. Suddenly, a player popped up on my left and took me to the ground.

"Let's go number two!" he said furiously. I wore this number because I always saw photos of people raising their fingers up to show number two. A referee dragged him away. My hands were shaking, and my heart was beating a hundred miles per hour. Yet, I popped up and kept on playing. We began the drive with a run play. I stood in the backfield nervously waiting for the quarterback to snap the ball. I saw defenders approaching the line of scrimmage aggressively. Immediately after the handoff, two defenders came in unblocked and tackled me for a huge loss. The hit caused the crowd to erupt with applause and loud whistling. My teammates came to help me up.

The quarterback called another run play, and I gained five yards. A defender wrapped his arm around the ball and ripped it away from me as my knees hit the ground. But the play happened so quickly that the referees didn't see that I was down before they ruled it a fumble.

"My knee was down. It's not a fumble," I said anxiously to a referee.

He ignored me and pointed his hand to the opposite direction, indicating that the opponent now possessed the ball.

I ran to the sideline and explained to Coach Foster. He went up to the officials and tried to talk to them. But the referees didn't change the call.

"Hold on to the ball!" the quarterback screamed at my face.

"I was down."

"I don't care. Hold on to the ball until the ref blows the whistle."

I walked away. I knew he was right. Protecting the ball was my most important job.

I continued to make errors as the game went on. During a punt-return, I struggled to catch the ball, allowing it to slip through my arms. I tried to recover, but it rolled farther away and ended up in the opponent's hands. Some of my teammates were cursing at me as we jogged off the field. Others encouraged me to get back in the game.

"Take a deep breath. You need to focus," said Mason. I stood there quietly, staring at the ground. "I believe in you, man. You're better than this."

Mason was one of the best teammates I ever had. But no matter what he said, I continued to struggle. During an offensive play, the quarterback tossed the ball to me. My mind was distracted by the intensity of the defense and I forgot to pay attention. The ball hit my left knee then bounced away, allowing the defense to recover once again. At this moment, everyone lost their trust in me.

"Cham, why don't you sit out for a few series. Try to relax," said Coach Foster.

I stood on the sideline watching James take over my position. I looked to the bleacher and saw Jeff was no longer holding his camera. I was devastated. For the second time in my life, I was a failure. Worse, I had let my team down, especially those who believed in me. All season long, I attempted to push myself to become a better player so I could help my team win. It was a horrible feeling to know that I came up short.

Late in the fourth quarter, Coach Foster put me back in the game. I ran hard trying to make up for my mistakes. However, there was not enough time for us to bounce back. We were trailing by three touchdowns. Our opponent was able to score after each of the turnovers that I had created. I was the reason we lost that playoff game.

Despite my terrible performance, I was thankful for the opportunity to play this amazing sport before heading back to Cambodia.

# 17

# A NEW OPPORTUNITY

SINCE I HAD left Oue Bram, the arguments between my parents were becoming more frequent. My siblings in Cambodia intentionally hid stories from me. They were afraid it would distract me from school. And yet, no matter how hard they tried, I found out eventually.

I heard that Mother had gotten in a quarrel with Father for using food money to buy equipment for a house project. The rest of the food money ran out before Chai and Kesor could send more. Father's poor money management upset Mother so much, she argued with him and cursed at him constantly. The fights became more serious, Father considered moving away. I had to call and beg him to stay and look after the family.

"Father, please, don't go. The family needs you. I need you. Please. Don't leave us," I said, shedding tears. "You're the leader of our family. Without you, our lives would be miserable."

Father listened but was still heartbroken by Mother's criticism. I called more frequently to cheer him up. I didn't want my family to dissolve while I was away. More than anything, I wanted to see them together when I returned.

In the winter, St. Luke released the second round of report cards. As usual, I sat at my desk biting my nails, nervously waiting for Ms. Russell to announce my name. I knew my performance was worse this semester. My mind kept visualizing C's in science, social studies, and literature. Even in my second year, these were still the most challenging classes.

I opened the folder and saw an A in math, PE, spelling, and English. The rest were all B pluses and B's. I was stunned. I had not expected to do this well. I folded the report card with pure joy. It was a special feeling, reminiscent of when I passed second grade in Khmer school.

"Hello! Hello!" said Jeff cheerfully when he picked me up in his new Mini-cooper. "How was your day?"

"Great, I have a good day."

"Good!" Jeff slowly drove off the playground. We waved at Ms. Russell as we were passing by. She waved back.

"Do you have her as one of your teachers?"

"Yes, that is Ms. Russell. She is my homeroom teacher."

"Oh, do you like her?"

"Yeah, she's really nice to me."

Jeff looked at me with a smile. "Your English is getting much better. Good for you." He turned the steering wheel. "You need to work on your accent though. Stella worked really hard on getting rid of her accent. Now she sounds like an American."

"Okay, I will." I knew Jeff's intention was to help me speak English fluently.

"So, anything exciting happen at school today?"

"I got my report card."

Jeff gazed my way. "How did you do?"

"I did okay, I get mostly A and B."

"That's good! A's and B's are always good. That's better than what my kids usually got." He laughed. "So, are you enjoying going to school here?"

"Yes, I really like it here."

He put his elbow on the window, turning to me. "Do you want to go to high school?"

I hesitated to reply. I was not sure if he was joking. When I looked at his face, I knew he was dead serious.

"I don't know. I have to ask my parents."

"Well, if you do, Wanda and I are happy to continue sponsoring you. We enjoy having you around."

"Thank you. I want to continue going to school here. But I have to talk to my parents."

"Well, just let us know so you can start applying."

I nodded silently. I was blown away by the offer. I did not think that Jeff and his family would allow me to stay in America beyond two years. My grades weren't perfect. I felt that I was not a well-behaved kid. Wanda frequently got mad at me for not cleaning my room. I did not believe that I had impressed them enough to earn a new opportunity. On the other hand, I was looking forward to seeing my family soon. Being away from them was tough, especially hearing about the issues they faced on a daily basis. Many thoughts ran through my mind. I had a difficult decision to make.

One quiet evening, I sat in the office upstairs, reflecting on Jeff's invitation. It had been one week since Jeff offered to send me to high school in America. I had not told anyone in my family about it. I couldn't decide. Part of me wanted to stay. I really enjoyed the food, music, sports, and my friends at school.

Nonetheless, I still wished to return home. I visualized myself hugging Mother tight. *I am back, you don't have to worry about me anymore,* I would say. I imagined myself teaching Cambodian kids the American sports I had learned on my journey. This could be the first step to fulfilling my promise. Villagers would have so much fun learning western sports. Even better, I pictured myself handing Father my diploma from St. Luke. He would hang my certificate on his gray cement wall to show my accomplishment to the rest of the family.

While lost in thought, I decided to call Father.

"Hello, Father! I have big news to tell you." I rubbed my forehead. "Jeff offered me to stay for high school. I don't know what to do. I don't know if I should continue going to school here or return home."

After a few seconds of silence, he asked, "when did he tell you this?"

"About a week ago. He told me that he and Wanda would continue to sponsor me through high school if I want to stay."

"That's a generous offer. This means that they like having you around." He talked in a low tone.

"Father, I want to come home, but if I go home, I don't know if the embassy would give me another visa to come back to America. You know how hard it was for me to even come here."

"If that's the case, I think you should stay. If Jeff and Wanda are willing to continue sponsoring you, then you need to take it. If you come back, what are you going to do here? No school in Cambodia is better than in America. You would have to attend the same school in Oue Pir. Coming back will only prevent you from moving forward."

"But staying for high school means that I would be here for four more years. I don't know if I want to be away from you and our family for that long. I don't think Mother would be okay with that. I don't want her to keep worrying about me. I don't want her to end up sick."

"Don't make this about your mother. There are a lot of us here to take care of her. Your mother will be fine. She will still be here when you're done. Now, you have to think of how special it is to study in America, especially at the high school level. You are the only one left with the potential to finish school. Attending an American high school is an honor for you and our family." He paused for a short while. "If Jeff and Wanda are offering you the opportunity to stay, you need to take it."

"But I'm worried about you, Father. Four years is a long time. I'm afraid that things will change."

"Everything is going to be okay. And don't worry, I can look after myself." He laughed gently. "I am so happy that Jeff and Wanda are kind enough to allow you to continue school. Tell them I say thank you for their kindness."

"I will. Take care of yourself, Father. Please look after the family and take care of Mother for me."

"That's my duty. As long as I'm here, everyone will be fine. We all will be here, waiting for you when you're done."

The next day, I told Jeff and Thalen that I wanted to stay. Thalen looked at me wide-eyed while sitting on the couch in the TV room.

"I thought you wanted to go see your family?" he asked.

"I do, but I see them when I'm done." I gathered my thoughts. "I talk to my father and he think I should stay. It's best for me and my family."

"Well, maybe you could visit them between schools. But thanks for letting me know," said Jeff with a slight smile. "I'll tell Wanda."

"What I have to do now? Do we have to let the US Embassy in Phnom Penh know I'm going to high school?"

"No," Thalen interjected. "Your visa is valid as long as you continue going to school here. But you do have to go back to the embassy if you leave this country." He looked straight at me. "Don't worry about that. The most important thing to do right now is find a school that will accept you. If you are accepted, that school will renew your I-20, and that's all you need."

"We need to start visiting high schools and figure out how to apply," said Jeff. "We probably need to do this soon."

"Talk to your teachers and your friends to see if you can find out more about private high schools and how to apply," said Thalen. "I would imagine that you may have to take some kind of test."

"Okay, I will."

"You need to continue working hard in school, man. If you want to get accepted, you have to get good grades."

I nodded. I knew Thalen was right. I never had perfect grades, and this could easily prevent me from attending a private high school. I was confident that Thalen was ushering me along the right path.

While still contemplating high schools, I ran into Coach Maul from Bishop Blanchet. He had a daughter enrolled at St. Luke. I had attended his football camp last summer. Coach Maul was impressed by my athleticism. He even talked to me about high school.

"Chom! How are you, bud? Did you figure out if you're gonna stay for high school?" he asked.

I was amazed that he could remember our last conversation. It had been almost a year since I attended his camp. "Yes! My guardian say I can stay. Right now, I'm searching for school."

"That's awesome! Is Bishop Blanchet one of your options?"

"Yes, I want to visit Blanchet, a lot of my friend going there."

"I think you will like Bishop Blanchet. And we would love to have you, not only as a football player but also as a student."

I nodded. "Yes, Coach. I think about it."

"Yeah, please do. It's a big decision, but just keep Bishop Blanchet in mind." He laughed.

"I will."

Within a week, Jeff and I managed to visit O'Dea, Seattle Prep, and Bishop Blanchet during open house events. Each one was crowded with students and parents. Posters, banners, trophies, and student projects were displayed in the schools. Each school had unique rules, traditions, and an overall feel.

Jeff and I had only visited those three schools. It seemed he expected me to pick one of them, but I was still interested in applying to Lakeside. The image of me wearing the maroon and gold uniform kept popping into my mind. I couldn't imagine how proud my family would be if I was accepted there. I knew Thalen and his brothers would be happy to see me attend their alma mater. "What about Lakeside?" I asked. "Can I apply there?"

Jeff hesitated for a long minute. "I don't know if Lakeside would be a good fit for you. It's a really difficult school. Now, I'm not saying that you're not smart enough to apply there. If you were to go there, you'd have to work really hard."

"I will. I work much harder than I am now. Can we visit Lakeside? I really want to visit it."

"Sure, but I think we might have to make an appointment. I can arrange a visit when we get home."

Jeff remained skeptical. After living with him for almost two years, I had heard stories about his children's academic struggles at Lakeside, a major reason why he thought the institution wasn't the best fit. Regardless, I was optimistic about overcoming any challenge. I was ecstatic that Jeff would at least consider giving me a chance.

The visiting day arrived. After exploring the campus, we returned to the administrative office where I was told I had an interview. Nervous, I looked through the open door and saw a middle-aged white man sitting in the office. He wore a brown sweater, khaki pants, and black shoes.

He conducted the interview in two parts: first with me and then with Jeff. My heart rate increased after hearing that I had to talk one-on-one with the interviewer. I did my best to stay calm and speak clearly. The interviewer grabbed the pen and paper attached to his clipboard.

"So, tell me a little about yourself? It says here that you're from Cambodia. How do you like studying in America?"

"I really like studying in America." I talked slowly. "School here is much better than in Cambodia. I'm learning more and more every day."

"What makes the school here better than in Cambodia?"

"Teachers here are much nicer and more helpful. In Cambodia, my teachers beat me when I do something wrong. There are more subject offer at St. Luke than the school in Cambodia. I think all of this good thing that make American school better."

The interviewer narrowed his eyes. "Is beating a normal thing over there?"

"Yes. Teacher hit students all the time. I think it's a way that make students work harder. It help me study more every day."

"Interesting." I could sense that the gentleman was uncomfortable talking about child beating, especially in a school environment. He changed the subject.

"In your opinion, why should Lakeside accept you?"

"I'm a good student and a hard worker. I know that Lakeside is a difficult school, but I will push myself harder so I can do well. I hope Lakeside would accept me because I come from a place without much to learn. If I study here, I think I learn a lot because Lakeside is a good school. I want to learn as much as I can before I go back to Cambodia."

"What is your plan after school?"

"I want to go back to Cambodia and help teach other Khmer students. Students in Cambodia need help. Most students don't know much about the world. I will do as much as I can to help, that is my plan."

"That's really cool, I'm amazed by your ambition. We have a program here that enables students to travel to different countries and help teach the native students. A significant number of students here sign up for the program."

"Do they go to Cambodia?"

"I don't think so. Students are only allowed to travel to certain countries. I don't think Cambodia is one of them."

"I think the students should go to Cambodia. It's a nice country, and people there need a lot of help."

The gentleman nodded. "Well, thank you, Chom-Ron. That's all I have for this interview."

I shook his hand.

"How did it go?" Jeff asked, a concerned look across his face.

"Okay, I think. But I'm not sure."

Jeff appraised my response in silence. He entered the room and sat across from the interviewer. I wasn't able to hear their conversation, but Jeff kept glancing over his shoulder when answering the questions.

I truly believed that I was a unique student that could enhance Lakeside's diverse culture. I didn't want to give up until I was denied.

I soon found out that Jeff and Wanda didn't want me to even apply to Lakeside. They told me, "it's not a good fit. You would have a difficult time attending this school."

I was especially disappointed that they wouldn't even give me a chance to apply. Perhaps, they didn't think I was smart enough or that I didn't have the foundation to be a successful student at this school. They were probably right. A school like Lakeside was no place for "a dumb kid" like me. My dream of being like my brother-in-law had faded.

# 18

# VISITING WASHINGTON, DC

AS THE TEMPERATURE reached the mid-60s, we were seeing the first signs of spring. A sunny day in Seattle is always beautiful, with the clear blue sky reflecting off the rippling surface of the Puget Sound. Staring out the window of Jeff's car on the way back from school, I could see far across the water to the peninsula. The snow-capped Olympic mountains stretched for miles, dominating the horizon. Cargo ships and small boats sailed north and south from the port.

"So, have you decided what school you want to apply to?" Jeff asked, as he glanced at me over his shoulder.

I wished I could say Lakeside, but I knew it wasn't the answer Jeff expected. Thalen and Blake didn't want to continue coaching, making my desire to play for them futile. A few seconds later, I turned and said, "I want to go Bishop Blanchet. I like it a lot, I think it's a good school for me."

Jeff nodded. "I think so too. The people there seemed really friendly. The culture of the school is similar to St. Luke." He paused then looked at me with a serious face. "I think it's a great fit for you and I think you will have a good time going there."

I was genuinely pleased to have Jeff's support. I was sure Thalen and his brothers would dislike me for attending another Catholic school. Worse, Blanchet was an archrival of Lakeside. Drew once told me that back when he was playing football, Bishop Blanchet had a terrible team. His school used to dominate them. His story had pumped me up, making me want to play for Lakeside even more.

Everything had changed now. I had to start cheering for a school I used to root against.

Most nights, I chose to study for a placement test for Blanchet's application rather than completing my class assignments. Trying to answer questions that were not taught in school was challenging. I often ended up looking at the solutions, but was still left confused. Sometimes, I had to ask Thalen to sit next to me in the TV room and help me with math and reading problems.

On test day, I sat quietly, tapping my fingers on the desk. I nervously watched as Ms. Russell passed out the exam. She placed a gray booklet and a test sheet near my arm.

I began to feel shaky and unsure of myself. Once every student had a copy, Ms. Russell stood in front of the whiteboard and announced we could begin.

I opened the booklet and read a question in the science section. The only sound I could hear was pencils scratching papers. Most students seemed to read and answer the questions much faster than me, whereas I often had to reread them. Some people turned to the next page while I was still on the first problem. I realized my pace was too slow. I forced myself to choose solutions more quickly.

The reading section was by far the hardest. Each problem had a long article with sub-questions. I spent roughly five minutes reading through the first report. I didn't get the content. I read it again. Like the science section, the multiple-choice answers in reading were often similar. I was stuck.

At that moment, the word failure kept on popping into my head. I envisioned myself being rejected by Bishop Blanchet because of a terrible score. My back was against the wall, and I really had no choice but to look at a brunette girl's answer. I shakily put my hand on my forehead to cover my eyes. I could still see her circling "D." Immediately, I marked "D" on my sheet.

In Khmer school, my action would be called, *may-chomlong*, which indicated that a person had no brain and could only copy others. For the moment, I didn't care about being a may-chomlong. What was worse, I didn't know that her exam was different from mine. American schools often issued multiple versions to prevent cheating. I was ashamed and couldn't imagine how disappointed Thalen's family would be. Father would whip me if he knew I had become a may-chomlong. But I was incapable of answering the questions. I feared that my limited English would cause me to fail this exam. Anxious, I kept on copying without realizing those answers were incorrect.

I was beginning to lose hope, knowing that this could be the end of my journey in America. So many doubts were running through my mind. I asked myself, *what high school is willing to accept a "dumb kid" like me with a bad score?*

A week later, Thalen and I had assembled my high school application for Bishop Blanchet. I was scared of being rejected. Because of this, I had also decided to start packing in case I had to return to Cambodia. One night, I knelt on the carpet in my room, folding clothes and placing them neatly into the bag that I had brought from home. I had to prepare myself for a departure because nothing was guaranteed.

As school progressed, the subjects were getting more interesting. Ms. Carter taught us about the wars in American history: World War I and II, the Korean War, and even the Vietnam War which had negatively impacted Cambodia.

I remember the frustration I had while listening to Ms. Carter explain the tragedy of the Vietnam War. She sat on a tall metal stool in front of the whiteboard.

"Guys, it was really a messy war. It got so bad, the US started bombing all over Vietnam, including the border of Cambodia." She glanced at me, showing regret. "It was terrible. It killed many innocent people."

It was an uncomfortable lesson for me to absorb. I stared at my desk, grinding my teeth. Part of me wanted to disturb the class, stand up, and yell, why did the US bomb Cambodia? Do you know what happened in the aftermath of the bombings? Yet, I forced myself to sit still, as my father's words, "America is not perfect" popped into my head. I didn't know much history of the war and thought it was wrong to fully blame America for causing the Khmer Rouge.

Regardless, many educated Khmers like my father, people who survived the Khmer Rouge, knew that America was partly responsible for the genocide. Rumor had it that if the bombings (between 1969 and 1970) hadn't happened, Lon Nol's Army (Cambodia's Army) could have stopped the Communist Regime from taking control of the country, preventing the genocide. But the bombings did happen, based on the belief that the North Vietnamese soldiers were fleeing west into Cambodia. They killed thousands of innocent villagers across the Eastern borders. Beyond that, it took a tremendous toll on Lon Nol's army, allowing the Khmer Rouge to beat a nearly defeated army.

Like my father, I respected America's role in being "the world's police," looking out for small countries and liberating people from oppression. But America's influence was not always positive. Sometimes, their actions led to wars.

In class, I was taught about the victories that America had over its enemies. Victories created a sense of patriotism. Students, especially boys, loved listening to war stories. I could see the joyful faces around me as we read about global wars. Studying in an American school, I was surprised to see how many wars the US was involved in. People talked of wars as if they were games. Most students didn't seem to care about how a war could ruin a country, let alone, one that killed thousands of men, women, and children.

Unlike other students, war stories absolutely terrified me. I always believed that killing wasn't the answer. In fact, it could deprive humanity of its potential. Growing up in Cambodia, I knew very little about the outside world, and yet, I understood how much a war could damage a nation such as my own. Cambodia was once a peaceful place, full of educators who thrived on guiding the nation toward success. The country could have become as advanced as our neighbors, Thailand and Vietnam. Sadly, this potential faded due to a civil war followed by one of the most horrendous genocides in the twentieth century.

I was disappointed that the class didn't cover much of the Vietnam War. Perhaps, it was a shameful chapter in American history that this "great nation" refused to accept. I wished Ms. Carter could teach us more of this war so my fellow students and I could know the ugly truth. I had many unanswered questions: why did the US invade Vietnam? How did the war end? Did the US know about the Khmer Rouge? If so, where were "the world's police" when millions of men, women, and children were slaughtered?

When I learned about the positive things America had done after WWII, it reminded me of when my father said that America had done many "great things." Ms. Carter once invited a guest-speaker, an old war veteran, who seemed to be in his 80s. He wore a worn-in black military hat, a gray vest over a blue shirt, and brown trousers.

He sat on a stool, holding a walking stick while telling his story. He talked about many battles in Europe and kept on mentioning, "the Nazi." Students' eyes lit up while listening to his struggles in the world war. Sitting in the back of the room, I could see faint tears at the corner of his eyes as he spoke of his fallen comrades. I couldn't imagine what it was like to fight in a war, let alone a world war. But to him, stopping an evil regime like "the Nazi" was necessary to defend America's principles of freedom, liberty, and human rights.

"Despite all the lives we lost, despite how much I and many others had suffered from that war, I think it was worth it to stop the Nazis." He pulled out a red swastika flag, holding it up with both hands. Students looked at each other, stunned to see the flag.

At the moment, I didn't know what the symbol represented. I was intrigued to see such a strange symbol.

"I need a volunteer," he continued. A few boys in front bravely raised their hands. "You," he pointed to Josh, sitting to his left. "I want you to hold this flag." He handed over the flag as the boy approached. "I want you to show this to the rest of the class." Josh stood tall, holding it slightly below his chin with confusion on his face. "I want you all to take a good look at this flag," the gentleman said, "because this flag represents the Nazi, the group that took many lives. They have done many, many terrible things that damaged the world until this day." He looked over his shoulder at Josh. "Now, I want you to drop this flag, let it lay on the ground." Josh did so. "Do me a favor, step on it!" Josh looked at Ms. Carter, his eyes open wide. She nodded. Josh placed one foot on the flag. "Stand on it! Walk all over it!" Josh stood over it, rubbing it back and forth over the floor. "Good!"

The gentleman brought out a folded flag, I peeked over my desk and saw a red, white, and blue American flag in his hands. He looked at Josh. "Now, I want you to hold up this flag." He unfolded the flag then handed it to Josh. "Hold it up with pride." He held it over his chest, smiling. "I want you all to take a good look at this flag." He glanced at us, in a serious tone. "This is the reason why I chose to fight." He looked at the flag and smiled.

I was honored to hear his story. Most of all, his comment made me proud to be in America. But I wasn't alone. I could sense admiration around the room as we stood up and applauded him. Some students left their seats, shook his hand, and thanked him for his service. I stood still, curious to learn more about the Nazis and why he disliked this regime so much.

I had read about the Nazi regime and the Holocaust in my textbook but still couldn't absorb the information due to my poor reading ability. His story helped my young mind realize the values of liberty and freedom throughout this nation. I was now beginning to understand why Father had said, "America has done many great things," and was excited to learn more about the principles of this country.

A couple weeks later, spring break had arrived. This was the time for us to visit Washington, DC. Flying on airplanes always terrified me, but thankfully this trip was much shorter than coming from Cambodia.

Once we arrived, all of us grabbed our luggage, hopped on a tour bus, and headed to a nearby hotel. Ms. Russell handed out room keys while Ms. Carter announced the roommates. Each room had roughly four people. Boys and girls were separated. I got to share a room with James, Gary, and Phil.

"Okay everyone!" Ms. Carter shouted. "When we get to the hotel, we're all gonna head straight to our rooms. We are not going anywhere tonight, so everyone must stay in their rooms. Please respect your roommates and others around you. We're all tired and need a good sleep tonight."

However, some students didn't listen. A number of boys, as well as a few girls, came over to our room to play cards with James and Gary. I sat on the bed, watching them dealing cards on the carpet floor. They played a game of War, talking and laughing loudly, attracting a few more people to come over. Within minutes, our small room with two beds was packed with students circling around, watching them play.

It was midnight, yet everyone was wide awake. We made so much noise, Ms. Carter came over and shut down the game.

"Guys!" she glared at us. "I told you all to not leave your rooms. What are you all doing here?" No one responded and quickly left our room. They left the cards piled on the floor. "This is unacceptable. You guys were making so much noise, I could hear you from my room."

Jack, Phil, and Gary didn't say a word, but they couldn't hide their giggling.

"Gather up the cards and go to bed!" Ms. Carter glanced at me, lowering her eyebrows, then left the room. James immediately did so. Phillip then hopped on the bed next to me, shutting his eyes, but he couldn't wipe the smile off his face.

"Goodnight guys," said James then turned off the light.

We had roughly four days in DC. This made our schedule busy because there was so much to see. Everyone got on the bus that was headed to the capitol building. The building was even bigger than the one in Washington State. The exterior was painted white, made out of brick and sandstone. It seemed so tall. My neck got tired of staring up. At the top, I could see a bronze statue of a person holding a sword. I had seen this building many times in Hollywood movies and on the back of a fifty-dollar bill. Yet, seeing it in person made my jaw drop. I was impressed by the detail of carvings all around the building. To me, the sculptures and artwork not only made it beautiful, but it also represented the capability of American ingenuity.

Our next destination was the White House. Unlike the Capitol, we were not allowed to enter the building. In fact, I was told this place was known as "the most protected building in the world." I held the metal fence, looking through the narrow gap. I could see heavily armed men, wearing black uniforms, positioned at the top of the flat roof, securing the property. I even spotted one person holding binoculars, pointed straight at me. Pulling my hands back, I took a few steps away from the fence. I told myself, *I'm not in trouble. I didn't do anything wrong.* Yet, my heart was pounding as I thought to myself, *he could be spying on me.* The White House was truly a fortress. Being there was nerve-racking. Regardless, I felt honored to witness it in real life.

As the trip continued, we went to see many more historical sites from morning until night. We rode down to Jamestown in Virginia, where I got to see reenactments of the daily life of the early colonists and their settlements that marked the beginning of America. We then came back and explored more of DC: the National Museum of Natural History, the Korean War Veterans Memorial, and the Vietnam Veterans Memorial. Lastly was the National Mall, a place that possessed iconic structures, including the Washington Monument and the Abraham Lincoln Memorial.

I remember looking up at the gigantic white statue of Abraham Lincoln, sitting on a chair underneath a powerful message carved on the wall: "IN THIS TEMPLE AS IN THE HEARTS OF THE PEOPLE FOR WHOM HE SAVED THE UNION THE MEMORY OF ABRAHAM LINCOLN IS ENSHRINED FOREVER."

Being an outsider, I didn't know much about the history of America, nor the accomplishments of its earlier presidents. Lincoln was my favorite figure due to his commitment to saving a nation. In class, I had been taught many significant lessons of President Lincoln's role during the Civil War. Ms. Carter addressed the tragic event: "Lincoln's mission was to save the nation," she said, "he would do it whether it meant ending slavery or ignoring it. Because to him, nothing mattered more than uniting this nation. But the people in the North wanted slavery to end and the people in the South didn't. So, the war was fought and won by the North."

Before leaving Washington, DC, we visited more tourism sites, including the World War II Memorial and the National Museum of American History. However, the most memorable destination of all was the Holocaust Memorial Museum. I remember listening to Ms. Carter's warning before entering the building.

"Guys, please be respectful," she said. "This is a really sensitive place for a lot of people. This museum contains many things that might not be appropriate for you guys. So, if any of you feel like you don't want to go in, please let me know."

No one said anything. I was confused. She never gave a warning at any of the earlier places. I thought to myself, *what's so bad here that would make people not want to go in? It can't be as bad as The Killing Fields, could it?*

As it turned out, I was dead wrong. I came in contact with many horrific objects that depicted one of the darkest times in human history. Walls were covered with thousands of pictures of men, women, and children, who were the victims of the Holocaust. As I continued to explore, I saw displays mounted along the aisles, filled with worn shoes in all sizes covered with dust, and piled on top of each other. The strong bitter smell of leather mixed with rubber, burned my nostrils. The smell didn't all come from the shoes. Ahead of me, there were hundreds of pieces of luggage containing clothes, hats, notebooks, and other items. I was heartbroken as I realized I was staring at another mass genocide. I shut my eyes, my body shook, and I was at a loss for words. The Holocaust was basically the same as the Killing Fields, except more people were slaughtered: roughly six million innocent lives were lost during the Holocaust. Jews were murdered simply for their religion, while Khmers were massacred because of their education. Millions of lives were lost under the hands of two men: Adolf Hitler and Pol Pot.

Coming from Cambodia, I was truly sorrowful to know that the Khmer Rouge weren't responsible for the only genocide that had occurred in human history. I looked around and saw signs asking people to remember this horrific event so we could prevent it from happening again. It was at this moment I wondered to myself, *how many people in this room were aware of the Khmer Rouge? And if the world had experienced a brutal genocide like the Holocaust before, how did we allow another mass genocide to occur?*

When we got back from Washington, DC, I found out that I had been accepted to Bishop Blanchet. I received a package which included an acceptance letter, a student magazine, and a planner.

I was told that one of the reasons I got in, despite my poor exam score, was because many students don't do well on the placement test. The exam wasn't the only factor that Blanchet looked at. Grades, personal letters, and cultural backgrounds were also significant parts of the high school application. Nonetheless, I was extremely honored to continue my journey in America.

On the other hand, my time at St. Luke was running out as we reached the end of the school year. My classmates and I had signed each other's yearbooks. Like most people, I knew my relationships with some of my friends were coming to an end because we were attending different schools. I had a sense of melancholy over leaving St. Luke. It was a special place that had created many memories that would stick with me forever.

On our graduation day, eighth graders dressed in blue caps and gowns sat among their families in the church, waiting to receive their diplomas. It was a cheerful moment; the room was filled with people singing along with the choir, following the Catholic tradition.

Everyone in Thalen's family, Chai, and Kesor came to support me on this special day. I stood tall among them, listening to the blessings from the choir. The Father who led the ceremony gave a speech as we all took time to reflect on our journey. Individual students went up to the podium and delivered meaningful messages regarding the teachings of the Catholic Church. Living in an atheist family, none of us took those words seriously. In fact, Drew kept on looking at me, rolling his eyes. I knew he was not enjoying the singing and praying, but still, I was happy to have him there.

Soon, it was time to receive our diplomas. Students aligned in the back, and boys and girls stood in two rows then began walking down the aisle toward the podium. Within seconds, I got there, smiling widely at the principal.

"Congratulations!" he said, then shook my hand and gave me the diploma.

"Thank you!" I turned around to see my family admiring me. Thalen and Kesor raised their hands, giving me a thumbs-up. I smiled and felt extremely thankful to be in this position.

# 19

# HOME OF THE BRAVES

AFTER BEING AWAY from my family for two years, I was getting more and more homesick. Sitting in the dining room in Jeff and Wanda's house, I dialed Father's number as a feeling of elation rose in me.

"Chamroeun! How are you? I haven't heard from you in a while. Chai told me that you have graduated. I am so proud of you. We're all proud of you. I'd give you a hundred riel if you were here next to me." He laughed over the phone.

"Thank you, Father." I giggled. "But I still have a long way to go. High school will be even more challenging than middle school."

"Yeah, but that's how school works. The higher the grade, the more difficult it becomes. As long as you study hard, the teachers will not punish you."

"I know . . . I will do my best. How's Mother? Can I talk to her?"

Father paused. "I'm not home right now."

"Are you at the market?"

"No, I'm in Prey Veng."

"Why are you in Prey Veng?"

"Don't worry, I'm only here for a few days. I just wanted to get away from all the drama happening at the house. I just can't stand your mother anymore."

"But Father, you know that's how she is. Why are you mad at her? She says mean things sometimes, but she doesn't really mean it."

"Yeah, but it still hurts my feelings. Your mother is so difficult to be around sometimes."

"The family needs you. I don't want to return home without seeing you there with the rest of us."

"Like I said, I'm only here for a few days. I'll be back in no time. But regardless of what happens between me and your mother, I will be there when you return."

It seemed like my parents' relationship had been getting worse since the day Sokha got in a bike accident. They often argued. Mother frequently cursed Father, calling him names: "crazy dog," "moron," or "dumbass." She blamed him for not maximizing our small budget for food, rent, and electricity.

"Since the day I met him, I've known nothing but struggles," Mother once said over the phone. "He always does stupid things and puts the family in debt again and again. I don't want to be with him anymore."

"Don't say that, Mother," I said. "Father did a lot to help our family. He cares about us."

"No, he doesn't! He only cares about himself and playing the lottery. He uses food money to gamble and always puts us in desperate situations. He doesn't care about the family. He has beaten me and damaged my body in ways that have never been fixed." She paused. "He broke my heart. I've had enough of it."

I was crushed to hear how hurt Mother was. I couldn't imagine the pain that she had gone through. Mother had been abused physically and emotionally by my father during arguments. I didn't blame her for disliking Father. Mother wasn't alone. My siblings and I deeply resented him for his mistreatment of her. We didn't have to be educated to know that domestic violence was wrong. I loved my father and viewed him as an educator and leader, who guided our family. Despite all of that, Father still wasn't perfect.

On the other hand, I couldn't imagine how it felt to be Father. Sometimes, I sat next to him, telling him, "don't get offended, Father. Mother only does that when she's mad. She didn't mean what she said."

Father often listened, saying, "if it wasn't for you and your sisters, I would've left her a long time ago. But don't worry about the things between your mother and me. Your job is to focus in school. I won't go anywhere. I won't do that to you all."

I wasn't surprised to hear Father wanted to move. I knew his feelings had been hurt. He wanted to move away months ago. I was disappointed that my siblings didn't stop him. At the time, I knew he would've listened. Truth was, Lab didn't appreciate how Father kept on spending money meant for food on the lottery and cigarettes. She even dared him to leave, knowing that he wouldn't survive without us. Lab's comments were often cruel, and they only seemed to add fuel to fire.

It broke my heart to hear that my family was falling apart. As much as I wanted him to return, it felt like the best thing I could do was leave him alone so he could find peace. Nonetheless, I hoped he would reunite with our family.

About one week before school started, freshman football practices began. Practice ran from Monday to Friday, three thirty to five thirty in the evening. Jeff and Wanda took Gary and I that day.

"A lot of teenagers make bad decisions in high school," said Jeff, looking at us through the rearview mirror. "Just be careful."

"High school kids often want to have fun. But you guys know that underage drinking is illegal and so is doing drugs," Wanda added, turning her head toward us. "You know that, right?"

"Yep, I am aware of that," said Gary, rolling his eyes at me.

"And what about you, Chamroeun?" said Jeff. "Do you understand what Wanda meant?"

"Yes, I understand."

"You have to be really careful, Chamroeun. Your status is not the same as other American kids at your school. If you get caught drinking or doing something illegal, you could get deported," Wanda said.

When we arrived, I saw Caucasian boys mixed with a few people of color, wearing shorts, t-shirts, and cleats, playing catch all over the turf field. On the right sideline, there was a metal bleacher with, "Home of The Braves" written in large letters on a banner. Brave was the school's mascot.

"Hey, you wanna run a route for me?" I asked a boy named Ty.

He nodded and got in position then started sprinting straight ahead. I took a few steps back and delivered a bullet to his chest.

"Hey Cham! Can you stop showing off now?" said Gary, laughing with a few other boys. "I'm kidding . . . That was a nice throw though."

I laughed. "I'm just practicing."

"I'm Jake," said a boy, standing to Gary's right.

"Matt," said the other boy on Gary's left.

"I'm Chamroeun, call me Cham."

"Can I call you Chamwow?" Jake asked, smirking.

I chuckled. "Sure. You can call me that."

"Dude, I got a perfect line for you," said Gary. "You can say, girls call me 'Cham-ron' but when they look down at my pants, they call me, 'Chamwow'." He dropped his jaw, raising his eyebrows. They all laughed.

Jake nodded with a big smile. "That was a good one, you should do it, Chamwow."

I shook my head, grinning to myself. "That's nice but I'm okay."

On that same day, I got to meet many people in my class. I even met a girl named Lenny. She had white skin and black hair. Lenny and I got to talk for a bit during our freshman dance welcome rehearsal. All incoming freshmen gathered in the big gym. We stood in small groups on the shiny basketball court, watching our mentors teach us the dance moves.

"You're good at this!" she giggled while watching me move my feet.

"You can do it too," I said, "try it!"

"Oh, no. I can't dance very well. It's not really my thing."

"Not with that attitude." We glanced at each other, then laughed.

Shortly, boys and girls separated into two long lines, facing each other. We now had to do the dances on our own. I stood near some of my football friends. Across from me, I could see Lenny and her friends, giggling while attempting the moves. Within seconds, the music hit, and "Call me Maybe" by Carly Rae Jepsen started playing. Loud beats hit the room. We started dancing, moving our feet back and forth, shaking our shoulders, spinning our bodies, and sliding side-to-side on the smooth floor. My friends and I didn't remember all the moves, but we kept on dancing, blending with the rhythm of the song. People were laughing while shaking their bodies. As for me, I was thankful to be at this place and was proud to call Blanchet home.

The first day of high school was frightening. I remember riding with Gary and his brother, Samuel, on the freeway in his black Chevrolet SUV. Samuel turned up the music, playing the rap song, "Bring em Out" by TI. I could feel the bass shaking the entire car as we sped up, changing lanes, passing other vehicles.

"Woo!" he yelled, rolling down his window, putting his hand on top. He steered with one hand. I could feel the car swerving. "How are you feeling back there, Chamrock?" he yelled over the wind. "Are you excited for high school?"

"Yeah!" I said, holding onto the door.

"Damn right!" he laughed, looking at me through the rearview mirror, seeming to pay less attention to the road. "You're gonna like Blanchet. It's a fun school."

"Okay!" I forced a big smile. My legs shook. Cold air made my face numb. I was more concerned about Samuel's driving skill.

I began my high school day with a math class. It was a large room with many glass windows and white walls covered with religious posters. Lenny sat across from me, giving us an opportunity to know each other a little more.

Seconds before class started, pop music erupted on the speakers and a number of students were rocking their heads to the beat. The song was cut off by the announcers, "good morning, Braves!" said a male and a female student. I could hear them giggling over the speakers. We laughed. The announcers gave us a quick report: students' birthdays, sports, and other extracurricular activities. Like St. Luke, they ended their report with a prayer. People bowed their heads and closed their eyes, saying, "hail Mary," softly.

Bishop Blanchet was a two-semester school. Class days were separated into two categories: green day and gold day. On green days, I had math, pottery, Spanish, and PE. As for gold days, I had 3D modeling, language arts, homeroom period, and religion. School ran from eight in the morning to two thirty in the afternoon. There were four classes in each day. Each one lasted roughly eighty-five minutes with ten-minute passing periods.

I remember sitting at a long rectangular table with a lot of people during my first lunch. The cafeteria was crowded, students sat in groups, and chatted while shoveling food into their mouths. In the middle of the room, I could see two long lines of students waiting to buy cafeteria lunches. I brought my own food which was packed with applesauce, a banana, snack bars, and a turkey sandwich. While unzipping my lunch box, I could see some of my football friends sitting in a corner of the room, but I chose to stay where I sat. I wanted to meet new people, especially those who didn't play football. I overheard a conversation to my right.

"What d'you got there?" asked a boy with brown skin and a straight nose. "It smells really good." I could also smell the sweet tomato sauce.

"Spaghetti with meatballs. My mom packed this for me," said a Caucasian boy with light blonde hair.

"It looks really good. Can I take a bite?"

"Sure," the boy gave him half a meatball, covered with tomato sauce. He noticed me watching them. "Do you want some?"

"I'm okay. I bring my own lunch. Thank you though."

"What's your name?"

"Chamroeun, you can call me Cham. What's your name?"

"I'm Andrew."

"I'm George," said the boy with brown skin. "Are you the one they call 'Chamwow'?"

I laughed, covering my mouth full of food. "Some people call me that, yeah. But I prefer, Cham."

We continued to talk over the noise surrounding us. I thought Blanchet was a relaxing place. The school occasionally provided a few late starts (nine thirty) on gold days, allowing students to sleep-in. Students were also allowed to wear casual clothes: jeans, shorts, t-shirts, and sweaters. But yoga pants and basketball shorts were prohibited.

The highlight of my first day was meeting my PE teacher. His name was Mr. Morris. He seemed so friendly: talking, laughing, and making jokes with us. I remember being struck by his humor as he was trying to get to know us.

"Who here plays sports?" he asked, leaning on a student's desk. A number of boys including myself raised our hands. "What sport do you play?" he pointed at a boy near him.

"I play football," he said.

"All of you play football?"

"No," said a skinny boy who sat in the corner of the room. "I play soccer. But right now, I'm doing cross country."

Mr. Morris laughed, shaking his head. "Don't tell me you play soccer."

"What's wrong with soccer?"

"I'll tell you what's wrong with soccer. It's a communist's sport." Students including myself started giggling. "When I was young, I played soccer too. But only because they were a player short. Now, I'll tell ya, I didn't know what the hell I was doing. All I did was kick the ball as hard as I could. Didn't matter what direction. The ball came to me, I kicked it." He nodded, smiling. "I even won an award for doing the easiest thing." He looked at the skinny boy in the corner. "One day, I drove by a soccer field. I saw little kids practicing kicking soccer balls around. I thought to myself, one day, this sport is gonna destroy America."

The whole class laughed even harder. I was stunned to hear such a disparaging statement coming from an American teacher, but I still found it funny. I knew Mr. Morris was only giving him a hard time. The skinny boy had none of it though. He crossed his arms and stared down at his desk.

My favorite part of freshman year was attending football games. I remember riding on a bus, heading to an away game. Blanchet played Bellermine Prep that week, a school roughly fifty minutes south. The bus was loaded with each seat holding three to four people, squished together on the worn leather. People were talking all around me while music echoed loudly, playing "Dynamite" by Taio Cruz. People clapped and sang along with the music the whole way.

One Friday evening at a home-game at Blanchet, I saw Lenny approach the field with a guy. They talked and laughed along the way. Within minutes, they stood below me on the bleacher and started cheering. I waved at her, but she didn't say a word.

My heart fell. After the game, I approached her as she was talking to some of her friends.

"Hey, can I talk to you for a second?" I asked.

"Sure," she said. We stepped away from the group.

"What's going on? You don't like talking to me anymore?"

"Cham, you're a great guy. But I don't think I'm ready for a relationship right now. I just want to enjoy high school and see what it's all about. I'm sorry."

I walked away, embarrassed. I was disappointed, but I respected Lenny's decision. I also thought that it was best to enjoy high school first.

As the year went on, Thalen had gotten tired of driving me around, so after I turned sixteen years old, he signed me up for a driving class.

Attending driving school also meant adding more workload to an already busy schedule. Once again, my life was dominated by classes and extracurricular activities.

One morning as Jeff was driving me to school, I sat in the passenger seat, yawning repeatedly.

"Did you get all of your homework done last night?" he asked.

"Yeah . . ." I lied. I didn't finish math and was planning on doing it at school.

"I feel bad for you, Chamroeun. You looked exhausted last night. You know if you are feeling overwhelmed with school, maybe you shouldn't play football." He adjusted his glasses. "Football is not that important, you know. It's not like you're gonna go pro, so if you feel like you need more time for homework, then maybe you can stop playing football for a while."

Jeff was right. I did struggle to keep up with school while playing football. I often wished I had more time to breathe and call my family. But in my heart, I knew I must not quit. "I'm okay. I can do it," I said.

"I know you want to play football. But school is more important. You know that, right?"

"Yeah, I know, but I can do it."

Jeff didn't say anything further. He knew it was my decision to make.

But even facing difficulty, quitting wasn't an option. I remember on one Thursday afternoon near the end of practice, the coaches made us run from one sideline to the other. At that point, we had already run back and forth roughly five times on a hot sunny day. There was no sign of when the drill would end. My body was exhausted, sweat dripped down my helmet, making me lose vision. My hamstrings cramped, begging me to stop. After completing the sixth time, I leaned forward, hands on my knees, breathing heavily. I could see people struggling, but most stood tall, hands on their hips and helmets.

"Okay, get ready," said the head coach, holding his whistle.

"Coach!" I yelled. "Coach, my legs are cramping. I don't think I can run anymore."

"Okay, then go sit down!" I walked slowly and sat on the bench near the bleacher. "See that!" he said in front of the team. "We're only halfway through but we already have one person tapping out."

"Come on, Cham! Get up!" said Jake. I bit my lips, staring at the turf in shame. My heart dropped, hearing a teammate calling my name.

The coach blew the whistle. Everyone ran. Most of my teammates stared at me, shocked to see me sitting. Some people had considered me one of the leaders on the team due to my ability to make plays in practices and games. At the moment, I felt that I was betraying them. It reminded me of the moment I let my eight-grade teammates down during the playoffs. Within seconds, I got up and walked toward the sideline.

"No!" said the head coach, approaching me. "You sit down! You told me you're hurt."

"Coach, I can run now."

"No! Go sit down. You're a quitter! I'm not looking for quitters. You understand?"

I nodded. My teammates rolled their eyes and looked away. The word "quitter" stuck in my head. From that day on, I promised myself that I must not be a quitter no matter how tough the situation was. This was a valuable lesson I learned from football that would help me overcome challenges in school and in life.

Despite my toughness, my performance in class dropped significantly. In pottery, I received a terrible score, 55/100, on my gallery paper. The teacher had to talk to me after class.

"Your paper didn't meet the requirements," said Ms. Miller, looking at my paper through her glasses. "Did you read the instructions?"

"Yes, but I don't understand some of it."

"Well, then you need to ask questions. Because I'm telling ya, this paper is a huge portion of your grade. If you don't get higher than a 70, you won't pass my class."

My hands shook. I hadn't failed a class since first grade. "Is there extra credit I can do to bring my grade up?"

"No, I don't do extra credit." She turned to me. "But since you're a freshman, I'm gonna let you redo this."

"Okay, thank you." I smiled with a wave of relief.

"Here's the deal, you have to pick a different piece of art, and you have to rewrite the whole thing. Okay?"

I nodded.

"And please follow the directions. Everyone else seemed to do pretty well, except you."

I looked down with shame.

"You have two weeks to complete this and come see me if you have any questions."

This was a time-consuming project. It took me three days to find the artwork, *The Fin Project*, located near Lake Washington, which was about a thirty-minute drive from home. Jeff was kind enough to take me there, allowing me to absorb the project in person, making it a little easier to report on.

"I think your teacher is going to like these sculptures," he said, while driving the car back home. "They're pretty cool. They look like shark fins. But do you know that those fins are a part of submarines?"

"No, what are submarines?"

"They are big battle ships that can go underwater." He smiled. "You know, I think your teacher will love it if you share your experience of being here."

"You think so?"

"Yeah, I think you should add this experience to your report. You can talk about where you're from and how things here are different from Cambodia. Say that you never see these kinds of things when you were over there." He nodded lightly. "I think your teacher will be delighted to read your story."

I followed Jeff's advice and wrote roughly three pages about my journey in America, but Jeff was dead wrong.

"What is this?" said Ms. Miller, circling that portion in red.

"It's a short story about me coming from Cambodia."

"Get rid of it! It's not relevant!" She crossed it out. "This is a gallery paper. It's about art, not your life story. If I was grading this, I would give you an F. Go home and fix this, okay?"

My eyes narrowed. I left the room with disappointment.

During dinner, Jeff was excited to hear about the meeting with my teacher.

"How did it go?" he asked, while squeezing lemon over a juicy salmon.

"She don't like it. She want me to take the part about me out." I took a slow bite into the cornbread mixed with honey. "She said the paper would get an F if she grade it now."

Jeff paused. Wanda glanced at Thalen with worry but didn't say anything.

"What class is this again?" Thalen asked, while chewing roasted asparagus.

"Pottery," I said.

"This is ridiculous," said Jeff. "She can't fail you. No one should get an F for trying." He wiped his mouth with a napkin. "I'm gonna go talk to her."

Jeff wasn't joking. He went in with me after class. "Chamroeun is trying very hard in your class. He works on his report every day. Now, I don't know how you do things around here, but he does not deserve an F."

"I understand," Ms. Miller said, "my class is hard. It's supposed to be for juniors and seniors, not freshmen. But the school allowed that to happen and that's why I gave him another chance to fix his report." She pulled out my paper. "There are some mistakes in his paper, but it's good that he is coming to see me because the more he does then the better his paper will become." She turned the page, skimming through it. "Now this story of him coming from Cambodia is fascinating, but it's not related to the project. If he wants a higher score, just follow the instructions. I'm only giving him points for what's on the rubric. The rest doesn't matter."

Jeff turned to me then looked at the paper. "So, if he follows the instructions and keeps coming to see you, he won't fail your class?"

"I'm gonna be honest with you. I'm not gonna fail a freshman. But that doesn't mean he should stop trying. And yes, doing those things will definitely help."

I breathed smoothly, relieved knowing that I wasn't going to fail. My teacher might seem harsh, but I was thankful for her willingness to guide me.

My hard work had prevailed once again. I had gotten a high enough score on the report to pass pottery class. I might not have earned the best grades, but it was rewarding to know I had made forward progress. I could not wait to share this excitement with Father.

Father had returned home. He didn't want me to worry and knew our family needed his leadership. My family and I were thankful to have him back. Nothing made me happier than hearing my family was back together. I missed them deeply and wished to reunite with them soon.

On a Sunday evening in mid-spring, I sat outside, calling Father. I hadn't called home in two months due to my busy school schedule. I tried again and again, but there was no answer. Fortunately, Lab had another cell phone at the moment. I dialed her number, hoping she would pick up.

"Brother! Haven't heard from you for a long time. I didn't know you still care about our family." She paused. "I'm kidding." She laughed. "How are you? Kesor said that you're done with school now. Are you coming to visit us?"

"I want to, but I have to check with Thalen first. You know it's difficult for me to travel back and forth."

"Yeah, Father told me about it. But it would be nice if you can come. We miss you."

"I miss you guys, too. Speaking of Father, where is he? I tried to call, but he didn't answer."

"He went to the market." Lab hesitated. "I have to tell you something, but you have to promise me to not ask him any questions, okay?"

"What is it?"

"I think Father has been cheating on Mother. I saw him riding a bike with another woman the other day."

"She could just be his friend."

"His friend? No, I don't think so. Father doesn't have any female friends. If he does, he knows that it is inappropriate to be that close with another woman knowing that he has a wife." She paused. "Don't forget that in our culture, it is wrong to be spending time with another woman. And he knows that."

I didn't say anything, stunned by the news.

"Don't worry about it, okay," she continued. "Ruat and I will get to the bottom of this. As for now, find out if you can come visit."

# 20

# BECOMING AMERICANIZED

THREE WEEKS HAD gone by since Lab asked me to visit home. I had talked to Jeff and Thalen about going back. Yet, they had some hesitation about it.

"I've talked to a lady at your school," said Jeff, opening a jar of olives. "She has experience dealing with international students. She said that you won't have any problem getting the visa. So, if you want to go home, there's a possibility that you could come back."

I nodded, then looked at Thalen, who sat on the couch, watching the evening news. It was an overwhelming decision. Should I go? Should I stay?

"Nothing is guaranteed, Chamroeun," said Thalen, over the noise of the TV. "Every time you go back, you would have to visit the embassy. They are the ones that get to make the decision about whether you can come back or not."

Part of me wanted to stay, I liked Blanchet and was looking forward to sophomore year. But I deeply missed home. Kesor told me that Lab and Ruat saw Father with the same woman once again. Even though I was only sixteen, I wanted to take leadership and solve issues that ran rampant in my family. "Is school more important than family?" Chai once asked me. The answer might be obvious to some people. To me, education was something I didn't know how to give up.

After a few days of thinking, I chose to stay. I wasn't happy with my decision, but I knew I was doing what was best for my family and myself. I was the last hope of finishing school, let alone having the potential to graduate from an American high school.

But I didn't make this decision alone. Father shined the light. "You have to stay, you will find a good job in Cambodia if you have an American diploma," he said over the phone. "Most people would hire you, knowing that you studied in America. Stay, Son. You will have a successful future if you study there." I listened to Father's advice, knowing that this commitment would divide me even more from my family. In my heart, I knew I must be strong to achieve my goal.

One midsummer evening, Jeff and Wanda picked me up from a football weight room session at Blanchet. We stopped by McDonald's on the way home.

"It's pretty cool that you can just drive in and order food, huh?" Jeff asked, looking through the rearview mirror.

"Yeah, that's pretty cool," I said.

"Your English is getting much better, Chamroeun," said Jeff. "Pretty soon you'll be like a native kid."

"He dresses like one too!" Wanda added, turning her shoulders. "Look at him, he's wearing shorts and a t-shirt just like an American kid."

What Wanda said was true. I often wore these kinds of outfits. I even had a buzz cut so I could blend in among most American boys.

"You know, maybe one day you can write a book about your life," said Jeff. "I think it would be interesting."

I was shocked by Jeff's comment. I thought to myself, *how could I write a book if I couldn't even read well?* I thought that asking a boy who spoke broken English to write a book was insane. On top of that, I disliked reading and writing and always found books boring. Jeff's words seemed to come out like a joke because me writing a book seemed impossible.

When we got home, I walked up the stairs toward my bedroom. My heavy footsteps caused the wood floor to creak, but I could still hear shouting coming from Thalen and Kesor's room. At first, I thought they were playing around. I lay on my bed, scrolling through my phone. Suddenly, I heard a door open and footsteps stomped across the hallway.

"How could you do this to me?" Thalen shouted. A door slammed shut, shaking the walls.

I turned off my phone and went across the hall toward Kesor's room. I entered and saw Kesor kneeling on the floor, folding her clothes, putting them neatly in her luggage. "What's going on?" I asked. She glared at me and continued folding. "Kesor?"

"Don't worry about it! And leave my room!" she shouted.

I went downstairs and saw Thalen in the dining room, rubbing his forehead, talking to Jeff and Wanda. Thalen didn't want to tell me the truth, but his parents forced him to.

"I just found out that my wife has been hanging out with another guy," he said. "It's pretty messed up." Thalen's face was red.

Thalen's comment shook me. My heart dropped to my guts. I breathed rapidly. I felt terrible for Thalen. I stood there in silence, at a loss for words.

I pulled out my phone, calling Chai. She was on a date with Ryan that day. He had returned from Iraq and wanted to spend as much time with her as he could before leaving for another tour. I called repeatedly but Chai didn't answer.

Without knowing what to do, I sat on the couch in the TV room, hoping that Chai would call me back soon. What does this mean? Is Thalen going to divorce Kesor? Is school over for me? Are they going to send me back?

Within seconds, Jeff came over to me. "Chamroeun, I want you to know that whatever happens between Thalen and Kesor, it doesn't affect you staying here." He forced a smile. "Wanda and I will continue to sponsor you. We want you to stay until you finish school."

I was incredibly pleased to hear Jeff's words. I didn't know how to handle this situation. Deep down, I was afraid to lose Thalen. He gave my family hope and helped us escape poverty. The most important lesson I had learned from him was something he had said during a car ride.

"What's important to me is impacting other people's lives," he said in a serious tone. "You know, if you can help someone, if you can impact someone's life in a positive way. If you do that, I think that's more important than making a lot of money."

"Yeah." I nodded. "I always want to help other when I go back."

"Well, you gotta help your family first before you can help other people." He grinned. "You know that, right?"

"I know." I never heard him say anything like this before. I would never imagine a person would choose to help others rather than being wealthy. Thalen had spent some of his salary supporting my family over the years. He even once made a plan to build a dream house for us in Oue Bram so we could live better together.

Thalen and Kesor's relationship had become complicated. Lab and Lane told me that Kesor thought Thalen was still a drug addict, using behind her back. She also didn't like how Jeff and Wanda always interfered with their relationship. She didn't think that Thalen was capable of handling dilemmas on his own. Whenever his relationship went wrong, Thalen always reported the news to his parents, and they in return would confront Kesor as a result.

But not all of this was Thalen's fault; Kesor cheated on him and couldn't take responsibility for her actions. Perhaps, she felt betrayed by Thalen's addiction. Or maybe, the love that she once had for Thalen was fading away.

Thalen did what he could to prevent Kesor from cheating. He went and told the guy to stay away, and this seemed to work.

To save their marriage, Thalen and Kesor moved out of Jeff and Wanda's house. Thalen, along with Drew and Blake, bought a house a few blocks away. Only Thalen, Kesor, Chai, and Drew moved in together. Blake and Krystal continued to live in their old place. As for me, I kept living with Jeff and Wanda. Jeff was concerned that I wouldn't have a place to study at the new house. Jeff and Wanda were also my sponsors. They thought it was best if I stay with them.

Thalen and Drew bought me an old blue Subaru station wagon, two weeks after I got my driver's license. It was a manual. Driving to school was one of my favorite pastimes. I took the shortcut, cruising through the narrow curvy roads. I turned the music up, listening to rap songs, rocking my body from side-to-side, feeling the vibration. My old speakers were blasting, causing the windows to rattle. My music was so loud a few pedestrians glared at me as I drove by. I didn't care. There were hardly any cars on this route, so I sped up through the chilly morning.

Most of the subjects I took my sophomore year were a continuity from freshman year. However, some teachers were a bit more aggressive. I remember sitting at my desk during history, preparing to turn in my map assignment. I looked across the room and saw my football teammate, AD, coloring his map. We were studying the ancient Roman civilization and their conquered territories.

Ms. Cook went around, collecting the papers. She noticed AD was doing his homework in class. Ms. Cook grabbed the map from him then ripped AD's paper in pieces. The whole class was in complete shock. Our eyes lit up, but no one had the courage to say anything. I had never seen an American teacher do anything like this before. She reminded me of my fifth grade teacher, especially when he tossed students' notebooks on the floor.

Despite the brutal treatments, I liked my fifth grade teacher and had learned tremendously from his class. Strangely, I had respect for cruel teachers. Mean instructors pushed students to the limit. There was no guarantee of passing the class, but there was higher certainty that students' knowledge would improve. The punishment might seem brutal, but without it students could become lazy.

On an evening during a school day, I came home after football practice, placed my duffel bag in the laundry room, then entered the kitchen. I saw Jeff and Wanda sitting on the couch in the TV room, eating dinner, with the news flashing.

"This is just terrible," said Jeff. I looked over my shoulder and saw him shaking his head at the screen. I could hear the sound of the news announcing, "one of the worst school shootings in US history." I picked up a bowl then scooped up some of Wanda's soup: broth mixed with chicken breast strips and vegetables. I grabbed a spoon then carefully carried my bowl to sit near Wanda. I took a sip of the warm broth, glanced at the screen, and saw pictures of children posted on the news. The video showed parents crying, hugging each other as the headline appeared, "Sandy Hook Elementary School Shooting." Below was a report, "At Least 27 Dead."

"Where is this?" I asked.

"It's in Newtown, Connecticut," said Jeff.

"This is awful, Chamroeun," Wanda added. "Most of the victims were children, kids in first grade."

"Ugh!" Jeff looked away with disgust. "It's just terrible." He walked to the kitchen. "Terrible thing." He put his bowl in the sink.

I continued watching the news, speechless. My skin crawled seeing pictures of children shown in the footage. After being in America for nearly four years, I had seen news reports of school shootings. The Sandy Hook shooting was different though. Children from ages six to seven were slaughtered by an insane gunman. If children that young weren't safe in a school environment, then how safe are American schools really?

I left Khmer school to escape the beatings from teachers and threats from gang members. I knew American schools would offer greater knowledge and always thought it would be a much safer place for me to pursue education. At St. Luke, I didn't have to worry about brutal punishments. Western teachers didn't beat students. There were no gangs at St. Luke nor at Blanchet. Yet, it was terrifying to see shootings occur in American schools throughout the country. At Khmer school, I feared gang attacks and teachers' beatings, but I still walked out alive. In America, many students lost their lives during school shootings. It became a norm reported on national news almost every year.

No student should have to worry about losing their lives while attending class. School should be a safe environment, not a killing field.

While absorbing Blanchet's culture, I learned that attending parties was a popular event. I was never interested in underage drinking or smoking weed. I didn't want to be addicted like Thalen or end up smoking like Father and my brothers. I wanted to be myself, choosing to be different even knowing I was losing popularity. Most of my friends didn't want to chat with me. Even if they did, they frequently talked about attending parties, making me wish I had gone. Sometimes, I wished I could go to parties so I could become as cool as them. It felt like every time I was about to take a risk, warnings I'd been given popped into my head.

"Don't do anything illegal or you could get deported," Wanda told me.

"You not American," Chai told me with her broken English, "those kids can drink and smoke, but they still be here. You not them."

Following their advice was the right thing to do, but it isolated me from my friends. I often stayed home, scrolling through pictures of my friends attending parties on Twitter, feeling like a loser.

I had thought I was one of the popular kids during freshman year. People referred to me as "Chamwow." It was strange how I lost fame just for being myself. Regardless of what people thought of me, I didn't let their criticism change me.

As life went on, I focused more on football. After Samuel graduated, I was committed to do whatever it took to be the starter. Some coaches didn't believe in me, especially Coach Collins, the offensive coordinator

"Listen Cham, I don't want to doubt you, okay," he said, "but if you can't show me that you can play, then you're not our guy! Being a running back is tough. You have to earn it, all right?" He shook his head. "I know Coach Maul believes in you, but I can't let you play if you don't look ready."

I always thought he hated me. There were times Coach Collins intentionally ignored me. Sitting next to my teammate Harley in the film room, he often greeted Harley and other people but didn't say anything to me. It seemed like he had no interest in talking to me.

I wanted to become a starting running back on the varsity team. More importantly, I wanted to overcome Coach Collins' criticism. Since I was a child, I had tried my best to ignore negative comments toward my family. This time was different. It felt like if I didn't stand up to defend myself, people would continue to judge me. Hearing players make fun of me was one thing but feeling like a coach doubted me was another.

At that moment, I was more committed than ever. I was willing to push myself to not only earn the starting job but also to prove to my team that I belonged.

Over the summer, I woke up early, driving to the morning weight room sessions at seven in the morning.

I met a friend that had the same passion as me. His name was Ramsay. He had brown hair, a light beard, and wide shoulders. His first name was Andrew, but people called him Ramsay because there were a few Andrews on our team.

Ramsay and I challenged each other every weight room session. We tried to beat one another by lifting heavier weights or doing more reps. Coaches noticed our competition. They even put Ramsay and me in the same group so we could keep pushing each other. We worked side-by-side as sweat dripped down our faces. Progress was made. My body was transformed as my shoulders broadened and muscle mass increased all over. My arms and legs were growing. I felt stronger than ever.

Football season had arrived. We had our first game at home, playing Ballard Public High School. The field was packed with students and parents, gossiping while sitting on the home and visitor bleachers. All kinds of music was playing, including rock and rap, boosting the players' energy. We stood on the field in rows, stretching. We wore white pants, green jerseys, and helmets. The coaches had given me the number twenty-six that year.

"It's gonna be a great day, gents!" Coach Maul shouted. "It's all about the freaking Braves today!" He smiled widely. "Am I right, Nikola?" He approached a teammate, positioned to my left.

"Yes, Coach!" he said with a straight face.

Coach Maul moved farther back into the stretching lines. "Ramsay! How many tackles are you gonna make today?"

"As many as I can, Coach!" said Ramsay. I glanced at Ramsay. He noticed me then nodded. I nodded back. I was glad to be playing by his side. All of the sweat and tears in the weight room had earned me a top spot on the depth-chart. All the hard work was meant for this moment.

Coach Maul walked toward my area.

"What's your story today, Cham?" he asked.

"I'm ready!" I yelled. "I've been waiting for this moment!"

"I like it." He laughed then moved on to the next person.

Parents and students filled the bleachers as we were getting closer to game time. The atmosphere came to life as the crowd started to cheer while the school band began playing the Blanchet fight song.

Before kickoff, we stood on the sideline, shoulder to shoulder, and removed our helmets.

"Ladies and gentlemen," said the commentator, "at this moment, I ask you to please stand up and remove your hats for the national anthem." Everyone did as he asked, placing their right hands over their hearts. I stood calmly, respecting the tradition. Everyone was staring at the American flag in a corner of the field next to the scoreboard.

After a short silence, a girl standing in the press box started singing over the microphone.

"Oh say can you see, by the dawn's early light . . ."

I rocked my body slightly, glancing at the American flag. Seeing the red, white, and blue stripes waving and twisting reminded me of the moment I was in the US Embassy, looking at the large picture of the American flag. Listening to the girl's singing gave me goosebumps. I realized at this moment that I didn't feel like an outsider anymore. I now understood what Thalen meant by "your life will change." I was becoming Americanized.

Everything felt natural to me. I was comfortable with the food, weather, and driving, and I even behaved like an American teenager. I didn't know if my family would be proud or disappointed if they could see how much I had changed.

I glanced at the stand where Kesor, Thalen, and his family stood. I smiled and turned toward the flag as the girl continued to sing. I raised my right hand and placed it on my heart. I shut my eyes, shedding tears, thinking to myself, *thank you America, you changed my life.*

# 21

# REGRETS

MY FIRST GAME as a varsity starter was brutal. Every time I touched the ball, defenders rushed in and tackled me immediately. During one play, a defender hit me so low, my body spun in the air and I landed on my stomach. Yet, I got up, pounding my chest. My effort sparked my teammates energy. Players on the sideline jumped up and down, shouting, "let's go, Cham! I see you, baby!" All of which inspired me to keep pushing.

Late in the fourth quarter, I finally scored my first varsity touchdown, putting Blanchet ahead by four points. The crowd erupted, cheering me on. My teammates were tapping my helmet. Ramsay and I gave each other a chest bump. Thanks to our defense, we protected the lead and ultimately won the game.

Being a starting running back suddenly gave me recognition. I received a few recruiting letters from small colleges: Linfield College, Puget Sound University, and more. At school, I felt included, bonding closer with my football friends. During lunch, I sat with my teammates among what I thought were a number of popular students.

I heard them chat about parties that I never attended. Listening to their conversations made me lonely. I sat there quietly eating my fries with ketchup.

Sometimes, I wondered, *if I didn't play football, would anyone notice me?* I certainly wouldn't earn the nickname "Chamwow" that Gary gave me. During sophomore year, the fame faded when people found out I wasn't a party boy.

At Blanchet, I didn't think playing sports would make students popular. I played football and competed in track and field from freshman through junior year. Still, I was never invited to any house parties.

I never considered myself a popular kid because I was a brown boy who spoke broken English with a thick accent. Yet, most people welcomed me. During home games, some students on the bleachers shouted my name, without ever having talked to me before. Furthermore, one of the cheerleaders had written my number on her cheek, a tradition that they followed. I was thrilled seeing my number on a girl's cheek, never thinking I would be one of the players they picked. Even better, I once saw my number on two cheerleaders' cheeks.

In our entrepreneurship class, Dalia, one of the two cheerleaders, talked to me about the number mix-up.

"I picked your number first," she said, typing the keyboard. "I even had it painted on my face." She turned to me. "That girl came to me and was like 'hey, I'm picking Cham's number. Can you change yours?' I'm like hell no! I'm not gonna wipe my face and redo it. You pick a different number, girlfriend." She rolled her eyes.

I chuckled. "What did your coach say about this?"

"She didn't say anything. Even if she did, I wouldn't care. I'm a senior, so whatever." We both laughed.

"Class! Can I have your attention?" said Ms. Bennett. "We have a guest speaker coming today. Please be respectful and please pay attention." She checked the clock on the wall. "He should be here any minute now." Ms. Bennett went back to her desk. We turned off our computers and rotated our chairs toward the whiteboard.

Seconds later, I saw Jeff enter the room, wearing his usual khaki pants, button-down shirt, and a brown sport coat. He greeted Ms. Bennett.

I didn't expect Jeff to be our guest speaker. Last class, Ms. Bennett mentioned "a successful entrepreneur" was coming to our class, but she never said it was Jeff. He was, as she described, having run his business since 1972.

Jeff sat down on a stool in front of the whiteboard, checking around the room with a smile. He saw me but didn't say anything. After living with him for nearly five years, I hardly heard him talk about his motivations for managing a company.

"The most important thing about starting your own business is believing in yourself," he said. "You have to believe in yourself if you want to achieve a goal." He looked around the room. "When I started my business, some people didn't think I could do it. Some people said I would fail. But all of that didn't matter because I believed in myself. Yes, there were some failures I faced at the earlier stage of my business, and I am still facing failures today. But that's okay. That's how businesses are supposed to work. Failures and successes are a part of the nature of business." He took a deep breath. "It's common for most entrepreneurs to face challenges while starting a business. Failure could be a wonderful thing that allows people to learn from their mistakes." He smiled. "As long as you believe in yourself and trust that you know what you are doing, you will overcome any obstacles."

Everyone stood up, applauding once he finished.

In junior year, I took challenging classes: entrepreneurship, English, advanced algebra, men's choir, modern chemistry, US history, and theology. Each class gave me a tremendous workload, forcing me to stay up late almost every school night.

I remember sitting in the TV room, typing an essay for my English class. It was twelve midnight and still I was only halfway done with my writing. The house was dead silent. I could hear the clock on the wall ticking.

*Tick-Tock. Tick-Tock. Tick-Tock.*

I felt like I was in my freshman year all over again. I rubbed my eyes, wishing I could head to bed. In addition to being challenging, junior year was the most important year. Most colleges would review this year's performance. Many students started to build their applications: writing their college essays, taking SAT or ACT exams, and visiting campuses. As for me, attending college was an uncertainty. Jeff and Wanda made it clear that they didn't want to help with tuition.

"If you want to go to college, we would sponsor you, but we will not help you with tuition. So, you're on your own," Jeff once told me.

I wasn't mad at Jeff and Wanda's decision. They had done more than enough by providing the opportunity for me to continue my education in high school. For the past five years, they had spent a lot of money on not just my tuition but also on food and clothing. In high school, they consistently gave me money for lunch and gas every week. Sponsoring me was expensive, costing thousands of dollars each year. I could understand that they didn't want to help with college tuition.

Without Jeff and Wanda's help, I didn't think there was a chance for me to continue my journey in America. My grades weren't decent enough to receive scholarships from universities. Worse, Jeff told me international students were not qualified for scholarships or allowed to work. There really wasn't much hope for me to continue on. My only option was to do my best in school and learn as much as I could before returning home. Drew told me to, "just enjoy it while you can," and that, "high school doesn't last forever." So I did.

My performance on the field made me popular. My name was consistently called during the school announcements. Most students including a few teachers recognized me as a "good football player" rather than a good student.

I appreciated the sincere compliments, but part of me preferred the latter. I knew education would secure a brighter future. Knowledge shaped my way of thinking, allowing me to use my brain to determine what was right and wrong for myself. American education allowed me to understand the world through multiple perspectives, but more than that, I learned how to draw my own conclusions. Studying at St. Luke and Blanchet enlightened the dark mind I once had. I could now truly see what it's like to be educated.

At the moment, it was clear my performance on the field was better than in the classroom. My GPA was slightly above a 3.0, heading into the middle of the school year. I wasn't alone. Most of my teammates focused more on football, spending time reviewing the playbook and studying film rather than completing homework. A lack of effort in the classroom impacted a student-athlete's eligibility to play on the field. From game to game, a few players were banned from competing due to their low grades. Coach Maul did his best addressing the situation to the team.

"Gents! You have to compete in the classrooms if you want to compete on the field," he said after a practice. "Football is important, but school should be your priority." He rested his hand on a player's shoulder. "I would hate to pull you guys from games. But if your grades aren't good enough, then I can't let you play. So, take care of your grades."

I respected Coach Maul not only for his coaching ability but also on the way he motivated people in life. Coach Maul often picked themes from week to week that encouraged players to stay out of trouble. Themes like, "Compete," and "Together as One," were chosen to bond us. One of the most important lessons I learned was from listening to his speeches on "Love."

"Love is the most powerful tool in life because love conquers everything," he said during one practice. "Love your family. Love your friends. Love your teammates. If you love your teammates, you will have each other's backs on and off the field." He paused, looking at the team. "Love will make us stronger. It will make us an unstoppable force."

One day after my football game, Thalen called and asked for a ride from work. Kesor had gone home early that day.

When I arrived, I saw Thalen near the bus stop, staring down with a frown on his face. He opened the door and sat down without even a hint of a greeting.

"Where am I taking you?" I asked.

"Just drive home." He rested his head on the seat. His eyes shut.

I accelerated down the road. "Are you okay?"

He didn't respond.

"Thalen!" I shouted, "are you all right?"

"No!" He glared at me over his shoulder. "I'm not all right! I just saw Kesor posting some pictures of herself with some guy." He rubbed his face. "This is super messed up." He took a deep breath as he stared at the ceiling. I continued driving in silence. "You don't have anything to say about this?" he asked then looked straight at me.

"I don't know what to say. Kesor is a big girl. I can't tell her what to do." My head throbbed in pain as I struggled to find a way to calm Thalen down.

"So, you're not gonna help me at all? I've helped you a lot, man!"

"I want to help you, but I'm having a terrible day. I played horribly and my team lost." I sighed. "I don't know what I need to do to help you."

"Just talk to her. Tell her what she's doing is wrong."

"She knows that, Thalen."

"Well, just talk to her anyway. Do whatever you can to help."

We got to the house. Thalen went inside in a hurry. To ensure everything was all right, I got out of my car and limped toward the house. Once I got inside, I heard Kesor's voice shouting. I stood at the bottom of the stairs, listening to their conversation. I hardly heard Thalen talk. Kesor was yelling, cursing at him. Hearing Kesor's words was unsettling. I bit my lip. I knew I shouldn't interfere with their conversation. In my heart, I hoped Kesor could change.

A few weeks later, Thalen went to Cambodia. He couldn't handle the situation with Kesor and wanted to be away for a while. Thalen and Kesor's problem wasn't the only dilemma occurring in my family. Chai told me, "Lab kicked Father out. She and Ruat saw him hanging out with a girl at the beach."

I was heartbroken to hear that Father was continuing to cheat on Mother. I knew Father was lonely. His love for Mother was fading away due to her unrelenting attitude. I didn't know what to say nor who to blame. Part of me was angry that my family kept hiding stories from me until they got bigger. I was convinced that I could've solved the issue if I'd known about it earlier.

On a late school night, I sat in the TV room at Jeff and Wanda's house, typing my English paper. I couldn't concentrate. I kept thinking of Father. Frustrated, I put my laptop aside then grabbed my phone. The phone rang forever, but there was no answer.

I dialed the number one last time. Just before I hung up, Father answered.

"Hello," he said.

"Hello, Father. It's me, Chamroeun. Where are you right now?"

He sighed.

"Can you hear me?"

"Yeah, I just don't want you to worry about this kind of thing."

"This is important. You're my father, I want to know where you are. I want to make sure you're okay."

"I'm fine. I'm living at a farm right now, growing potatoes and lettuce."

"Why are you living at a farm? We have a house in Oue Bram. Chai and Kesor sent you money for food, there's no need to grow vegetables." I could hear him breathing heavily over the phone. "Where are you right now?"

"I'm in Kandal Province." Kandal Province was located southeast of Phnom Penh.

"Who are you living with?"

"I'm living by myself. I don't need anyone to stay with me."

"Father, could you please go back? I don't want you to live alone."

"It's not that simple, no one respects me over there. I think it's better if I live alone for a while."

"You're our Father. We do respect you." I cleared a lump in my throat. "Please go back. Our family needs you."

Father paused for a few seconds. "Okay, but I'm not going anywhere until I'm finished with farming."

The call dropped as the minutes on the phone card ran out. I banged the phone on my forehead repeatedly. I wished I could go back so I could be with Father in Kandal Province. I opened my eyes and stared at the computer screen while the clock on the wall kept ticking. It was twelve thirty in the morning, but I was still a long way from finishing my paper. At this point, I didn't bother typing the essay. I kept thinking of home. Without the energy to finish the assignment, I went on the internet and copied some paragraphs then pasted it in my paper.

A few days later during English class, I sat at my desk watching Ms. Anderson return our assignments. My heart pumped a hundred miles an hour. I knew I would receive a terrible score because nearly half of the paper was from the internet. After handing back everyone's paper, Ms. Anderson went back to her desk and opened the class lesson.

"Seventy-five?" said Ramsay, sitting to my right. "I for sure thought I was gonna get mid-eighties." He glared at the teacher then turned to me. "What did you get, Cham?"

"I didn't get mine."

"Did you turn yours in?"

"Yeah, I did."

"Ask her, maybe she forgot."

I raised my hand, looking at Ms. Anderson as my heart kept beating faster than normal.

"Yeah?" she asked while looking at the computer's screen.

"I didn't get my paper."

"I need to talk to you about your paper." She looked at me with a serious face.

"Ooh . . ." said a few boys.

I cleared my throat then asked, "when can I talk to you?"

"After class."

My body shook, I knew I was in trouble. I glanced to my right and saw Ramsay looking at me with sorrow.

"You'll be all right," he said with a smile. I nodded to keep myself calm.

After class, I waited for everyone to exit the room before approaching Ms. Anderson. "Okay, Cham. Here's the problem," she said. "I read your paper and noticed that you copied it off the internet." She handed it to me. I saw many sentences underlined in red with feedback, indicating the sources. My palms sweated and my chest tightened. I didn't have the nerve to admit my cheating.

"I have a lot of homework and I didn't have much time to finish this," I lied, not wanting to tell her the truth about the family issues that overwhelmed me. "Writing is difficult for me . . ." I paused then looked at her. "Can I redo this to get some credit?"

"No, I can't let you redo this! I'm gonna have to report it to the dean." She scanned the paper. "This is plagiarism. You're a junior, you should be aware of this."

At this point, I knew there was nothing I could do to escape trouble. My only option was to accept my mistake.

When I got home, I saw Jeff and Wanda in the TV room looking at their laptops. Wanda stared at me worryingly as I walked by.

"Hi, Chamroeun," said Jeff in a low tone.

"Hi." Something was wrong. They didn't have the TV on and Wanda kept looking at me.

"Chamroeun," said Wanda, "do you have something to tell us?"

My mind told me to come clean because they already knew the issue. I put my backpack down then sat at the end of the couch. "I got in trouble at school," I said quietly. "I made a silly mistake, but I am responsible for it."

"Could you tell us what you did?" Wanda asked.

"I, umm." I swallowed. "I got caught copying some stuff from the internet."

"Chamroeun, cheating is not 'a silly mistake'. It's a big deal!" She turned to Jeff. Her face turned red. "This is like plagiarism. Do you know what that is?"

"Yes."

"People can get kicked out of school because of it. You need to be really careful with this kind of thing."

I rubbed my forehead. I knew Wanda was right.

"What class is this?" Jeff asked.

"English."

"Did you talk to the teacher about this?"

"Yes. She told me that she has reported it to the dean." I looked up, seeing both of them glancing at each other with concern. "I'm getting a detention."

"You're very lucky," Wanda interfered, "other schools could have expelled you."

I took Wanda's words to heart. Plagiarism was a serious topic discussed in every American school. Cheating off someone's work and claiming it as my own was stealing. After being at St. Luke and Blanchet, I often heard teachers encouraging students to work on their own assignments. A student would get a zero on the homework if he or she got caught cheating. Ms. Anderson didn't even give me a score on my report. In fact, the paper went on my high school record. The dean had told me, "you now have one strike on your record. Two more and you will get expelled." It was nerve-racking to hear those words.

As days went by, Thalen came back from Cambodia, bringing presents for Chai, Kesor, and me, sent from my siblings. Lab bought me some polo shirts, but they all were too small to fit my growing body. No one knew about my size and thought I was still a small boy. Nonetheless, I was really happy to receive gifts from them. Above all, I was thankful to have Thalen around once again.

With him back, we went to a few Khmer parties on the weekends as we approached Khmer New Year. One night, Thalen, Kesor, Chai, Ryan, and I went to an indoor event located near downtown Seattle. There were so many Khmer people there. Some women even dressed up in traditional Khmer outfits, wearing *sampot chang kben* (traditional skirts) and *av pak* (traditional shirts). The place even hired famous artists from Cambodia who sang on a stage with the band. The dance floor was crowded. Chai and Ryan stood near the edge, dancing along to the music. Thalen asked Kesor to dance.

"No!" Kesor said, "leave me alone." She rolled her eyes and sat still at the table with me. Thalen reluctantly went in alone, dancing near Ryan and Chai.

Kesor still resented Thalen. She didn't share the bed with him anymore and often slept in her closet to stay away from him. What was even worse, Kesor saw a picture of Thalen when he was in Cambodia with another girl.

I remember hearing them argue in their bedroom. Kesor was cursing loudly. She even blasted bowls full of water at Thalen. I could see water dripping down the doorway. I entered the room and saw that half of their bed was soaked. A picture of Thalen and Kesor was torn to pieces on the floor. Kesor saw me then slammed the closet door shut.

"What's going on?" I asked.

"Nothing. Kesor is mad at me for something that isn't true." He walked downstairs.

I went to the closet door, knocking with rage.

"Who is it?" she asked.

"It's me! Open the door!"

"Go away!"

"Kesor, open the door, now!"

She opened the door halfway, glaring at me. "What do you want?"

"What the hell is going on?"

"It's none of your business." She pushed the door back, but I reached out, stopping her from shutting.

"I need to know! Tell me!"

"Why don't you go ask him? Ask him how he feel about hanging out with that girl in the picture?"

"Why does it matter? You cheated on him before, too!" Kesor scowled at me then slammed the door shut. I then went downstairs, sitting next to Thalen in the living room.

"Kesor said you hangout with another girl, is that true?" I asked, breathing fast.

He sighed, looking at me over his shoulders. "I don't know, man. She went in my computer and saw some pictures of me in Cambodia. I don't know what she saw."

"Well, did you hangout with another girl or not?"

He rubbed his forehead, inhaling deeply. "I love my wife, but I think she hates me. Everyone hates me."

"Not everyone hates you. I care about you. My family loves you."

He scoffed. "Your father changed the title of the land in Oue Bram. He changed it from Kesor and my name to his."

My eyes narrowed. "When did this happen?"

"A couple of months ago, I found out about it when I was there. I spent a lot of money to change it back to our names."

"Why would my father do that?"

"I heard that he has a girlfriend now." He laughed. "Maybe he wanted to sell it and live with his girlfriend, I don't know."

I leaned forward, looking at Thalen in the eyes. "My father wouldn't do that."

"I don't know what to tell you, man. Your family has changed." He looked at me with sorrow. "Things are different now than they were before."

I wasn't surprised by Thalen's words. I knew "things" were falling apart especially for Father. In my heart, I trusted that he wouldn't do anything to harm the family.

At the moment, I wasn't given an explanation for why Father changed the title of the land. The rumor of Father having a girlfriend kept spreading. Lab even warned Chai and Kesor to not send him money. She was convinced the money would go to supporting his girlfriend. Chai didn't listen, however. She occasionally sent him roughly 200 dollars for food and medicine. Chai's heart was too big.

Despite all the drama back home, my biggest concern was for Thalen and Kesor. Thalen started using again, causing Kesor to despise him even more. Every day, Kesor treated him terribly, throwing water and swearing at him.

I remember one day, Kesor was shouting at Thalen, using profanity in almost every sentence. He couldn't take it anymore, leaving the room soaked.

"What the hell is wrong with you?" I shouted to Kesor. "Why do you have to do this?"

Kesor looked at me with a straight face. "Yeah, you would defend him. You would pick him over me."

"Why should I pick you? You're stupid! You're worthless! I don't give a crap about you!"

Kesor frowned.

"Sometimes, I wish you could just die! Without you, my life would be much better!" I added then walked away. I looked out the window for Thalen and noticed his car was gone. I thought of the words I said and realized I had gone too far.

I approached the room, knocking on the closet door, but there was no answer. I opened it and saw Kesor lying on a thin mattress, her arm covering her forehead. I could see tears on her cheeks.

"Kesor, I," I hesitated. "I'm sorry."

"Get the hell away from me!"

"I'm sorry, I . . . I didn't mean it."

"You're an asshole! You would never pick me! You would never defend me! No matter what, they will always be right to you!"

Looking back, I knew Kesor was right. I couldn't think of a moment when I had picked her side over Thalen's. I always blamed her without fully understanding the story.

My anger led me to do terrible things toward my sister. I even packed her clothes in black garbage bags a few days later. "You need to leave," I told her. "I don't need you here. You only cause trouble. My life would be better if you were gone."

"If I leave, would you still love me?" she asked. "Would you still accept me as your sister?"

"No. When you leave, you and I are done!"

Soon afterwards, I deeply regretted the words I had said and the things I had done toward Kesor. I had always wanted to live with my sister and wished she could maintain her relationship with Thalen.

Being young, I didn't realize that my words had broken her. Anger forced me to lose my head, not caring about her well-being. I treated her like an animal so she could feel the pain Thalen received.

"No one is perfect," Jeff once told me. I was certainly not perfect and never will be.

A few weeks later, Kesor left the house and rented a place without telling anyone. Chai also moved out, living with Ryan in a small house roughly thirty minutes away. Without my sisters there, Jeff and Wanda let me stay with Thalen to keep him company.

# 22

# DEFEAT

A FEW WEEKS later, Chai told me that Father had returned to Oue Bram.
I was relieved and called him.

"Father! Thank you so much for coming back!" I said with pure joy.
"I'm sure the family is happy to have you once again."

"They don't seem like it," he said. "Lab barely talks to me and your
mother still seems mad. But that's something that I can't control."

"You know how they are. They might not show it, but I'm sure they
are happy to see you."

"I hope so." He laughed over the phone. "But this is nothing new. I'm
used to it."

After our conversation, I called Lab, begging her to change her behavior toward Father.

"Lab, please!" I said, "there's no need to be mean to him. He's our
father. He deserves better."

"So you expect him to cheat, leave, then come back, acting like nothing
had happened?" she replied. "I don't think so."

"Well, what would you have him do? Live on a farm, alone?" I paused.
"Before I left, you told me that you will look after the family. The family is
now back together. Please don't break it." I could hear Lab breathing on the
speaker. "How's Mother doing? What does she think about this?"

"I don't know. Why don't you ask her yourself?" I heard footsteps. Lab shouted for Mother. "It's Chamroeun."

"Hello, Chamroeun!" said Mother. "How are you my son?"

"I'm doing well, Mother! How about you?"

"I'm hanging in there. My hips are sore. My legs are numb from hours of sitting and cooking. There's hardly anyone here to help me with chores anymore."

"What about Hou? Is he helping you?"

"Sometimes, but he has school. So, all the duties fall on me." She sighed. "Now I have to make more food because we have an extra mouth to feed."

"I know you're mad at Father but please . . . He belongs with us."

"Yeah, well, I don't belong with him. I think I'll be fine living alone. I don't need a man in my life to survive."

"But I need him. I never wanted our family to separate. He's back now. Please don't push him away."

"I'm not going to do anything. As long as he doesn't touch me, I couldn't care less if he stays here or elsewhere."

Lab made it clear, if Father wanted to stay, he must not talk to any woman. She wanted him to earn the family's trust and be loyal to Mother. Father had agreed.

At the moment, I didn't have any way to influence this problem. Being the youngest, I didn't have the authority to set policies in my family. Worse, I didn't know who to believe. Father often told me the rumors of him cheating were false. Lab would say the opposite. Regardless, I was thankful that my family was together once again.

On a Thursday evening, I sat in the living room at Thalen's house, working on my philosophy homework. While typing, I could hear the noise of dishes clanging from the kitchen.

"Chamroeun!" Thalen yelled, "do you want dinner?"

"Sure!" I put my laptop aside, "what are you making?" I headed toward the kitchen.

"I don't know, there's not a whole lot." He opened the fridge. "There's some chicken, but we don't have any vegetables." I could see him staring at a pumpkin, sitting on the counter that Drew had used as decoration. "Do you like pumpkins?" He giggled.

"No, dude. I'm not eating that!" I shook my head. "That pumpkin has been sitting there for months now."

"Well, we don't have a whole lot of options and I don't have any money to buy food. So, pumpkin and chicken are all we got." He turned to me. "I'll cook. It's gonna be good."

Thalen was a good cook. He peeled the pumpkin then chopped it into small pieces. He cut up the chicken and fried it. I stood there quietly, watching Thalen cook. I was fascinated to see him crafting something out of nothing. He put in all kinds of ingredients: salt, pepper, sugar, chili, and more. Minutes later, we got ourselves a fried chicken pumpkin dish.

"Here you go." He handed me a bowl. The spicy steam burned my nostrils.

"It smells good. Thank you." I took a bite.

"How is it?"

"I can live with it."

He tasted it. "I think it's a bit dry." He laughed. "I should've added more water." He swallowed. "Have you heard anything from Kesor?"

"No. I don't think she wants to talk to me."

"Has anyone in your family talked to her?"

"I think Chai talked to her sometimes. Lab may have talked to her." I set the fork down. "I don't know, man. She's a difficult person to talk to."

"Keep reaching out to her because she won't talk to me." He blew on his food. "Just do whatever you can to help."

"Maybe, I can ask my father to call her. He's back now."

Thalen lowered his eyebrows. "He's back in Oue Bram? Why didn't anyone tell me?"

"He came back a few days ago."

Thalen set his plate on the counter. "That's not okay with me!"

"What do you mean?"

"Dude, your dad changed the title of the land to his name. Now that he's back, he gonna change it again. I'm not okay with that!"

"He's my father, Thalen! Where would you have him go?"

"Anywhere, but not there! I don't want to spend any more money just to fix things that your dad causes." He rested his arms on his lap. "I might go to Cambodia soon. I don't want to see him there."

I sat speechless. I didn't want to tell Father to move, knowing that doing so would crush him. At this moment, I had no choice but to do what Thalen asked.

Later that evening, I sat in my bedroom, calling Father.

"Hello," Father mumbled, "why you call so early this time? What's going on?"

"Sorry if I woke you up. But I have something to tell you." I took a deep breath. "Thalen doesn't want you to stay there. He's afraid that you're going to change the title of the land again."

"So he's mad at me about that, huh?" He inhaled. "I did it because the government was strict about having a foreigner owning land in Cambodia. I didn't want him to get in trouble, that's why I changed it to my name."

"But it was under Kesor's name too, and she is Khmer."

"Kesor is not here. If the government wanted to meet the owner, it would be inconvenient to fly her back just to handle the paperwork. It's my job to look after the family. I changed the name for their sake."

"He's really mad, Father. Even if I explain this to him, I don't think he would listen. He's in a deep mess right now. His relationship with Kesor is falling apart. He told me that he's going back to Cambodia soon. He doesn't want to see you there." I rubbed my forehead. "I'm sorry, Father. But I think it's best if we do what he asked."

"Chai told me about their situation. I tried to call Kesor, but she won't pick up her phone." He paused. "What would you have me do, Chamroeun? I have no place to go."

My heart sunk to my stomach. I cleared a lump in my throat. "Could you temporarily stay with Ruat? You could move back after Thalen leaves."

"It's not that simple. His place is small and his wife would not be okay with this."

"It's only for a short while. I'll talk to Ruat."

"Don't. It's okay. I'll figure something out."

I sat on my bed, staring at the wooden floor, not knowing what to do. In my heart, I knew I had made a mistake by asking Father to move away.

The next day, Jeff and Wanda invited Thalen and me for dinner. We gathered in the living room, eating grilled steak, mashed potatoes, and asparagus. Thalen obliterated his plate, chopping the meat in large pieces and chewing them at a fast pace.

"Slow down, Thalen," said Wanda, "there's plenty of food." Thalen kept eating.

"How's school going, Chamroeun?" Jeff asked.

"It's okay. I'm hanging in there."

"You're almost done with the semester, right?" Wanda added.

"Yeah." I felt my phone vibrate and pulled it out to see Chai calling. I pressed decline. "I only have a couple of months left," I continued. My phone vibrated again. "Hold on, Chai is calling me." I went to the laundry room. "Hey, can I call you back?"

"No!" she sobbed. "What the hell is wrong with you? Why you kick Father out? Tell me!"

"I . . ." I exited the house, "I didn't kick him out, Chai. Thalen didn't want him there, so I asked him if he could live somewhere else for a while."

"And you listen to Thalen? You do what he ask!" She sobbed even louder. "Do you know how hurt Father is right now? He is brokenheart, Chamroeun. He just got home and now you asking him to move out. How could you do this?"

I sat down, tears falling down my cheeks. "I didn't mean to push him away. I thought he could just live with Ruat for a short while until Thalen leaves."

"You tell him to live with Ruat for a short while? You want him to pack his clothes and go live with Ruat? Just like that? Are you kidding me?"

I didn't answer.

"This is so wrong. I'm really disappointed in you. I don't want to hear from you again." She hung up.

I heard the door open. I wiped my cheeks.

"Chamroeun, are you okay?" Thalen asked.

"No, man," I mumbled. "I did what you asked, now Chai is super mad at me. She doesn't want to talk to me anymore."

Thalen sat near me, rubbing my back. "I'm sorry, Chamroeun. I didn't mean to push your dad away. It was in the heat of the moment." He bit his fingernails. "I just don't want him to change the title of the land again, you know."

"He did it to protect you, man. The government didn't want barang to own land in Cambodia. My father thought it was best to change the name to his."

Thalen scoffed. "I don't know if that's true. But I don't want to talk about it anymore."

"So, can my father stay?"

"Sure, as long as he won't change the name."

I called Father and apologized for my action. I begged him to stay and told him that Thalen didn't mean what he said. Father listened. He talked in a low tone and repeatedly said, "I'll do whatever you want me to do." It was clear from his quiet voice that his feelings were damaged beyond repair.

The summer of 2013 was my last chance to improve my football skills. Playing this sport could open the door for me to study in college. I even had a mohawk that year so I would look tougher. I was willing to give it my all, working out almost every day. Thalen mentioned, "if you want to get better, you have to get bigger and that starts with eating a lot more." Following his advice, I ate five times a day. I often grilled a plate full of chicken breasts with BBQ sauce then wolfed down the meat even if I was full. There were times I ate so much food I ended up vomiting. But I would continue eating, following the five meal a day routine.

Due to the consistent workout, I gained roughly twenty-five pounds that summer. The majority of my clothes didn't fit me anymore. I had to wear sweatpants and sweaters. Even worse, I lost my speed. I could barely beat the fullback, Nikola, in a 40-yard dash.

"Dude, I almost had you!" said Nikola, "and I'm much fatter than you." He laughed.

"Yeah. I had a bad start," I lied. I was shocked to find out how slow I had become. In football, weight and strength were important, but speed was just as crucial. Being fast was one of my talents that allowed me to start as a running back.

One morning, after the weight room session, my phone rang. It was Chai. I hadn't heard from her in months.

"Hi, Chamroeun," she said. "I don't see you call anymore. How are you?"

"I thought you didn't want to talk to me. I thought you hated me, so I didn't want to bother."

"Chamroeun. You're my brother. I always want to talk to you."

I opened my car door and sat down. "What do you want, Chai? There's gotta be a reason you called."

"I just want to talk to you. I don't want you to think that I hate you. You're my little brother. I will always be there for you." She paused. "If you want to come over later tonight, I make chicken curry."

"I think I'm okay. I already have plans."

"Okay," she paused. "I'm going to Cambodia in less than a month. Is there anything you want to send with me?"

"No, I don't have anything."

"Well, you can send pictures and some of your old clothes for our nephews."

"I'll see what I got. Why are you going to Cambodia?"

"Lane is getting married. I think Kesor and Thalen are going too."

"Wow, she is. No one told me anything about this."

"We don't want you to feel bad for not going. We don't want to distract you from school." Her tone changed to sorrow. "But I wish you could join us, Chamroeun."

It broke my heart hearing that I couldn't reunite with my family. I could only imagine seeing everyone's faces. It would have been a great homecoming.

While Thalen, Kesor, and Chai were gone, I continued to live with Drew and his girlfriend, Annica. She had smooth brown hair, white skin, and was a bit shorter than me. We often went to dinners and saw movies.

Two weeks later, Thalen, Kesor, and Chai returned. I went to Chai's house later that day to receive my gifts: a button-down shirt, trousers, t-shirts, and even underwear. Just like the last gifts, none of the clothes fit.

"Did you tell them that I've grown?" I asked, folding the clothes neatly on the couch.

"I did," Chai said, sitting next to Ryan, "they got large for you."

"Their large is our small. You know, everyone is tiny over there."

Ryan glared at me over his shoulder. "I think you should appreciate what you got."

I leaned on the couch, watching ESPN.

"Mother miss you, Chamroeun," said Chai. "She always ask about you. She's so tiny now. I feel so bad seeing her."

"Did you tell her that I'm fine? And not to worry about me?"

"Of course, I did. I told her you can take care of yourself. That you big now and there's nothing to worry about." Chai patted my back. "You know how she is. She just miss you, that's all."

I sighed. "I miss her too. How's everybody else doing?"

She paused for a long minute. "Father is sick."

I sat up straight. "What do you mean?"

"He been complaining about a lump growing under his chin. He said it hurt when he chew and swallow." She hesitated. "Ryan think it could not be serious."

"That's one possibility," Ryan added. "But there's no way to know right now." He rubbed the back of his neck and turned to me. "It's probably a lymph node. If so, he needs to keep an eye on it to see if it gets better or not."

"Father asked if he could go to Vietnam and get checked out," Chai spoke in Khmer, not wanting Ryan to know the situation. "But I don't have the money. Maybe I can borrow some from Ryan."

"Did you talk to Kesor?" I asked in English.

"She doesn't have the money either," she continued in Khmer. "She's working at a coffee stand, earning like thirteen dollars an hour." Chai rested on the couch. "Lab thinks that he's only trying to get money to help his girlfriend."

"But I thought he stopped talking to her."

"No. Lab told me that she tried to call him all the time. She snuck through Father's phone and setup a ringtone specifically for her number. That ringtone rang three to five times every night." She stared at the TV. "Lab said she answered the phone once and talked to her. She told her to leave Father alone, that he has a family. But she kept calling."

After a few minutes of silence, Chai went on in English. "I really want to help him, Chamroeun. I know it sound bad, him seeing another girl. But he's our father, I don't want him sick."

Ryan gently rubbed Chai's arm as she cried.

My heart sunk, yet I kept thinking positively. I told myself, *Ryan could be right. This lump might not be serious.* I felt helpless. Yet, the only thing I could do was to focus on school and football.

Blanchet played Lakeside at home on our third game of the season. During the unity dinner, Coach Martin gave an inspirational speech, *I Am a Champion.* Players were pumped up, shouting and applauding. Other coaches got up, shaking his hand. We were ready to battle.

I was nominated as the honorary captain that week, raising the wooden axe while charging with my team onto the field. Blake and Drew came to watch me play, sitting on the Lakeside bleacher. Thalen, Chai, and Ryan came too, but they chose to stay on the Blanchet side, supporting me.

It was the second quarter, and Blanchet led 24-3. Our offense was playing so well, scoring touchdowns in every series.

"If it gets out of hand, I'm gonna have to pull you," said the running back coach. "We want to keep you fresh. We have a long season ahead of us."

"Don't pull me yet, Coach," I said. "I haven't scored. At least let me get a touchdown."

He laughed, shaking his head. "All right. But this is your last series."

I nodded. "Yes, Coach."

I got in my position. Eyes focused on the center. Within seconds, the quarterback hiked the snap, handing me the ball. I ran to the right, following a tight gap, but there was no room to go. I cut left, hurdled over a defender who was lying on the ground. I could see an open field ahead. Suddenly, a defender came up and wrapped my ankles. I reached out my left arm to break the fall as I was hitting the turf.

*Pop!*

I could see the joint of my elbow slightly bending the opposite way. Freaked out, I punched my joint back while a sea of pain hit me. I lay on the ground, holding my arm, rolling back and forth. My eyes shut as I stomped my feet and yelled at the top of my lungs. "Ahhhh!"

"Cham! Are you okay?" I opened my eyes and saw a teammate standing over me. "Get up, man, we gotta go!" He handed me one of my cleats. I didn't even know my shoe had fallen off. I got up, still holding my arm, grabbed my cleat, and jogged toward the sideline. I ran straight for the trainer.

"Help!" I said, "I . . . I think I broke my arm!"

"Let me see," said the trainer, checking my elbow. "Can you move it?"

Fighting the pain, I tried to move my arm but couldn't. "I don't think so."

"Here, try pressing against my arm. I want to see if you have any strength." He opened his palm. I slowly raised my arm up, putting my fist on his hand. I bit my lips, pushing with everything I had, but his hand didn't move. The trainer looked at me. "It could just be a really bad sprain. Don't worry, okay? We're gonna have you go get an MRI to see what's wrong with it." He went to grab his aid box.

I stood there, holding my arm. Meanwhile, the crowd had gone wild, cheering for a sophomore, O'Neal, who rushed for a long-distance touchdown.

"Chamroeun!" a voice shouted over the crowd. I looked over my shoulder and saw Thalen with Ryan. "What's wrong with you?" Thalen asked.

"I don't know," I hesitated. "I think I broke my arm. But the trainer said it could be a sprain."

"Can you move it?" Ryan asked.

I shook my head. Thalen and Ryan looked at each other with a frown on their faces.

"Okay, Cham," said the trainer, "I'm gonna have to take you to the locker room, get you out of that shoulder pad, and have you wear a sling. Okay?" He looked at me through the face mask. "You're done for today."

After the game, I drove to Chai's house and lay on the couch. My elbow was swelling, becoming almost as big as my leg. Ryan grabbed an ice pack from the freezer. He placed it on my arm and secured it with an ACE wrap.

"It's burning my skin," I said, squeezing my eyes.

"You have to tough it out, man," he said. "This will help the swelling."

Exhausted, I lay there quietly. Within minutes, I fell asleep.

I heard noises and felt the floor shake. I opened my eyes and noticed Chai and Ryan were watching a movie. Ryan always had the volume up high for his intense action movies. I slowly got up.

"How are you feeling, Chamroeun?" Chai asked. Ryan paused the movie.

"I'm fine." I pulled the ice pack. I could see my skin was peeling off. Bruises and blisters were popping. "What's wrong with my skin?"

Chai came close. "Oh my god, Chamroeun!" Her eyes lit up. "Ryan, look how bad his arm is."

Ryan got up. "You got an ice burn. You left it there for too long."

I got up, frustrated that my arm had gotten worse. Irritated, I drove home.

Looking back at it, I probably overreacted about the ice burn. At the time, I was angry and may have been looking for other places to lay blame. I didn't realize I should've taken the ice pack off earlier.

Entering the front door of Drew's house, I saw Annica and Drew rinsing the sink. As I was walking upstairs, Annica heard my footsteps and came following.

"Hey, Chamroeun," she said, "we heard about your arm. How is it?"

"Umm, I don't know, it got worse. I iced it too long, now I have blisters. It hurts really bad." I took off the sling and showed it to them. To my shock, Annica immediately dropped on the floor in horror, covering her face as her eyes watered.

"I'm sorry, Chamroeun," said Drew. "That looks really painful. Did you take any pills?"

I shook my head.

"We should give him some Ibuprofen," Annica added, still covering her face.

Drew gave me two Ibuprofen pills. I glanced around the room. "Where is Thalen?" I asked.

"I don't know," Drew answered. "He went somewhere earlier. But don't worry about him, you should take care of yourself."

I nodded then went upstairs to my room.

I remember lying on my bed, grinding my teeth. It felt like my arm was on fire from multiple stab wounds.

I had dealt with injuries from football before. In the past, I had ankle sprains, which were always painful. Playing running back, my skin often got scratched from the face-mask, and bruises formed all over my body from the hits I received. Nothing came close to the pain I was in now. It truly felt like my left arm had gotten cut off.

The next day, Wanda and Thalen took me to see the doctor. We sat in a room, waiting for the results from the X-ray. Nervously, I waited, picking my nails. My heart was pounding against my chest. The trainer's word, "sprain," kept coming up in my thoughts. I hoped he was right. Minutes later, the doctor appeared and sat on a stool, looking at the computer screen. I could see black and white images of my elbow.

"The X-ray is showing that a piece of bone has gotten detached from your tricep," he said. "Well, it looks like only a tiny portion of it is still there, but ninety-nine percent of your tricep tendon is torn. This is why you don't have any strength."

"What does that mean, Doctor?" I asked, "will I get a chance to play again?"

He paused. "No, I'm afraid not. Your elbow is damaged pretty bad. You're going to need surgery as soon as possible." He tapped me on my leg. "I'm sorry."

The doctor's words struck me like lightning from Cambodia. I felt cheated from the benefits of all the hard work I'd done preparing for this season. Wanda patted my back.

"When can we schedule the surgery?" Thalen asked.

"Well, his skin is really weak right now. I gotta tell ya, that's the worse ice burn I've ever seen." He turned to Thalen. "Let's wait and see if the blisters will go away. We can schedule an appointment for him two days from now to get his arm cleaned up so it can heal faster. Then we'll go from there."

"Thank you, Doctor," said Thalen.

I didn't accept the doctor's words and went for a second opinion a few days later. I didn't want this injury to crush my chance to play college football. There, a doctor made me do a few tests by straightening my arm and pressing it up against her palm, testing for strength. Both of which I failed to do.

"It seems like your arm is getting weaker and weaker," she said. "The best thing you could do is to get the surgery."

Disappointed, I stared at the floor. In my heart, I knew I had no choice but to accept the truth.

On a Friday after school, I approached Coach Maul in the locker room before the team's chapel.

"What did your doctor say?" he asked.

"Not good, Coach," I said, looking down. "The doctor said ninety-nine percent of my tricep tendon got detached. I'm gonna have to get a surgery." I inhaled. "I'm done with football."

Coach Maul gave me a hug. "I'm sorry, bud." He looked me in the eyes. "Hang in there."

In the chapel, I sat in the corner of the room among my teammates. Coach Maul stood in the front, delivering a speech.

"Gents, before we get started, I have terrible news to announce," said Coach Maul. He turned to me. "Come up here, Cham."

I stood near him, looking down. Coach Maul put his arm over my shoulders.

"Today, Cham found out that he cannot compete on the field anymore." He cleared his throat. "It's tough because I know that Cham has been working so hard in the weight room over the summer. I know that he's a warrior and would do anything to be out there, competing. But sometimes, when adversity hits you, you just have to be strong." He looked at me sincerely. "We'll miss you out there, Cham." He tapped my shoulder, nodding, eyes watery. "Do you want to say anything to the team?"

Holding back tears, I took a deep breath, looking around the room and seeing all eyes on me. "I . . ." I cleared a lump in my throat. "I don't know what to tell you. I didn't see this coming. My advice to you all is to keep fighting. Play every down like it's your last because you don't know what's gonna happen next." I took a deep breath. "But this won't stop me. I will continue to be there, doing whatever I can to support you all."

"Thanks, Cham." I went back to my chair, listening to Coach Maul as the chapel went on.

When we returned to the locker room, I sat on a wooden bench wearing my jersey over my hoodie. I looked up and saw my teammates getting suited. The music hit, sound track blasting around the room, playing, "When The Levee Breaks" by Led Zeppelin. The song gave me goosebumps. My heart dropped to my feet. I pulled the hoodie over my head and stared down at the tile floor. I felt players tapping my head as they walked by. I couldn't keep myself from crying. I was defeated.

# 23

# A LIGHT FADED

THREE MONTHS HAD gone by. My arm finally healed after wearing a long cast from palm to shoulder. With barely any muscles between my thin bones and brown skin, I could hardly move it. The doctor recommended that I see a physical therapist so I could get full rotation back. But it would be expensive. I didn't want to ask Jeff and Wanda, especially knowing they had spent a lot of money on my insurance for the surgery. Coming from Cambodia, I also didn't think it was necessary to see therapists. People there often toughed it out when they got injuries because most couldn't afford to pay for medical care.

Following the Khmer way of living, I told myself, *I don't need to see a therapist. I'm going to tough it out and fix my own arm.* So I did.

Day by day, I sat on the couch, downstairs, moving my elbow joint, inch by inch. Grinding my teeth all the while, I used my right hand to hold the top of my left fist, then slowly pushed it back. It felt like I was moving a wall. My arm joint was so tight it refused to bend. After minutes of pushing and straightening every morning, I gained some rotation back, allowing me to drive and write normally again.

Entering the second semester, most of my classes were a continuation from the last term. One of the most intriguing subjects I took was marine biology. Every morning, Mr. Ford went around the room, quizzing students from the prior lesson.

"Andres," he called to a boy sitting near me, "a zone that's considered as the foreshore or the seashore is also known as?"

"The intertidal zone," said Andres.

"Excellent!" Mr. Ford applauded, "could you name a few creatures living in this area?"

"Sure. Starfish, crab, and snails."

Mr. Ford gave him a thumbs-up. "Cham!"

"Ahh, crap," I whispered to myself. People who sat near me heard my reaction and chuckled.

"Cham, what are some challenges that most creatures in the intertidal zone faced?"

"Umm," I looked at Andres, who smirked but didn't give me an answer. "I'm not sure."

"I'll help you out. A few of the challenges are high tide and low tide. Could you name a few more?" The class was dead silent. All eyes were on me. "Cham, if you were a crab, what would you fear the most?" He walked closer to me. "Let me put it this way, what would you try to get away from?"

"Ahh, water?" The whole class, including Mr. Ford, laughed.

"You would get away from water? But crabs do live in the water, Cham." He chuckled. "Let's try again. They are afraid of big and tall creatures, walking around the beach, flipping rocks. Those creatures are . . .?"

I hesitated, scratching my head. He then pointed at each one of us. "People?" I guessed.

"Yes! Cham!" The class laughed again. "Humans are one of the biggest threats to life in the intertidal zone." He came close. "Cham, when you were a kid, didn't you go around the beach, flipping rocks, looking for life underneath?"

"Sure," I lied. I didn't want to say that I didn't have time to flip rocks. Instead, I sold bracelets and chips to learn English. Not only that but beaches in Cambodia weren't the same as the ones in America. Ochheuteal Beach was covered with pure white sand and blue warm water. There weren't small rocks for us to flip.

One late night, Ruat called with concerns about Father's illness. I had butterflies in my stomach afterward. I didn't sleep well. The next day, I dialed Father's number.

The phone rang for a few seconds. "Hello," said Father.

"Hi, Father. It's me. How are you feeling?"

"I'm fine. What's going on?"

"Ruat told me that your neck is still bothering you. Is it getting better?"

"Don't worry about that. It's just a small lump. I'm feeling a bit better now. It will go away." He laughed. "How's school going? You're almost done, right?"

"Yes, Father. I have about three to four months left then I'm done."

"Excellent! I'm excited for you. Finally, a person in this family will earn a diploma, let alone graduate from an American high school. Your future will be bright. You'll find a good job. You'll be successful."

"I want to be back home. I can't wait to teach you all the sports I played over here. I'll bring the coconut ball with me. We can go to an empty field and I'll teach you how to throw just like when Thalen taught me."

Father laughed over the phone. "That sounds great. I'm looking forward to it."

We continued talking without worrying about anything. Speaking to Father always cheered me up. It seemed like he had the best way to help me reduce stress, encouraging me to work hard in school even if it was difficult.

When spring arrived, I attended a school retreat known as Kairos. It was a place where students could bond together. There, we were separated into small groups of five to seven people. Each group went to a different room, sat in a circle around a lit candle, and listened to one another's stories.

Hearing people talking about their alcoholic and addict siblings hit me. All this time, I thought I was one of the few who was living a life full of obstacles. Their stories gave me a better understanding of who they really were. It persuaded me to realize that I couldn't judge a person based on their looks. We had different appearances and beliefs, but everybody had their own story.

Kairos not only bonded students closer, but it made us appreciate the value of family. I remember sitting at the table with my group in a large cafeteria, the instructors went around, handing out letters from our loved ones. A pile of notes was placed in front of me. I was shocked to see so many people involved: Annica, Jeff and Wanda, Coach Maul, and more. Every letter was heartfelt and full of love and support. I was beginning to realize how a little thing could impact an individual's life.

A few weeks later, I started visiting colleges. Ryan and Chai took me to Puget Sound University, a school that sent me a recruitment letter for football. While walking with a group of visitors, I could see the beautiful campus: mowed grass, flower gardens, and tall trees along the entryway. Ahead of me was a large brick building, surrounded by hedges. A huge water fountain shot up water while students sat around reading and chatting. All of this made the school's atmosphere astonishing.

"I really like that school," I said from the backseat on our way home.

"Yeah, I like it too. I thought it's really pretty," said Chai, turning to Ryan. "What do you think, Ryan?"

"It was great, but I think it's too expensive." He looked at me through the mirror. "Tuition is over forty-four thousand a year. Your sister and I can't afford that."

Ryan and Chai were my last hope of attending college. I had to follow what worked best for them.

Thalen also said he would help with college. However, he had recommended I apply to a community college in Bellevue because it offered some four-year programs. I thought about it, but my desire was the University of Washington. It was Blake, Thalen, and his parents' alma mater. Seeing their degrees hung on the walls at Jeff and Wanda's house made me want to attend this university. Therefore, I applied even though I knew that Chai, Ryan, and Thalen couldn't afford tuition.

The University of Washington had sent me emails, asking for additional information. Annica always helped me reply, figuring out the best way to respond.

"This is huge, Chamroeun," she said. "The fact that they are reaching out to you means they are interested."

Regardless, I didn't think there was a way for me to enroll in UW. Jeff and Wanda had said they would never support it. Furthermore, Thalen, Ryan, and Chai made it clear that they couldn't afford the high tuition. It really felt like my back was against the wall. The only option I had was to follow Thalen's advice and enroll in Bellevue College.

On a quiet evening, I received a call from Chai.

"Hey, Chamroeun," she said in English with a low voice. "How are you?"

"I'm good. What's up?"

"I call to let you know Father left and went to Phnom Penh. He been gone for almost two week now."

"Wait, what? Why is he going to Phnom Penh?"

"He feeling sick. He want to get his lump check out. He's not getting any better."

"But I just talked to him a couple of weeks ago. He said he was getting better."

"He probably don't want you to worry, Chamroeun. The lump never go away. I have to send him money for medicine almost every month." She sighed. "Lab said he's staying in a hospital, somewhere in Phnom Penh. She gonna go see him."

"They let him go alone? Knowing that he was sick?"

"Everyone is busy. Lab and Lane have to keep their hair shop open. Lim has work and so did Ruat."

"You think all of this is more important than Father?"

Chai didn't reply.

"When is Lab going to Phnom Penh?"

"She going tomorrow. She let us know what going on with him. Don't worry, okay? Lab will take care of him."

I wanted to call Father, but I didn't have any phone cards. It was eleven thirty at night. Every store that carried the cards was closed at this hour. I took a few long breaths, trying to calm myself down, but my heart kept pounding in my chest. I hoped Father would be okay.

In the morning, I went and bought a five-dollar card, stood in my room, and called Father.

"Hello," he said. His voice sounded croaky.

"Hello, Father. What's going on with you? Are you in the hospital?"

"They told you. Yeah, I'm in a hospital in Phnom Penh. I'm just trying to figure out what's going on with me. It's nothing big. I'll be out of here soon."

"Can you please stop lying to me? Tell me the truth, I want to know what's really going on! How bad is your neck?"

He paused. "I don't know, that's why I'm here. I couldn't eat well and couldn't swallow anything. I was hoping the doctor could figure out what's wrong with me."

"Lab is coming to see you tomorrow, so please call her and tell her where you are."

He made a sound, as if he was considering the best way to reply. "She really doesn't have to come. I can take care of myself."

"Father, stop it! You're not okay! This lump is not going away anytime soon. You need someone to take care of you."

"I understand that, but this is Phnom Penh, everything is expensive here. You don't need Lab to come and spend money on a hotel. That money is more useful toward medicine."

"For once, could you please let us take care of you! If you don't want me to worry about you, then let Lab take care of you. If you want me to focus in school, then you can't be in Phnom Penh alone. Especially when you're sick." Tears filled my eyes. "I'm coming home soon. I don't want anything to happen to you."

"Everything is going to be okay, Son." He sighed. "When you come back, I'll be okay. I'll be waiting."

Two weeks later, I found out that he had lung cancer. The news forced Kesor to return home to find a better hospital for him. I remember sitting on the couch at Chai's house, listening to Ryan's conversation with Kesor over the phone.

"I met a foreign doctor," said Kesor. "He said he know a hospital in Thailand that could treat my Father cancer. He getting weaker and weaker every day. I have to do something."

"I don't know if that's the right thing to do," said Ryan. "There's no guarantee that this hospital in Thailand can cure your father. I think it could only make it more difficult for you and for him."

"Well, what you suggest us do?" Chai interfered, "give up?"

"No, babe. It seems like his condition is getting worse. You don't want to take him to Thailand without even knowing that he could be cured. With this condition, it's best if he could be with your family."

"What did the doctor say?" Chai ignored Ryan.

"He said there's a chance because they have better technology over there. They could fix him. But he ask for 2,000 dollars if we want him to take Father to that hospital."

"That's ridiculous!" Ryan snapped, "2,000 dollars just for taking him there?"

"Stop it, Ryan!" said Chai. "Do you have any other way? Or do you want my father to die?"

"This doctor is good," said Kesor. "He's really famous in Phnom Penh. That's why he's so expensive."

"Take him, Kesor," said Chai. "I'll help you with some money."

"Okay," said Kesor, "I gotta go. I'll talk to you guys later."

Chai left. Ryan scratched his head.

"What do you think is best for my father?" I asked. "I mean you're a doctor, what should we do?"

"It sounds like he's really weak right now. It might already be too late. If that's the case, I don't think going to Thailand will help. If the cancer is already spreading through his body, then there's nothing we can do."

"Can he have surgery? Can they remove his lung?"

"It's possible but unlikely. Surgery is not the usual treatment for something like this. It seems like there's a really low chance they can stop it at this point."

Ryan could be right, but I didn't want to lose hope. I still visualized Father's face, smiling when I returned.

Kesor took Father to Bumrungrad International Hospital, located in Bangkok. There, the doctor was able to give him treatment, taking fluid out of his lungs and prescribing all kinds of medicine that would give him a chance to live longer. But no matter how hard the hospital tried, Father wasn't getting any better.

For the second time in my life, I had to choose between family or school. My heart told me I needed to go home.

Coach Maul gave me his advice. "In this situation, Cham. I think there's no other option. Family is important. Your father needs you. You don't want to do something and end up regretting it for the rest of your life." He tapped me on my shoulder. "Go home. And be with your father."

Thalen agreed. "You need to go, man. I'll talk to your school. We'll figure out something. We'll submit the application for Bellevue College. But don't worry about that. Pack your clothes and let's go see your dad."

Fortunately, Blanchet allowed me to graduate early. The school knew about my situation and thought it was best to give me my diploma now. Coach Maul helped set up a mini-graduation ceremony for me in the chapel. He gave me a white football jersey, with a number two on it, signed by everyone on the team. The assistant coach, Coach Henderson gathered pictures of me during games, then put them in a booklet along with a heartwarming letter, wishing my family and me the best.

During the ceremony, many students and teachers showed up. I was honored to see so many people come support me. Chai sat next to me, holding flowers and graduation balloons. Thalen and his family sat behind us. Within minutes, Coach Maul approached the podium.

"Good morning, everyone," he said. "Thank you for coming to support Cham and his family." He scanned the room. "I've known Cham for a long time. I know that he's a competitor on and off the field. I know that he has a great heart and I know that going to see his father is the right thing to do." He glanced at me. "I just hope that your family can still recognize you after we turned you into a monster." The whole room laughed quietly. "We'll miss you, Cham. I'll be praying for you and your family. And I'm sure that everyone here will be doing the same."

The next morning, after gathering my luggage, I went to Jeff and Wanda's house, leaving them a thank-you note. I wanted to show my appreciation for everything they had done. I then called Ramsay.

"Hey bro, I need you to do me a favor," I said.

"Yeah, what's up?"

"I need you to do a fundraiser for me. My father is gonna need all the help he can get. It would mean the world if you could help raise some money so I could help pay for his medicine."

"Yeah, let's see what I can do. I can ask George and other people if they want to join. We can start something."

"That would be great. Anything would help. Thank you, bro."

Ryan picked me up later in the afternoon. The ride was dead silent. Sitting in the backseat, I looked out the window, staring at the tall skyscrapers as we approached downtown Seattle. I knew this could be my last time seeing this city. *Thank you for everything, Seattle*, I thought to myself.

I heard Chai sobbing and wiping tears off her cheeks. Ryan held her hand but didn't say anything.

I leaned forward, patting her shoulders. "It's gonna be okay, Chai," I said with tears slowly falling. "Stay strong."

After a nineteen-hour plane ride, we arrived in Bangkok. Stepping out of the airport, I could feel the extreme heat, making me sweat from head to toe. Thalen came to get us. We had to catch a train to the hospital.

"Hurry up," said Thalen, dragging Chai's luggage.

Chai and I sped up, following him alongside the crowded streets, jam-packed with motorbikes and cars. We walked about one mile until we reached the train station.

"It's too hot here," said Chai, holding onto the metal post. "They need to turn on the AC."

Thalen smirked. "You guys are from Cambodia. You'll get used to it."

Minutes later, we exited the train then walked for another mile until we reached the entrance to the hospital. The building was massive. The gateway was busy with cars entering and exiting. There was a large cafeteria on the main floor.

We took an elevator, heading up to Father's room. My heart was pounding in my chest like it was about to jump out. We followed Thalen into the hallway and then through a door. I saw Kesor in the room, wiping Father's head. His eyes were half-open, tubes attached to his nose and arms. His body was so thin I could see his collarbone and the bones of his chest underneath the hospital gown.

"Father, Chamroeun and Chai are here," Kesor said in Khmer. He turned his head, blinking slowly. My heart dropped to my stomach. Words couldn't come out. Tears dripped as I approached him. "He said don't cry, Chamroeun," Kesor continued. "It's gonna make it hard for him to breathe."

I wiped my cheeks, went in close, and gave him a gentle hug. "I'm here, Father," I mumbled in Khmer. "I'm not going anywhere."

I stayed up late, holding Father's arm and watching him breathe through the tube. Kesor and Chai lay behind me, sharing a small sofa next to the wall. Thalen slept on the floor in a corner of the room. There came a knock on the door and a few nurses along with a doctor entered the room.

"Hi," said a nurse wearing gloves and a gown, "we need to do the treatment."

"Move, Chamroeun," said Kesor, "let them do their job." I stepped away, sitting next to Chai.

"What are they gonna do to him?" I asked.

"They checking his tube that connects to his lung. They need to make sure it's still there before he sleep," Kesor answered. "He have a lot of fluid in his lung. It's important that it come out."

I watched the doctor turn Father to his side. Father squeezed his eyes in pain, his hands gripped the bed sheet.

I felt helpless. I wanted to hold his hand, but I didn't want to be in the doctor's way.

"It's okay, Father," said Kesor, "they're almost done."

Soon enough, the doctor moved him onto his back and injected some medicine into the IV fluid bag, making him fall asleep.

In the morning, I sat on the sofa, watching my sisters wipe Father's arms and legs with a towel soaked in lukewarm water. The liquid made him look fresher. His eyes were fully open. He even tried to talk.

"How," he spoke with a croaky tone, "much . . . longer . . . do I have to be here?"

"We don't know yet," said Kesor, "the doctor hasn't told us anything."

"Don't worry too much, Father," Chai kept wiping his arms, "just try to rest."

Father rolled his eyes in my direction.

"He wants to talk to you, Chamroeun. Come closer," Chai continued.

"How are you feeling?" I asked, patting his hand.

"A little . . . better . . ." He gripped on my fingers. "Are you . . ." he paused, struggling to talk, "are you . . ." He stared at the ceiling and breathed at a quick pace. He raised his hand, scribbling.

"Chai, get him paper and pen," said Kesor, "he wants to write." Chai handed him a pen and a notebook. Father took his time, writing words in Khmer.

I stared at the words in shock. I couldn't recognize any of the letters Father wrote. After studying in the US for six years, I couldn't read Khmer letters anymore.

"He's asking if you're done with school?" Chai translated.

"Yes, Father," I said, "I finished." I got up. "I want you to see something." I opened my luggage and showed him my diploma. Father attempted to get up but he couldn't. Chai and Kesor assisted him, leaning him on the headboard of the bed. Father wore his glasses, staring at my diploma for nearly five minutes. He couldn't read any of the writing. Everything was in English. But that didn't stop him from reviewing my accomplishment. He then wrote on the paper.

"He said very good," Chai translated. Father nodded, with a slight smile.

"Yes, Father," I said. "I couldn't have done it without you." I paused. "I'm going to finish my goal. I'm going to try to finish college."

Father didn't write anything. He turned to me, shaking his head slowly. "Stay . . ." he spoke, "I want . . ." He took a deep breath then wrote on the paper.

"He says he wants to spend time with you," Chai said, looking at me in the eyes. I nodded, rubbing his arm softly. Father kept writing. "He wants to be here with us. He doesn't want you to go."

"I . . ." he spoke, "want . . . to be with you . . . all . . ." I could see tears in his eyes.

"You're not going anywhere," said Chai, combing his hair. "You're going to get better soon." Father didn't say nor write anything else. Chai and I lay him back, letting him rest.

Later that day, Thalen told us that the hospital wouldn't allow the four of us to stay in the room together. Thalen and I had to rent a hotel nearby.

Worse, the hospital bill was getting expensive. We were thousands of dollars in debt as the days went by.

I contacted Ramsay through Facebook. He was able to raise roughly 1,000 dollars. Unfortunately, that wasn't enough. Chai spent all of her money and had to ask Ryan for help. Thalen did too, providing us with everything he had. He even asked his parents to help, but Jeff and Wanda wouldn't do so unless Kesor would promise to pay back the money.

"They want you to write them an email, saying that you will pay them back," said Thalen.

"No!" said Kesor, walking away from Thalen.

"You don't understand, there's no other way. We owe the hospital over 10,000 dollars right now. I don't have that kind of money. Without my parents' help, we're screwed!"

"Calm down, Thalen," Chai interfered, "let me talk to her."

Kesor listened to Chai and agreed to send Jeff and Wanda an email, saying she would take responsibility. Even with the agreement, there was no guarantee that Thalen's parents would help. I didn't think they would trust Kesor because when dealing with financial problems, she always relied on Thalen to bail her out. They knew Kesor was a hardheaded person who might not follow through with her words, all of which could have convinced them to say no. But they instead chose to send the money.

I was relieved. Without Jeff and Wanda's help, we really didn't have a way to pay the debt. Chai asked Ryan's mother, but she refused. Ryan was incapable of paying for the whole bill. If it wasn't for Jeff and Wanda, I truly believed the hospital would have put us in jail.

A few days later, the doctor broke the news, telling us, "there's nothing we could do to save his life. His time is running out. He has roughly one month left."

At this moment, it seemed like all hope had faded. The best thing we could do was take Father home.

"Father, we have to go home now," Chai said in Khmer, slowly patting his head. "We're going to join the family."

Father leaned his head forward. "Am . . . I . . . healed . . .?" he mumbled. Chai didn't reply. She didn't want to lie. Father rested his head, looking at the ceiling. He knew the truth. It crushed my heart seeing him lie there, breathing calmly, knowing his time was coming to an end.

We took Father back to Cambodia via ambulance. After hours on the curvy and potholed roads, we reached Sihanoukville. Ruat took Father to a Chinese-owned hospital that was decent enough to look after him.

Having my elder siblings take turns caring for Father gave Thalen, Chai, Kesor, and me a chance to go home and rest. Sitting in the back seat, I couldn't see anything. It was seven thirty in the evening and the road was pitch-black without any street lights. Within minutes, the driver stopped.

"This doesn't look like Oue Bram," I said.

"It's not," said Chai in Khmer, "we have to pick up Mother. She came to wait for us here." Chai and I got out of the vehicle. To my right, I saw Lane walking out of a coffee shop with Mother.

"Chamroeun?" she asked, "is that you?"

"Yes, Mother!" I gave her a big hug. "I'm home . . ."

Mother was so tiny. Her head rested on my chest. I could see her looking up at me through the dark and she kept holding my arm. She was overjoyed having me back.

When we got home, I saw the wooden house had been torn down. Everyone stayed at the cement house. I sat next to Mother on her bed, talking to her for hours. Mother kept telling me to shower and to eat dinner, but I didn't listen. I continued speaking, patting her shoulder and kissing her forehead. I then heard the sound of a motorbike approaching.

I walked out and saw Lab and her boyfriend, Dara, on motorbikes. Lab took off her helmet. I went out and hugged her. Lab started crying.

"It's okay, Lab," I said in Khmer, "I'm back now."

Lab wiped her eyes. "Brother, I'm so happy to see you. I'm happy that you're back." She paused. "But I think you came a little late."

Her words gave me goosebumps. I bit my tongue, knowing that Lab was right. I knew my return didn't mean much because "things" had changed. Everything I had dreamt, a joyful reunion with my family, had faded.

The next day, Chai and I went to the hospital, taking turns with Ruat. While wiping Father's arms, I thought about Lab's words, and the sense of regret was unbearable. I wished I had come home sooner, but nothing could change that now.

"Go dump the water outside," said Chai. "We're done. Let him rest for a while."

I did so, then stood at the corner of the bed, staring at the ground. Father was sleeping, breathing oxygen through the tube. Chai could see right through me.

"What's wrong, Chamroeun?"

"Nothing." I sat down. "I'm just thinking. I wish that I could've come back sooner, you know."

Chai sat next to me. "Don't worry too much, you're back now."

Tears fell on my cheeks. "I messed up. If I came sooner, I would at least get to have a conversation with him." I inhaled. "But I didn't and this is what I get." My eyes became watery. "It hurts, you know. It feels like a bullet hitting my chest. Leaving a hole that can never be fixed."

My head lowered and my vision blurred as tears kept dripping. Chai wrapped her arms around my head but remained silent.

Later in the afternoon, Mother came to visit, standing at the side of the bed. She didn't say a word, but the doleful look on her face gave it all away. She was downcast. After moments of quietness, Mother finally spoke.

"Are you feeling better, Pen?" she asked, holding onto Father's palm.

Father nodded, slowly. Mother stood by his side, watching him.

It was a heartwarming moment. I haven't seen my parents getting along since living in Oue Muoy. Yet, I couldn't tell if Mother forgave Father for the beatings that she received. I didn't think that she would ever want to talk to him again after hearing the rumor of him cheating. Nevertheless, I was happy to see Mother there, holding Father's hand. I wanted my parents to be together.

Day by day, Father was getting worse. He couldn't speak anymore and could barely move his arms. Even in this condition, Father attempted to communicate, writing notes with shaking hands.

"Love you all," Chai read the note in Khmer, "forgive you all." She turned to us. Her eyes turned red as she relayed Father's words.

My skin crawled hearing those words. I had never heard Father say anything like this. Perhaps, he knew his time was coming to an end. Or maybe, he didn't want us to think that we were terrible kids, mistreating him and breaking his heart. I knew I did, when asking him to move out and not returning home when I had the opportunity.

As Father's condition weakened, our finances were draining. The hospital bill increased each day, leaving us no choice but to take Father home. We still hired the doctor to come see him to provide the necessary equipment to keep him alive as long as possible.

Being away from the hospital was difficult. Father didn't get enough treatment and was often in pain. I remember one night, he was groaning repeatedly while lying on the hospital bed. Sleeping near him on the ground, I watched him moving his fingers.

"Ah . . ." he moaned. "Argh!" He moved his arm again. I got up and saw him staring at the roof, steadily moving his head as he kept groaning.

It was two thirty in the morning. Everyone was asleep. Lab, Chai, and Kesor all slept close to one another. Our house was packed. The hospital equipment took up most of the space. Lab had to rent a place nearby for the rest of us. My siblings and I had to alternate duties from day to day.

"Argh . . ." Father moaned and kept moving his arms.

I pulled a chair and sat near him. "Rest, Father," I said, patting the back of his hand. "The more you move, the more painful it gets."

Father breathed deeply and made less noise. His eyes opened, staring at the wall. I continued rubbing his hand and was able to calm him down. The night was dead silent. I could hear insects crying all around me. "Try to shut your eyes."

He turned to me, blinking his eyes and taking long breaths. "Get some rest. It's late." He kept staring at me. "You know, Father. I'm glad that I'm here with you." I rubbed my thumb on his skin, gently. "I'm glad that you got to see my diploma." I smiled. "I did it for you." I cleared a lump in my throat then looked him in the eyes. "No matter what happens, Father, I'm going to finish it. I'm going to do whatever I can to be the one to finish school. I promise . . ."

Father appraised me, breathing calmly, then nodded. I patted his hand late into the night until he fell asleep.

The next morning, I hopped on a motorbike with Lane sitting behind me. We had to find Father a new hospital. He was always in pain and wasn't getting enough treatment at home. I started the engine, glanced inside the house and noticed Father was looking at me.

We rode off into the narrow dirt road.

When we arrived, I parked the motorbike underneath a mango tree. Lane and I went from building to building, checking out the atmosphere of each place. Every room was filled with two to three patients, lying directly on wooden beds, hands covering their foreheads. I could see flies in almost every room. A strong, pungent smell of body odor hit my nose.

"This place is disgusting," Lane whispered to me, grabbing the tip of her shirt to cover her nose. "I don't think Father should stay here." We both walked out of the room, heading to another building. "What do you think?"

"I don't think we have a choice," I said. "Come on, let's go check out another building." As we walked back to the bike, I felt my phone vibrate.

"Hello?"

"Chamroeun!" Chai screamed. "He's gone! Father's gone!" She cried.

My mind froze. I dropped the phone, the screen hit a rock, shattering the glass.

"Chamroeun, is everything okay?" Lane asked.

I immediately picked up the phone from the ground. "Hang in there, Chai!" I mumbled, choking up. "We're coming back!" I hung up. "Father passed away!" I told Lane. "We have to go back, now!"

We rushed to the motorbike, speeding as fast as we could through the curvy dirt streets. Tears fell on my cheeks. I was heartbroken. I didn't get to say goodbye.

# 24

# HOMECOMING

WE WASHED FATHER'S body in water mixed with flowers and put a number of lit candles around his bed. We tied his hands with red strings to hold them together as if he was praying, combed his hair, then dressed him in a button-down shirt and trousers before putting him in a coffin. This ritual was to ensure that his soul would have a proper send-off in the afterlife.

We took Father's body to Wat Kroam, a nearby temple, and invited a number of elderly villagers along with a few monks. Everyone sat on the cement floor, listening to the monks giving Father blessings. In Buddhism, death didn't mean the end of life but only an end of a life cycle. My family believed Father's soul would be reincarnated.

After the blessing, we gathered, burned incense sticks, and prayed.

"Father. Go in peace," said Lim, then stuck the sticks into a pod of sand. "Go reincarnate into a better and wealthy life." She turned to me. "He's beyond our reach now. The only thing we can do is to give him a warm blessing."

I nodded.

The next night, Father's coffin was put up on a tall metal stage, roughly ten feet above ground. The stage was decorated with colorful lights and fabrics. A large photo of him, alongside flowers, was placed in front of his coffin. Beneath this was a pit, dug a few feet deep into the ground, and filled with wood blocks. The funeral planner opened the coffin, letting my siblings and I say our last goodbye. Everyone was in tears, circling around him.

"Goodbye, Father," Chai sobbed in Khmer, patting his head, "I will miss you."

I didn't say a word, but in my heart, I said, *if you can hear me, please forgive me. Rest now, Father. There's no need for you to be stressed anymore. You will always be in my heart.* I lightly kissed his forehead.

Within seconds, they closed the coffin, lowered it to the bottom, and burned his body.

I stood in front of his picture, staring at the image for a long time as dusk approached. I wished I could go back in time so I could have visited him sooner. As I descended the stairs, I saw my mother alone, staring at the stage in silence. I could only imagine how she felt.

We took Father's urn to Prey Veng, a place that he called home. Thanks to Ramsay's fundraiser, we were able to buy a small piece of land on the temple's property, where we built a spiritual house to keep his urn. There, we hosted a seventh-day funeral procession, a tradition in the Khmer culture.

I was surprised to see hundreds of villagers came to show their respect. I remember standing near the entrance, underneath a metal tent covered by a canopy. I saw kids and adults arrive with their old rusty bicycles, holding small bags of rice as gifts. Some wore worn clothes with sandals and didn't have anything to bring, but they still came to support my family. Seeing their condition reminded me of the life I had lived.

Despite our early struggles, most villagers still considered him as an honorable man, a person who would never forget Prey Veng. I knew Father's reputation would last forever in this village.

Chai hired a group of traditional Cambodian musicians to play, pin peat. They used all kinds of instruments: percussion, string, and woodwind. At first, it felt like I was experiencing my own culture as a tourist. My heart made a connection to a joyful memory I had a long time ago during Thalen and Kesor's wedding. Father loved pin peat. He paid the musicians to play all day.

Being in Prey Veng, no matter how hard I tried to be that village kid who drew cartoon figures in the dirt, I couldn't. I was taller and more muscular than any man in the village.

After the funeral, we returned to Kompong Som. Lab and Kesor sold the Oue Bram house because Mother didn't want to continue living there, especially after Father's death. We all moved into the rental house in Oue Pir.

Kesor went back to America a few days later. Even in Cambodia, Kesor and Thalen's relationship was not improving. Thalen often went out drinking and didn't come home until late. My family and I felt terrible seeing him in this condition. We tried to help but no matter what we said, he didn't listen.

"Don't go out, Thalen!" Lim said in Khmer, holding his arm while he was on the motorbike. "It's dangerous to drink and ride."

"I won't be drinking. I'm only going to see my friends." Yet, he would return late, his face all red before passing out on the floor.

I remember hearing Lab checking on him.

"Thalen! Have you eaten?" she asked in Khmer. "You're all dirty! Go take a shower before you sleep!" Thalen kept sleeping.

"Let it be, Lab!" Chai shouted. "He's an adult. He knows how to take care of himself."

As days went by, Chai stayed in Cambodia a little longer. She and I often went to the beaches, having lunches, and enjoying our homecoming.

I deeply loved standing in the shallow water. The white sand made my feet look dark. The sun was shining brightly, causing the surface of the sea to sparkle. Small waves washed up against my ankles while a warm breeze gently grazed me, putting a smile on my face. Even at age nineteen, I still felt like a little kid, wishing I could jump into the water and lie there for hours.

One night, while sitting at a restaurant at Ochheuteal Beach with some of my sisters, Dara, and Lane's husband, Charaka, kids approached us, selling bracelets, potato chips, and sarongs (traditional skirts).

"Aunt, do you want to buy chips?" asked a small girl in Khmer, holding a tray full of chips. Her shoulder carried a coat hanger, holding a variety of bracelets.

"No, thank you, Niece," said Lab. "We already have food."

"Doesn't she remind you of when you were young, Chamroeun?" Chai asked in English.

"Yeah, a little bit."

The girl heard Chai, then came to me. "Mister, mister," she spoke in broken English, "do you want buy bracelet? I make them for you!"

"I'm okay, thank you." I chuckled.

"Don't speak English to him, he's Khmer," said Lane.

The girl's eyes narrowed at Lane. "He not Khmer. He too big and strong." She switched to English. "You are handsome man. This bracelet make you handsomer." She picked out a red bracelet.

I wanted to tell her to go away, but I knew how it felt to get denied by a tourist.

"How much are they?" I asked. I spoke in English because I wanted her to keep practicing her speaking ability.

"One for two dollar. But I can make you a cool one for five dollar."

"No, I won't do that to you. It's already late. You need to be home. You have school tomorrow, right?"

"I have school in afternoon."

"If I buy one from you, would you go home? You shouldn't be out here selling at night."

"Yes, okay. I go home."

"Okay, I'll buy this one." I picked a blue one. It was my favorite color.

She tied the bracelet around my wrist. "Here, bracelet mean friendship. You and I are now friend."

I chuckled. "I'm glad to be your friend. What's your name?"

"Chan."

"How old are you, Chan?"

"I am ten year old."

"You're a smart kid. I wish I was as smart as you when I was your age." I paused. "Would you believe me if I told you that I used to sell bracelets and chips on this beach?"

She lowered her brows.

"My sister and I were once just like you when we were young," I spoke in Khmer.

She turned to Chai, seeing Chai smile and nod. "You can become like us too," I switched to English.

"Keep practicing your English and work hard in school," I added. "Your future will be bright."

A few days later, Chai and Thalen had to go back to America for work. With Chai gone, I tried to see more of Kompong Som. Lab's boyfriend, Dara, came too because he didn't want me to travel alone. We went to an island, Koh Rong, located about an hour away by boat. The island was cleaner than the peninsula. Walking on the beach, I hardly saw any garbage. The place was full of locals including tourists: Khmers, Westerners, and even Chinese. People were tanning in the sun. Others played volleyball on the soft sand. There were all kinds of restaurants and bars alongside the shore. Khmer music played from shop to shop. I even saw fishing boats anchored in the clear blue water.

Later in the evening, we went to a crowded western restaurant and bar. Every table was taken. Khmers and foreigners sat in groups, eating steak, burgers, and more.

We sat on tall wooden stools next to a few foreigners. Some were speaking French, leaving me clueless.

"You guys know what you want?" a Caucasian waitress asked in English. She was tall, wearing a black dress. I could see tattoos covering her white skin.

"Yes! We'll have grilled steak, please. Thank you." I handed her the menu.

She wrote the order then appraised me. "You're American?"

"No, no," I chuckled. "I'm Khmer."

She raised her eyebrows. "You have an American accent."

"That's funny. No one has told me that before, but I don't think I have an American accent though."

She giggled and took the orders to the chefs.

Minutes later, we got our food: thin sliced grilled beef and fried tomatoes. I remember chewing the meat, my jaw getting sore because the beef was too chewy.

"This is hard to eat," I mumbled in Khmer, "how are you eating this?"

"Cambodian beef is always like this," Dara answered.

"How's the food?" asked the waitress.

"Good. Really good," I lied.

"Uh-huh. You don't seem to like it." She looked at my plate and saw most of the beef still there.

"Oh, I'm a slow eater."

"Where you learn your English? You sound like an American."

"I went to study in America." I smiled. "I lived in Seattle for six years. And I just came back for a visit."

"Nice!" she nodded, "welcome back."

"Thank you."

As I continued to chew, my gums got so sore, I could only eat half the plate. I gave the rest to Dara.

"Check, please!" I signaled the waitress.

"Check?" she giggled. "This isn't America. We don't do checks here. You can say, I WANT TO PAY NOW."

"Okay, I WANT TO PAY NOW."

She shook her head with a smirk then handed me the bill.

"Where are you from?" I asked.

"Holland! Do you know where that is?"

I put some money on the table. "Europe, right?"

"Yes, but where in Europe?" She turned to a large map, hanging on the wall. I peeked at it up close but couldn't spot Holland. "It's right here." She pointed at a region next to Germany.

"It says Netherlands?"

"It's the same thing, Holland. Netherlands. Like America. USA."

"You guys speak English there?"

"No, we speak Dutch. But English is an important language that most people have to learn."

"How long have you been here?"

"Almost one year now."

"Wow, that's a long time. Do you have any friends here?"

"No, I did a while ago, but they all left." She sat on the stool then lit up a cigarette. "I love this place. I don't think I'm leaving here anytime soon."

"Aren't you afraid to be here alone? Don't get me wrong, you're a girl. Don't you think it's dangerous traveling alone?"

"Not really. I meet a lot of female tourists traveling alone all the time. And the locals here are friendly. There's nothing to be afraid of."

"You're a brave girl." I paused. "I didn't catch your name."

"Natalie." She took a drag of her smoke. "You?"

"Chamroeun." I hesitated, distracted by the smoke. "This is probably none of my business, but you shouldn't smoke. I'm just saying, it's not good for you."

She glared at me. "What make you say that?"

I exhaled. "My father just died from lung cancer. He used to smoke a lot."

Her tone changed, looking at me with sorrow. "I'm sorry to hear that." She rubbed the cigarette into a bowl full of ash. "I didn't know. I hear people say the same thing, again and again. But there's still a lot of people smoking. They're still alive." She put the cigarette down. "People get too scared sometimes, you know. People talk about how dangerous it is to come here but everyone is friendly." She turned to me. "Most people are too afraid for no reason. I mean, what's the point of living, if you are scared to die."

I nodded.

"Look around you. These people didn't come because they were scared. They came here because they want to see the world. Experiencing new cultures, eating different food, talking to the locals. Not all of that can be taught in school."

I agreed that traveling could give people a sense of happiness. Seeing the wilderness of Koh Rong Island did make me feel relieved. I realized that because I had spent so much time in the classroom, I had a greater appreciation of being free. An individual had to experience pain to understand pleasure. Growing up, my family and I suffered from extreme poverty, but the struggles did make us stronger, forcing us to search for a better life.

When I returned, I met up with Ruat for coffee.

"My goodness!" he said, staring wide-eyed at my arms. "How did you become so fat?"

"I'm not fat." I took a sip of the iced coffee. "I just work out a lot."

"Not fat? Look at you! You probably ate a lot over there, huh?" He laughed.

Ruat wasn't the only one that called me "fat." Some people in the village said the same because of how big I was. Ironically, back in the states I was one of the shortest and the smallest among my classmates. I often looked up while talking to my peers. I thought of Coach Maul's comment and realized he was right. I truly felt like a "monster."

I had to be in Cambodia for roughly three months before reapplying for my visa. To stay busy, I found a job with a touring company.

Being a tour guide was a perfect job to meet new people and could give me a chance to travel more. However, I picked the wrong time to work. Cambodia was entering monsoon season, making tourism much more difficult.

I remember my first day of work, I sat in the back of the truck underneath the canopy among a number of foreigners, watching heavy rainfall with thunder. A Khmer coworker tapped me on my wrist.

"You're not going to like this job," he said in Khmer, over a noisy crowd.

"Why? Is it because of the rain?"

"Yes, rain is a part of it. But this job is exhausting. You barely have time to rest. You're not going to like it."

I cleared a lump in my throat. "Thanks for letting me know."

My coworker wasn't kidding. When we arrived at the dock, I could see big waves pounding on the shore. Water splashed against the pier as a gale came through.

"Is this safe?" asked a female tourist, holding her backpack. I could see her legs shaking.

To my right, I saw my boss signaling me to take the tourists on the boat. "We'll be all right," I said, "people travel in this condition all the time." I got to the front. "Everyone! Listen up!" I shouted as rain and seawater dripped down my face. "We're loading now! Please grab your gear and walk carefully to the boat!"

Fearful, they looked at each other but refused to move. Being a tour guide, I had to lead the way. I started walking on the dock to ensure safety. I turned around and saw a few people following me. Soon enough, everyone walked in a line, heading toward the boat.

Everyone sat in two rows on the sides of a big wooden boat, holding on to the posts as waves rocked us side-to-side.

"Tour guide!" the captain shouted from the upper deck. I climbed and saw a skinny Khmer man holding a walkie-talkie, turning the steering wheel. "Tell them we're leaving now. Here are some bags just in case anyone throws up." He handed me some black plastic bags. I went down, standing in front of the crowd.

"Okay, everyone!" I shouted. "We're leaving now. This trip will take about thirty to forty-five minutes. Please hold on tight." All eyes were on me, I could see water dripping down their faces as their lips turned white. I sat down as the boat slowly left the dock and pushed against the strong wind. A canopy tied on the left side blew off.

"Whoa!" a girl sitting next to me yelled.

"It's okay," I tapped her shoulder, "it's just a canopy." I got up, holding a post, making my way to the sailor. "What's going on?" I asked in Khmer.

"The wind blew it off," he said, "it's nothing serious. I'll tie it back."

The man climbed on the side of the boat and tied the canopy back in. I sat down, surprised that he had the nerves to go out in the storm.

"Hey man," an elderly foreigner scooted in close. "Can you be honest with me? I know your job is to calm people down and all, but is this normal?"

"Umm, I'm not sure. It's my first day."

He laughed. "Are you kidding me?"

I shook my head.

"Well, you picked the wrong day, my friend."

"Yeah, the thing is, I don't even know how to swim. So, if the boat sinks, I'm screwed."

"Brother! If the boat sinks, we're all screwed! I mean, look, there's nothing near us!"

I peeked out and saw an island through the heavy rain, miles away.

"Is there a rescue team?"

"I don't know. I don't think there's any. They didn't tell me anything."

His eyes opened to the size of eggs. He went back to his seat.

I saw a girl sitting to my right with her mouth covered. Her face turned purple. I grabbed a plastic bag and crouched toward her. "Are you all right?"

She kept covering her mouth. Within seconds, she gripped my hands and puked. I looked up and saw everyone staring at me, some even smiled. "Are you feeling better?" I asked, patting her back.

She nodded. "Thank you."

"Sure," I smirked, "just doing my job."

The storm worsened as we reached the halfway point. The wind was so strong, our boat drifted sideways, blowing out the side canopies again. A few more people threw up, puking into the sea. A tourist in a blue shirt crawled to me.

"This is insane!" he yelled. "Why did you make us come?"

"Easy!" the elderly tourist interfered, "it's his first day. He didn't know."

The man in the blue shirt glared then went back.

"Thanks for that," I said.

"Yep! You know, I was asking myself if flying is more dangerous than boating?" He paused. "After seeing this, boating is definitely more dangerous."

I didn't say a word. My body shook as wind and water droplets hit me. I could see the nose of our boat cut through the tall waves. Water splashed in, flowing on the floor. People screamed and clung to the posts for dear life.

At this moment, I wasn't convinced that we were going to make it. Our boat wasn't moving forward anymore. The storm got stronger, keeping us in the middle of the sea away from our destination. I could hear the captain, yelling on the walkie-talkie, reporting that we might sink. My heart shook, I looked around but didn't see any life jackets.

I shut my eyes and prayed to Father.

"Father, please help me. Please look after me and these people. Please make the storm go away. I don't want to die today. I still have a lot of things to do."

After Father passed, I thought the only way of communicating with him was through prayers. Khmer people believed that to talk to the dead, we had to burn incense, shut our eyes, and make the wish. Lim once told me that the smoke of incense would carry our message. I didn't have any incense with me, but I still hoped Father received my prayer.

By a miracle, the wind calmed down roughly thirty minutes later, allowing the boat to make headway once again. I never claimed Father's spirit as a supernatural being. Who could have the power to stop the storm? Being a nonbeliever, I didn't want to pray to God only in a desperate situation. I prayed to Father because he was an ordinary person who deeply cared about my well-being. I knew he would do anything to keep me safe. Perhaps Father asked God to help, or maybe I got lucky, but the strong wind finally stopped. Shortly after, we made it to the island. I was truly blessed to be alive.

# 25

# FULFILLING MY PROMISE

THE NEXT DAY, I asked my boss for a different job. He offered me a position working alongside the US soldiers. Apparently, the Marines were in Cambodia to train with the Khmer army for a few weeks. This would be a long shift: lasting from six in the morning to two the next morning.

I was thrilled about working with the US soldiers, but knowing that I would be in a twenty-hour shift gave me hesitation. I thought the hours were insane, yet it was still a better option than being on the boat.

I remember the morning of my first shift, I rode in a white van through many villages. The narrow routes were filled with potholes, and there were domestic animals and pedestrians on the sides of the road, making our commute even longer.

Minutes later, we arrived at the military base which was basically an abandoned school surrounded with tall trees. The place had a big empty space in the middle. Khmer soldiers ran in small groups. Others practiced rope climbing drills.

We went inside an office and saw a few Khmer soldiers dressed in green uniforms in the foyer. The room had two long wooden tables that faced each other. There were flowers in the middle, and near the wall was a large green board covered with writings and posters of the king. In the corners of the room were a cameraman and a videographer adjusting their equipment.

"Hello!" said a Khmer soldier in English, "welcome!" He shook the Marines' hands. "Please take seat! The Deputy General be here soon." A Khmer soldier looked at me from the corner of his eyes. He wasn't pleased to see my outfit. I was in shorts, flip-flops, and a t-shirt; underdressed for this occasion.

The Marines settled at the left table. I sat on a plastic chair behind them. Soon enough, a group of Khmer soldiers entered. I then saw two older men in black uniforms with stars pinned on their shoulders. They even brought their own linguist, who was much older than me. He translated their greeting with the Marines. After handshakes and pictures were taken, we settled in to begin the meeting.

"Good afternoon, Deputy General!" said Captain John. "It is an honor meeting you!" He turned to me and I translated.

Nervous, I spoke slowly and clearly, especially after seeing the Cambodian linguist watching me. I knew this was a special event and didn't want to misinterpret any words.

Captain John continued after I spoke. "My fellow Marines and I are thrilled to be here, and we are looking forward to doing some training drills with the Cambodian Army." He turned to me. Right before I spoke, he interfered, "could you move up and sit near me? I don't want to turn around every time I talk." I moved and sat on a big wooden chair near Major Harrison.

"He's just a translator, but he is sitting in a high-ranking chair," people whispered in Khmer.

I swallowed then began translating Captain John's words. The meeting went on for another two hours. The Marines talked about all kinds of training drills: running, climbing, hand-to-hand combat, and more. I did my best to translate. There were times I didn't know the correct Khmer words and let the other linguist speak instead. He spoke Khmer clearer, but his English wasn't better than mine. He often let me do the talking when it came to interpreting from Khmer to English.

After the meeting, the Marines and Khmer soldiers gathered for some more pictures. Meanwhile, I stood in the corner near the other linguist.

"You seem to have a little accent when you speak Khmer. Are you a foreigner?" he asked in Khmer.

"No, I'm Khmer. But I went to study in America for so long I forgot some of the Khmer words."

"Really? What state were you in?"

"Washington State."

"How long were you there?"

"Six years. I just finished high school. I'm here to visit my family for three months then I'm going to reapply for another visa."

"You've been away for six years? Don't you want to stay here longer?"

"I want to. But school starts in September. I have to be there and sign up for classes." It made me feel guilty discussing possibly leaving again after being gone for six years.

I remember getting back to the rental house at three in the morning after a rough night at work. Lim's husband always gave me a ride home. While putting the motorbike back inside, he made so much noise, Mother woke.

"Chamroeun?" she asked, opening her room's window, "is that you?"

I walked around Lim's sleeping net. "Yes, Mother," I said quietly, "go back to sleep."

"Why are you working so late?"

I entered her room and sat near her. "Work took a bit longer than usual."

"Can you find a different job? I hardly see you."

I nodded but didn't say a word.

"Have you eaten? There's dinner for you."

"Okay, I'll have some. Go back to sleep, Mother . . ."

I sat in the kitchen, eating fried lettuce with pork and rice at a fast pace. I had roughly three hours until work started again. While chewing, I thought of Mother's words. After working for nearly two weeks, I didn't have time to spend with my family. I worked seven days a week and always had to go right to sleep when I got home. I felt terrible leaving the house every day. This was no different from being in America. Part of me didn't want to quit, but this job wasn't worth being away from Mother. I chose family over money.

Without the job taking up my time, I was able to be around Mother, buying her fruit and snacks almost every day.

"Thank you, Son," she said, peeling a grapefruit. "This is my favorite. I don't often get to eat this." I sat nearby, watching her eat with pure joy. Mother turned to Lim, who was lying in a hammock near the entry door. "Lim, do you want some?"

"No, I'm okay. But if you could save some for Houd, it would be great." Since I was gone, Lim had another baby, Houd, who was three years old.

"Take your time, Mother." I rubbed her back then got up. "I have to do some laundry."

I went upstairs, grabbed my dirty clothes, then put them in the large metal bowl in front of our house.

"Chamroeun, just leave it there," Lim yelled, "I'll wash it for you later."

"It's okay. I can do it." I turned on the water to soak the clothes. We didn't have a well at the rental house. Instead, a water and electricity system were already installed.

I sat on a wooden block underneath an extended eave, cleaning a shirt with a brush, water, and soap. Suddenly, loud thunder crashed, shaking the ground. The atmosphere darkened as rain clouds covered the sky. Within seconds, a downpour of rain fell. I was soaked as the wind blew the water sideways. I took off my shirt, put it in the bowl, and kept brushing.

"Hey, Wrestler!" Lim shouted from the inside. "Why don't you pull the bowl further away from the edge of the eave, so you won't get wet." I did so.

Lim called me "Wrestler" because she saw muscular wrestlers on TV, especially those she saw on WWE.

While hanging washed clothes on the wooden rod, I saw my nephews, Hou and Houd, playing in the rain near the flooded street. Watching them blasting water at each other brought back memories of when I was young. I loved playing in the rain.

"Hou!" Lim yelled, "stop playing in the rain! Bring your brother inside." Hou kept playing.

"Ay!" I shouted, "did you hear your mother?" The two brothers sprinted inside. Weirdly, Hou and Houd were always intimidated by me. Maybe, they were scared of my size. Or perhaps, I was still a stranger to them after being away for so long.

Standing near the road, I saw a number of kids holding bags, walking alongside the muddy stream as they collected plastic bottles. It was pouring.

There were hardly any motorbikes on the street. Most people didn't bother going outside and stood underneath their shelters. Street kids didn't care about the rain. They all seemed thrilled to spot so many plastic bottles flowing down the road. As they got closer to me, I saw a kid as small as Hou, rush into the muddy water then grab an aluminum can. He put it into his bag with a big smile on his face. "Chamroeun!" Mother yelled, "keep an eye on our bucket and the bowl. I don't want those kids to steal anything."

It broke my heart seeing how small they were. I had seen street kids before but this time it felt different. Back in America, I didn't see any street kids. Children were always protected by their families, living in homes and attending schools. After living in the US for six years, I had forgotten how extreme poverty was in Cambodia. Thalen's family was wealthy, so I didn't have to worry about food. Seeing those street kids reminded me that I was once in their position. I had my family to look after me, but these kids did not. Most of them probably didn't have support of any kind.

I remember Mother said that street kids didn't have much to rely on. Most of their parents have passed. Selling bottles and cans was a way to earn money so they could buy food.

Part of me felt guilty knowing I had been so lucky, getting to study in the US and not having to worry about surviving. I could have been like them if I hadn't been given the opportunity. Guilt pushed me to do something for my community. After all, I did make a promise that I would do whatever I can to help.

I went inside and talked to Hou. "Tell your friends that I am teaching English for free, Monday to Friday, six to seven in the evening," I said. "If anyone wants to learn, they can come here. Okay?"

Hou did so, bringing three to five children around his age and younger to our house. I bought a small whiteboard, hung it on a window in the living room, and began teaching them the English alphabet. Some kids like Hou had attended English school and could recognize the letters. Others had never seen English letters and were fascinated to learn.

Regardless of their experience, I treated every kid as beginners. I started the lesson by reading the alphabet out loud and had them repeat after me until they became familiar with the letters. The next couple of days, I taught them greeting words for them to form into sentences. I even picked two random students to come up and have a conversation.

"Hi," said a girl, "my na—" She scratched her head staring at the board.

"MY NAME IS," I helped.

"MY NAME IS Davi." She then stuck in the next sentence. The boy giggled after seeing her struggle.

"Don't laugh," I said in Khmer, "you're not better than her." I got closer to Davi. "WHAT IS YOUR NAME?" I read the sentence. "Davi, if you don't know something, ask me. Don't just stare at the board." I switched to Khmer.

"I didn't want you to hit me for not knowing the words."

"Hit you?" I chuckled. "I'm not going to hit you." I then remembered that Khmer teachers physically punished students. I turned to the rest of the class, boys and girls sat on the tile floor. We had two sofas, but Mother didn't want to get them dirty. "Everyone, I won't use any kind of punishment here. So don't be afraid to ask questions, okay?"

They all nodded.

"Continue," I told Davi.

"What is your name?" Davi went on.

"My name is Leap," said the boy. "How. How—" He turned to me. "Teacher, I forgot that word," he switched to Khmer.

"See? That's why you don't laugh at people." I shook my head. "HOW OLD ARE YOU?"

"HOW OLD ARE YOU?" he repeated.

"I am," Davi paused, "I am—" she looked at me. "Teacher, how do you say eleven?"

"ELEVEN."

"I am ELEVEN. What about you?"

"I AM ELEVEN YEARS OLD. WHAT ABOUT YOU?" I corrected.

"I AM ELEVEN YEARS OLD. WHAT ABOUT YOU?"

"I am twelve year old."

"I AM TWELVE YEARS OLD," I corrected, "YEARS." I bent my knees. "You put 'S' on anything that is more than one."

"Yes, Teacher," he said, "I AM TWELVE YEARS OLD."

"Nice to meet you," said Davi. They shook hands.

On the weekends, I taught Hou and a few of his friends American sports, throwing a football near the house.

"Hold the ball with both hands," I said in Khmer. "Put your throwing hand on the laces. Bring it up to your chest. Eyes forward, lower your shoulders, raise your arm." I prepared to pass. "And release!" I threw to Hou who stood five-feet away.

"Uncle, how do you make it spin like that?" he asked.

"The rotation came from the twist of my fingers." I grabbed the ball. "As I release it, I mostly use my pointing finger to push the ball down." I demonstrated. "If you do it right, that causes the ball to spin." I tossed him the ball back. "Practice it." Hou and his friends did so.

After many attempts, they were able to throw with some rotations. It wasn't perfect, but it was a great start.

Sometimes, we went to a public college, Don Bosco, located five minutes away by motorbike. Don Bosco was sponsored by foreigners, offering technical programs and other educational approaches to help Khmer students succeed. The school had a courtyard, large soccer fields, and a basketball court. There, I showed Hou and his friends how to dribble and shoot the ball.

"Hold it with both hands," I said, gripping the ball. "Bend your knees, eyes on the basket, and shoot!" I shot the ball. It hit the rim and bounced off the backboard but didn't go in. "Practice that." I handed the ball to Hou.

We attracted a small crowd. A few adult students surrounded us and watched us play. One of them knew how to play. We even formed a three-on-three match, playing a few pickup games.

As I continued to teach, more and more kids showed up including an adult and a teenager. My class got so big, our small living room was packed with students. Some of them had to sit on the sofas because there wasn't enough room.

"Where did you get all of these kids?" Mother asked.

"They live in this village and they want to learn."

"Just make sure they won't make a mess on the sofas."

Since I had new students, I had to go back to the alphabet, refreshing their memory and also giving new individuals a chance to catch up. I even taught the world map. I knew they didn't know much about the world and wanted them to see places beyond our borders. I continued to select students to come to the board.

"Who here knows where China is?" I asked in Khmer but left the name, China, in English. I scanned the room with a bag of candy in hand.

"Me! Me!" said a few of them, raising their hands. Others remained quiet.

"You," I pointed at a smaller boy with a ruler, sitting near me. "Here," I handed him the ruler.

"China is right here!" he said in Khmer, correctly marking on the map.

"Very good! Here you go." I gave him a piece of candy. "Who here knows where India is?"

No one raised their hand.

"Really? No one knows?" I stood still, allowing them a chance to think. Seconds went by but still nobody knew the answer. "India is a neighboring country to Cambodia." I pointed at the map. "It's right here. Remember it, I might quiz you again." I paused. "Who here knows where America is?"

"Me! Me!" More students raised their hands. I knew America was one of the most well-known countries among villagers, but I was still shocked to see how many kids remembered. I picked Hou.

"Here!" he said with a big smile.

"That's correct." I handed him a candy. I continued to quiz them, but I couldn't stop thinking of America. I realized that I had been in Cambodia for almost three months and had to prepare for an upcoming interview soon. Thalen told me that he would return to Cambodia within a week to help me organize my paperwork.

One afternoon, I lay on Lab's bed alone, practicing for my interview. I wrote potential interview questions on notecards and quizzed myself.

"It says here that you would return after studying for two years. Why didn't you return?" I pretended to be the interviewer.

"I wanted to, but I was offered to continue my education through high school," I answered. "F-1 student visa status says that as long as I continued going to school in the US, I could legally stay. So I did."

"Tell me about your experience in America? And what did you learn?"

"At first, I thought I was on a different planet. People's lifestyle over there is easier than here. Seeing the tall buildings and riding on the highways full of cars almost seemed like a fantasy. The school system was more sophisticated too. St. Luke and Bishop Blanchet offered many subjects: science, art, technology, dance classes, and more. Teachers used a variety of tactics to teach students such as allowing us to watch movies, visiting historical sites, and doing class activities which helped bond students closer. Studying in American schools and being there for six years allowed me to see more of the world. Being over there changed my life and I have no idea how my life would turn out if I hadn't gotten the opportunity to study in America."

"How is your visit in Cambodia? And why do you want to go back to college?"

"I've been here for almost three months. I came to see my father, who recently passed away from lung cancer." I choked up. Every time I thought of Father, my chest tightened, my eyes watered. "It was tough, but I was able to be with him for a short while before he passed. I want to go back to college because I want to finish what I've started. I want to be the first person in my family to earn a degree from college. Above all, I made my father a promise that I would go back and finish school. So here I am."

Tears dripped down as I finished the sentence. I got up, took a deep breath and wiped my cheeks. I didn't want to continue practicing because doing so only made me cry more.

Stressed, I put the notecards down and went for a ride. I borrowed Lab's boyfriend's bike and rode into the narrow street, crossing through a few villages. Thirty minutes later, I found myself at Otres Beach. I rode alongside the white sand as a warm breeze hit me. I picked up speed. My hair and shirt flopped back as I cruised across the beach, approaching a narrower and curvy road. Past the road, I spotted an empty beach without any tourists. I parked the bike and sat on the grass, absorbing the wilderness of Kompong Som.

Far to my left, I saw many restaurants and bars with people playing in the sea. To my right, there were only trees with some birds flying above them. Ahead of me was clear blue water, with small waves brushing the shore. In the middle of the sea were fishing boats, floating on the horizon near an island. The wind carried the sound of the boats' motors mixing with the noise of waves slamming on the soft sand. I breathed in the fresh air and couldn't help but smile. I thought to myself, *what a beautiful place.*

# 26

# WANDA'S WORDS

THALEN RETURNED TO Cambodia and brought all the required documents with him, including a letter of recommendation from Jeff and Coach Maul. On the day before the interview, Thalen and I rode his motorbike to Phnom Penh. He didn't want to pay for a taxi. Therefore, I had no choice but to travel with him. It wasn't smart; Cambodia's highways were small, filled with cars and semitrucks. Our motorbike's top speed was roughly forty-five miles per hour given the traffic. Riding behind cars was difficult and dust blocked our visibility. Thalen and I only wore helmets without any other protective gear. At this speed, an accident would kill the both of us.

At one point, Thalen tried to overtake a semitruck.

"Hold on!" he yelled over the wind then accelerated. The engine roared. I wrapped my arms tight around his waist as we reached top speed, and yet, we still couldn't pass the truck. I looked up and saw another car approaching, coming in fast from the opposite direction.

"Thalen! Get back in your lane!" I shouted through my helmet. Yet, he kept on trying to pass the truck. "Thalen!" I tapped his stomach. "Get back in your lane! Now!"

He hit the brakes and got behind the truck just seconds before the other car came.

"What's the matter?" he slightly turned to me, "I almost had him."

"Yeah, you almost had us killed!"

"Dude, I know what I'm doing. Trust me."

"No, man! I don't want to die before my interview!"

"You're not gonna die!" He laughed.

We continued to cruise on the highway, crossing through many villages including a beautiful mountainous terrain full of trees. Hours later, we arrived in Phnom Penh, checking into a guesthouse near the embassy. I lay on the bed, practicing the questions, but I couldn't stop thinking of Father. I felt like the outcome of the interview process would be more assured if I had him by my side. Without him, it truly felt like I was walking in the dark without a light shining the way.

In a time like this, I told myself to *be strong and focus on my goal*. After all, I knew I needed to fulfill the promise I made with Father. With Father now gone, I had to be resilient so I could pursue my dreams.

Morning arrived. Thalen and I hopped on the motorbike, heading to Wat Phnom for my nine o'clock appointment. I sat behind Thalen, wearing the blue button-down shirt, red tie, and black trousers and shoes that I had brought from Sihanoukville. It was seven in the morning, but the streets of Phnom Penh were flooded with motorbikes and cars. Vehicles were honking as the roads jammed with traffic. Thalen had to take the back roads, riding past many shops and restaurants to get to Wat Phnom. About fifteen minutes later, we had arrived.

Thalen parked his bike on the side of the triangular median. To my right was the US Embassy. I could see the American flag waving on the metal pole behind the tall fence. Khmer policemen were guarding the entrance gate. My heart was pounding. I kept visualizing the interviewer asking me, why didn't you return after two years? Thinking about it made my stomach drop. I got off the bike, crossing the street to the other side.

I made my way up the hill, heading toward the temple at the top. I remember Father was praying before my prior interview. I wanted to do the same.

I put 500 riel into the donation pot then burned three incense sticks. I placed them between my palms and raised them in front of my nose. My eyes shut, I took a deep breath and prayed in Khmer. "Father, if you're out there listening, please help calm my mind so I can answer the questions clearer. Please help me pass. I'm doing this for you. I'm doing this for our family."

I opened my eyes, stuck the incense into a pot and headed back down. As time went on, my chest became so tight, I couldn't breathe smoothly. Thalen kept pacing back and forth in front of me, biting his fingernails.

"Can you stop walking around?" I asked, "you're giving me a headache."

Thalen stood still but kept biting his fingers. He pulled out his phone, checking the clock. "In ten minutes, you can go wait in line."

Finally, the time arrived. I got up, crossed the street and stood on the triangular median. We stood at the same spot as Thalen and Father waited last time.

"Good luck!" said Thalen, tapping my shoulder with a smile. I exhaled then headed to the entry gate. Waiting in line, I turned to Thalen as he stood alone. I looked to his right and visualized Father standing there. I stared at the spot where Father once stood. My eyes watered. I knew he was there somewhere, waiting for me.

I entered the building. The interview room seemed to be the same. Large pictures hung on the wall. Chairs were aligned in rows as people waited for their numbers to be called. I saw interviewers who stood behind individual glass window stalls. I looked for the lady who had conducted my prior interview, but it seemed like she wasn't there. I remained calm as the announcer continued calling the numbers. Soon, mine popped up, directing me to window five. I then saw a tall white guy, wearing a long-sleeved shirt and slacks.

"Hi," I said with a smile. "I'm a bit nervous but I'm excited for the opportunity." I repeated the same line I had used in the prior interview. I handed him my paperwork. The guy appraised me while opening the documents. He mostly reviewed my I-20, acceptance letter from Bellevue College, and a few other papers resting at the top of the package.

"How long have you been studying in the US?" he asked through the speakers.

"I've been studying in America for six years. I went to St. Luke Middle School and Bishop Blanchet High School."

"I see." He browsed through the computer screen and typed on the keyboard. My fingers tapped on the counter lightly as I waited for him to ask more questions. "Everything looks good here. Do you have your transcripts with you?"

"Yes, it should be toward the back of the package."

He pulled it out and scanned through.

"When does school start?"

"School will start on September 22nd."

"Will you be staying with the same family?"

"Yes, I will be staying with Jeff and Wanda Griffin, who are my sponsors."

"Got it." He gathered my documents and handed them back to me. Then he stamped my passport and gave me a purple slip. "Come back to pick up your visa tomorrow evening. Okay?"

"Yes, sir. Thank you!" I grabbed my paperwork and walked out. I was shocked to see how simple it was. Despite how thankful I was, a wave of sadness hit me. I was heartbroken as I now realized that I had made a huge mistake in being too scared to return home. The fear of getting denied by the US Embassy prevented me from coming to be with Father before he got sick.

I wept with nothing in my mind besides the thought, *I'm so sorry, Father. I should've come home sooner.*

A few days later, I had to leave for America. Mother and my sisters came with me to the airport to say farewell.

"I have to go now, Mother," I said, then kissed her lightly on her forehead. "I will call you more often."

"Take care of yourself, Son." She looked up to me with watery eyes. "Don't fight with your sisters, okay? Look after one another."

I nodded then gave Lab, Lane, and Lim a hug. "Please take good care of Mother. I'll be back when I'm done with school."

"We will. Don't worry," said Lim.

"Have a safe flight, Brother," Lab added but still held onto my arm. She didn't want me to leave. "We will miss you." Her face turned red as she let go. Holding back tears, I picked up my luggage and walked inside the airport with Thalen.

Thalen and I arrived in America in the evening.

"We're glad to have you back, Chamroeun!" said Jeff, looking through the rearview mirror as we approached downtown Seattle. I leaned on the window, staring at the skyscrapers. Towers were covered in yellow, green, and blue lights while the orange sunset appeared in the background, making the scenery astonishing. I had never been any happier seeing this city.

Jeff and Wanda took us to their house. We had to live with them now because Drew and Annica had gotten married when I was in Cambodia. Wanda thought they should have the place to themselves.

The next evening, I met up with Ramsay at his place. As I pulled the emergency brake, I saw Ramsay burst through the door and rush toward me.

He opened the door. "What's up, my brother!" he said, hugging me, "it's good to see you again!"

"Yeah, you too!" I grinned. "How are you?"

"I'm good. How was your trip? How's everything?"

"Good! Everything is a bit better now." I paused. "Hey, umm, thanks for everything that you've done, man. It meant a lot to me and my family. I really appreciate it."

"Of course! I'm glad I can help."

"What did you do to raise that much money?"

"I did a bunch of random stuff." He laughed. "At first, I went to Coach Maul and asked if we could do an announcement on the speakers, but the school didn't let us, because it wasn't for a charity or for an organization that was related to a school's program. So, I just walked around the hallways with a basket during passing periods and asked people to donate. Stephen donated a hundred dollars, which was pretty cool." He put his elbow on the window. "Joe helped too. During a track and field practice, while people were stretching, he got up on a bench and was shouting, 'Yo! Cham needs help with some money to help his dad.' People came in and donated a lot of money." He smiled. "I only did it for a few days and I was able to raise over a thousand dollars so that was pretty cool."

"That's awesome, man. Again, thank you."

I once told Jeff that my intention in America was to study and not to make friends. Yet, I was glad I met Ramsay. To me, he was more than just a friend and teammate. I knew Ramsay was special since the moment he sat by my side during the night of prom, one day before I left to see my father. The way I looked at it, when things went wrong and a person chose to be there for me, that showed they were a dependable person. Ramsay was that individual. When it seemed like all hope was lost, he was there for me. I was proud to call him my best friend.

Ramsay enrolled at the University of San Diego and had moved to California as we were getting closer to the start of the semester. Meanwhile, I tried to get more familiar with Bellevue College. Thalen and I drove there and explored the campus.

"This isn't too bad," said Thalen, "you'll have a great time here."

"I don't know. It's still school."

"Try to make friends." He looked at me. "Are you finally gonna get a girlfriend?"

"I don't know, man," I snapped. "Why do you care so much about this?"

"I'm just saying. I've never seen you with a girl before." He chuckled. "Just wanna make sure you're not gay." He paused. "If you are, that's totally fine. We would still support you."

"Dude, shut up! I'm not gay." I shook my head and kept walking.

The first day of school arrived once again. I remember waking up early and driving to Bellevue College at six thirty in the morning.

Going to school in the mornings was always the worst. I often got stuck in traffic. It took me roughly forty-five minutes to an hour to get to Bellevue College. Sometimes, I had to drive aggressively, switching from lane to lane to make it to my first class at seven thirty in the morning. Bellevue College was a crowded school. Most classes were full, I had to take what was available. Each class was about an hour long, and I had huge gaps between them.

As school progressed, I took more classes in the winter quarter: US history, geology, and American Sign Language (ASL). Learning a new language was always challenging.

I remember during finals week, I practiced ASL for so long, I almost abandoned dinner. It was Sunday night. I didn't have the test until Wednesday, but I wanted to study early so I could be more prepared.

"Chamroeun!" Jeff called from the TV room, "dinner is ready!"

"Okay!" I said but sat still and continued practicing the signs.

Five minutes later, Jeff approached. "Hey, Chamroeun. Wanda made a really nice dinner. You should come join us."

I closed my laptop. "Yes, I'm coming. Sorry."

Entering the kitchen, I saw Jeff, Wanda, and Thalen already sitting on the couch with their plates full. A rich smell of fried pork hit my nose. Wanda had made pork chops with mashed potatoes.

I grabbed a plate and scooped some up. "Thank you for dinner, Wanda," I said.

"Sure. Help yourself."

Sitting at the edge of the couch, I used a knife to cut the pork. We watched the evening news while we ate.

"Do you have a lot of homework tonight?" Jeff asked.

"No, it's finals week." I took a bite. "I was just studying for my American Sign Language class."

Jeff glanced at me while cutting the pork. "I want to let you know, Chamroeun. I've never seen anyone work as hard as you in school." He put the knife down. "None of my kids tried this hard when they were your age." He smiled. "Good for you."

I smiled back.

"When are your finals?" Thalen asked.

"I have one on Wednesday and two more on Friday. Then I'll be done with this quarter."

"Cool." He wiped his lips. "Can you help me this weekend?"

"Sure, what do you need?"

"I'm repainting some rooms at the store. I'm gonna need your help on Sunday morning, probably around eight."

I hesitated, knowing it was too early, but I didn't want to say no in front of Jeff and Wanda. "Okay," I said.

Finals went well. I was able to earn decent scores on each exam, advancing to spring quarter.

On Saturday night, I met up with a high school friend, Chris. He, a few of his friends, and I attended a party near the University of Washington's campus. Despite wanting popularity, I didn't like going to parties, but thought it was a perfect time for me to get some fresh air especially after all of those studies.

Walking down the street, Chris put his arm around my shoulders. "I'm glad you're back, bro!" He grinned. "A lot people said that you weren't gonna come back because they won't give you a visa or something."

"Yeah, I thought the same too, but I was wrong."

"Yo!" Chris' friend, Evan, interrupted. "I think we're here! Are you guys ready to party or what?"

"Yup!" another friend of Chris, Dillion, shouted.

We entered the house. Rap music blasted around the room. A strong smell of marijuana hit my nose, making me want to cough. The place was packed. We had to sneak through many people to find some free space. People stood all around the room, some were dancing while holding red cups. Others played beer pong near a wall. They were shouting and laughing.

I stood near the beer pong room, watching people play. To my right, I saw a darker skinned girl, standing near a few of her friends. She seemed pretty: brown hair with some highlights, straight nose, and big round eyes. My heart was jumping. I pushed through my nerves.

"Hi!" I said, looking at her friends with a smile, "do I know you from somewhere?" My chest tightened, but I forced myself to stay calm.

She shook her head with a laugh. "I don't think so."

"Are you sure? Your face seems familiar." I paused. "Do you go to H-square?" I guessed. H-square was the name of the gym that Thalen and I attended.

"Yeah." Her eyes lit up. "How do you know?"

"Uhh, I ran into you a couple of times." I lied, surprised to hear my guess was right. "I go there all the time."

"Huh, I see." She giggled. "So, if you go to my gym, how come you never come talk to me?"

"Oh, I don't like bothering people, especially during their workout. You know how annoying that is, if someone disturbs you."

She chuckled. "Yeah, I know what you mean." She touched her hair, staring at me. I could see her cheeks were turning pink. "So where do you go to school?"

"I go to Bellevue College. The commute kinda sucks, but the school is all right." I smirked. "What about you?"

"I go to Seattle U."

"Cool, I didn't catch your name. What's your name?"

"Anna! You?"

"Chamroeun." We shook hands and continued to talk. Unfortunately, our conversation was interrupted when Evan rushed in.

"Guys! Cops are here!" he said, "let's go!"

Anna looked at me with fear on her face. She and her friends walked out of the room in a hurry. So did I. My body was shaking. I didn't drink at the party but was still afraid of getting in trouble for being there. Wanda once told me, "you could get deported if you get caught at a drinking event." I wasn't sure if Wanda was right, but I didn't want to risk it anymore than I already had.

I rushed through the back door while Chris and his friends went through the front. I walked through an alley road in the dark. I could see the cop cars' flashing blue and red lights from the front of the house. My hands shook as I picked up my pace. I kept walking and finally met up with Chris a few blocks further away.

It was a long night. I didn't get home until two thirty in the morning.

The next day, while lying on my bed, I heard my phone ring. I got up, rubbed my eyes, looked at the screen, and saw a few missed calls from Thalen. My head hurt from sleep deprivation. I couldn't think of a reason why he called.

I called him back.

"Hey, what's up?" I spoke, "did you call?"

"Yeah, man! I've been waiting for you all morning! It's ten thirty now, where have you been?"

Immediately, I remembered that I was supposed to go help Thalen paint the rooms. "Crap. I'm sorry. I forgot. I'll be there soon."

"No! Don't come now! I already finished." I could hear him breathing heavily over the speaker. "Next time, when you tell someone that you will do something, you do it! You understand?"

"Yeah. Okay."

He hung up.

I felt terrible. I knew I had let him down because he was counting on me to help.

Minutes later, I heard the sound of rocks shuffling under car tires, a vehicle was approaching in our driveway. I looked out the window and saw Wanda in her white Subaru.

I put on some sweatpants and a jacket then went downstairs.

"Hi Chamroeun," said Wanda, standing in her room, wearing her tennis outfit. "What are you doing here? Aren't you supposed to be helping Thalen?"

I scratched my head, looking at her with guilt. "He already finished."

"Well, did you go help him like you said you would?" She glared.

"No, but I'm gonna go check with him now."

Wanda grabbed her phone and called Thalen. Meanwhile, I went in the TV room, putting on my shoes. I could hear Wanda's voice from her room but didn't understand what she said.

"Hey, Chamroeun!" she called.

I got up, clearing the lump in my throat. "Yes." I went to her room and saw her holding the phone.

"I just talked to Thalen. He was really disappointed that you didn't show up. He did the work all morning by himself!"

"I know."

"Why didn't you go help him?"

I hesitated. "I slept in and I forgot about it."

"I noticed that you came home pretty late last night. Were you out partying?"

I didn't reply. I leaned on the wall near her bedroom's entry door and stared at the floor.

"Chamroeun! I am really disappointed! I don't know if I want to do this anymore!" She walked away.

My heart dropped to my feet. I bit my lip, breathing unevenly. What did she mean? Is she sending me back? Is school over for me?

Speechless, I went inside the TV room and stared at the blank screen. Wanda's words stabbed me in the heart. I had never imagined this moment would come. Wanda was one of the people that held the key to my journey. She was my sponsor and had the ability to end this opportunity at any moment. After living with her for nearly seven years, Wanda was often upset and had said things to show her frustration. Yet, she had never threatened to end my journey. Until now.

I wasn't mad at her comments. She and her family had helped me a lot in the past years. They continued to support me in spite of Thalen and

Kesor's relationship failing. I would never forget them for bailing us out of trouble in Thailand. My family and I had no way to pay them back besides thanking them for all they had done.

Sitting on the couch, I told myself, *if this is the end of my journey, so be it. Regardless, I had to show my gratitude.*

I got up, took a deep breath and walked to Wanda's room. I knocked on the wall. She came and opened the door. There was a resentful look on her face.

"Wanda," I swallowed. "If you want to end this, it's really up to you . . . But regardless, I am thankful for everything that you and Jeff have done for me. I enjoyed this journey. And I wouldn't be the person I am today without your help." I choked up. "Regardless of how you feel about me, Kesor, or the rest of my family, that won't change anything between us." I looked at her in the eyes. "You will always be like a mother to me." Tears fell on my cheeks. "I would never forget you and your family."

I could tell Wanda had a sense of regret. Her face turned red, and she wiped the corner of her eyes. "Good to know," she said in a low tone, "I will think about it."

I walked away without saying anything else. In my heart, I hoped she would change her mind.

In moments like this, I wished Father was still alive so I could ask for his advice. Without him, I felt helpless about what to do next.

Later in the evening, I went to Chai and Ryan's house to report the news.

"Wanda told me that she might not want to continue sponsoring me anymore," I said while sitting on the edge of their bed. "If she doesn't, that means I have to go back."

"Why would she do that?" Chai asked.

"She was mad at me because I said I would go help Thalen with some work stuff, and I didn't. I went out last night . . . I slept in and forgot to go help him."

"She would stop sponsor you because of that?" Chai glanced at Ryan, who stood tall, leaning on the wall with his arms crossed. "Are you kidding me?"

Ryan looked at me with a sense of sorrow. "I think the only thing you can do right now is to be patient," he said. "Wanda might change her mind later, when she's more calm."

I nodded and tried to calm myself down. Wanda's words still hurt, but at this point, I had to follow Ryan's advice and hope that Wanda would change her mind.

A few days went by, Wanda hadn't said a word about sending me home nor keeping me in the US. Day by day, I was patiently waiting for her decision.

One evening, I went for a drive with Jeff in his new electric car, a Nissan Leaf. We didn't go far, cruising around the neighborhood.

"Pretty cool, huh?" he asked, turning the steering wheel.

I nodded with a smile but didn't say anything.

"I think this thing is pretty quick too." He stepped on the peddle and the car accelerated instantly, pushing my body back against the seat. He slowed down. "What do you think?"

"It's nice."

Jeff looked at me over his shoulder. He always noticed when something was wrong. "Are you doing okay?"

"Yes, I'm fine," I lied.

"I heard about what happened between you and Wanda." He glanced to me. "I heard that the conversation went far." He focused on the road. "She was upset that you didn't do what you said. She told me about what she said."

My heart started beating a hundred miles an hour.

"Those words came from frustration. Do you know what that means?" he continued.

"Yes," I cleared my throat. "And what do you think?"

"Well, Wanda was disappointed." He turned to me. "And I am a little disappointed as well." He exhaled. "But the conversation should never have gone that far."

"What do you mean?"

"We will continue to sponsor you, Chamroeun." He looked me in the eyes. "You are like one of our sons now. We won't send you home because of this."

I had goosebumps hearing Jeff's words. I never thought they would consider me as one of their kids. Since the day Kesor left, I felt awkward living with Thalen's family, knowing that Kesor had abandoned Thalen. But Jeff's words changed everything.

# 27

# PURSUING MY DREAM

SPRING 2015 WAS the last quarter of my freshman year. I took English, mathematics, and sociology, which were the prerequisites to my business studies in the upcoming year. To obtain my Associate Degree, I decided to study business because I wanted to follow in Jeff's footsteps and become an entrepreneur. I admired his ambition and ability to find ways of succeeding.

Entering my English classroom, I sat in the second row in the middle of the room among a few of my classmates. Seconds later, two tall white girls, looking almost identical, sat in front of me. One had blonde hair, and the other had brown.

The twin sisters, Amy and Alexa, were friendly. Amy even gave me her number in case I needed help with homework. I was pleased to make friends on the first day of the quarter.

One day, I texted Amy to play flag football because we were one girl short. She couldn't make it, but Alexa was interested.

"Thanks for coming," I said, walking Alexa to her car. "Sorry, that we lost, but you played well."

"It's all good. I had fun. Thanks for inviting me."

"Yeah, of course."

"This is my car." She unlocked her vehicle. "Thanks for walking me."

"Yeah, sure! Anytime." I gave her a hug. I had to go on tip-toe because she was taller than me. "Drive safe!"

I hopped in Thalen's car and put my duffle bag down.

"So, was that your girlfriend?" he asked.

"No, man. We're friends."

"Good, because I think she might be a little too tall for you." He looked at me over his shoulder. "But that's okay, I mean you're short, most people here are gonna be taller than you." He laughed.

I glared at him, shaking my head. He drove onto the street.

"A few rules about dating, Chamroeun," Thalen continued. "Don't ever talk about politics or religion." He glanced at me. "Are you listening?"

"Okay, why?"

"Because people will have different opinions than you, especially about these two things. It could create conflict. The moment you reveal your belief or your thoughts on these things, people will either like you for it or hate you for it. Just don't mention something like this, especially when you're with a girl."

I nodded. At the moment, I didn't think Thalen's comment was important because I never spoke to girls about these matters.

Alexa and I continued to talk. In class, we worked together during group activities and kept texting after school. I had a crush on her.

"Hey, we should hangout sometime. And I don't mean like playing flag football. Maybe like a date or something. What do you say?" I texted her.

"Sure, yeah I'm down," she responded.

"Awesome! Are you free Friday night?"

"Yes, Friday night works."

Like a gentleman, I picked her up early. I even dressed nicely, wearing a button-down shirt and khaki pants. When I arrived, I parked my car further from her driveway. I didn't want her parents to see me.

"I'm here," I texted.

"Ok cool. Come on in. My parents want to see you."

I hesitated. I was nervous knowing that her parents wanted to meet me. "Ok I'm coming." I texted and drove into her driveway.

Knocking on the door, my hands shook.

Alexa opened the door. "Hi!" She hugged me. "How's it going?"

"Ahh. Good." My hands were still shaking.

"Good, come on in, my parents are in the kitchen."

I took off my shoes and followed her. I greeted her parents politely, shook their hands and talked with sincerity.

Her dad stood in a corner of the room with his arms crossed and stared intently at me.

"So, you and Alexa are in the same class, right?" he asked.

"Yes, sir," I said, "we're in the same English class."

"How do you like it?" her mom asked.

"It's good. The teacher is really nice. I like it."

"Cham and I often work together during class exercises," Alexa added, "we help each other out a lot."

"I see," said her dad.

Alexa looked my way and noticed I was intimidated. "I think we're gonna get going, Dad. See you later."

"Have fun," said her mom.

I smiled then followed Alexa out the door.

We got in the car and drove south toward downtown Seattle. I wanted to show Alexa the city because she had mentioned that she rarely went there.

"Sorry if I made you feel nervous," she said from the passenger seat. "My parents just wanted to meet you."

"It's all good. They were nice." I handed her a cord wire. "You wanna play some music?"

"Sure." She pulled out her phone. "What kind of music do you listen to?"

"Everything really." I laughed.

She played "Often" by The Weeknd with Kygo remixed. The music hit, I moved my head side-to-side, feeling the tune.

"I like this song," I said.

She looked at me and giggled. Alexa played more music as we continued to cruise toward downtown.

About thirty minutes later, we arrived at a park, full of people taking photos of the city.

"Whoa, you can see the whole city," said Alexa, getting out of the car. "What is this place called?"

"Kerry Park. It's one of my favorite places."

Alexa pulled out her phone and took a few pictures. "It's really pretty." She smiled.

We sat on a cement wall, underneath a clear night sky. A light breeze made it colder. I took off my jacket and placed it on her shoulders. The moon was shining brightly in its crescent phase, high above the skyscrapers. The Space Needle stood in front of the buildings, looking like a giant mushroom covered with white lights.

"You know, I've been to a few cities," I said. "I've been to Bangkok in Thailand. I've been to Washington, DC, but none of those places were as pretty as this."

"Why were you in Thailand?"

"I was visiting my Father in a hospital in Bangkok. He was diagnosed with lung cancer." I turned to her. "He passed almost a year ago."

"I'm sorry to hear that."

I exhaled. "Yeah, me too. It sucks that he's gone because he was one of the people that always cared about me. He would always give me advice on things." I paused. "But I guess death is just a part of life, ya know?"

She saw the pain on my face. "You don't have to talk about it if you don't want to."

I nodded.

"So, what's your plan after Bellevue College?" Alexa asked. "I'm assuming that you're gonna transfer out, right?"

"Yeah, probably, but I don't know yet. I still have a long way." I rubbed my face. Cold air made my nose feel numb. "As for right now, I'm just trying to get my Associate Degree. What about you?"

"I don't know either." She chuckled. "I was thinking about applying to WSU, but we'll see."

"Oh, a party school, huh? Didn't know you're a party girl."

"I'm not!" she snapped. "Lots of people say the same thing, assuming that I like to party, but I don't. I don't even drink. I just like the school and I want to get away from my family for a while."

"I feel it. What about Amy? Does she want to go to WSU as well?"

"I don't think so, but that's okay, I guess. We've been going to the same school, doing everything together our whole lives." She inhaled. "Maybe, it's good that we're separating for a while. But it's gonna feel a little lonely without her, I really don't have anybody else."

"Well, you have me. I'm here." I smiled and held her hand. "I know I can't replace Amy, but if you ever feel lonely, I'm just one text away." I then untied one of the bracelets on my wrist that I bought in Cambodia. "I want you to have this." I handed it to her. "Where I'm from, bracelets represent friendships." I tied it on her wrist.

"Thanks, Cham." She rested her head on my shoulders.

Our moment was interrupted when Alexa pulled out her phone.

"My dad's texting me," she said.

"What does he say?"

"He wants us to move. He's probably thinking that we're doing something weird."

"Your dad is tracking you?"

"Yeah, he does that sometimes." She looked at me. "That's so strange, he never texted me during a date before." She got up. "All right, we gotta move."

We hopped in the car, grabbed some food, and drove back north. Along the way, I showed Alexa my neighborhood in the hope that she wanted to know more about me.

"This is where I live," I said. "It's a pretty small town, but I like it here."

"Where I live is pretty small too. I love small towns. It's more peaceful than crowded areas."

We approached St. Luke. "This is my middle school." I parked the car. "This is where it all started for me."

"What is it called?"

"St. Luke. It's a Catholic school." I drove out of the parking lot and headed back to Alexa's home.

"So, are you Catholic?"

I hesitated. I knew it wasn't a smart idea to talk about religion during my first date. Yet, I wanted to be honest. "I'm not. I don't even know if I have a religion actually."

"So, you're like an atheist?"

"Umm . . . I would say I'm agnostic. But my family are atheist. Living with them, kind of makes me think that way though." I licked my lips.

"Going to school shaped my way of thinking too. If you look back at history, millions of people died during the Holocaust. I came from a country where innocent people were killed in a genocide. I mean, I could be wrong, but if there is god, how could he or she allow something like that to happen?"

Alexa didn't reply.

"I'm not against religions, Alexa," I continued. "I think everyone has the right to choose their own faith. But I just feel like people have the ability to impact the world instead of waiting for God to save us."

"Well, if you think like that, then I don't think we can be together."

"What do you mean?"

"I want to be with someone that I can read the Bible with and who can discuss the topic with me."

"I can discuss the topic with you. I mean, I went to Catholic schools. I took religion classes. I know enough about Catholicism principles."

"Yeah, but it's still hard that you don't feel the same. I mean, what if we have kids? How are we gonna raise them with you having different thoughts?"

I hesitated. "Uhh, this is our first date. I'm not thinking that far. And if we do have kids, then they can decide to be whatever they want."

"I just don't think something like this would work out."

"So . . . I'm willing to accept you for who are, and you're not willing to do the same?"

"I don't know, it's hard to say right now. I'll think about it."

The next school day, Alexa arrived in class, sitting a few rows farther away from me. However, Amy sat in the same spot right in front of me. Glancing at Alexa, I noticed that she still wore the bracelet, but her behavior had changed. She didn't say a word to her twin sister. I knew something was wrong.

After class, I went to talk to Alexa. "What's going on?"

"I'm sorry, Cham. You're a nice guy, but I don't feel it."

I bit my lips. "It's about my belief isn't it?"

"No. It's not even about that." She paused. "It's just, I don't feel it. Normally, I feel something when I'm with a guy, but I don't feel it with you. And you can't pressure that, you know."

"I get it." I nodded.

"You can have your bracelet back, if you want."

"No, keep it. It was a gift."

I walked away. My heart sunk hearing her words, but there was nothing I could do to make her like me. The only thing I could do was focus on school to pursue my dream. So I did.

Without any distractions, I was able to pass all three classes, earning a 3.68 GPA in that quarter. I could now call myself a sophomore in college.

Midsummer 2016, Thalen and his parents met up for dinner with Chai, Ryan, and me. I had to inform them about my future after Bellevue college. I wanted to study marketing. I asked them if I could transfer to a university, but they couldn't afford to pay more than the current tuition. Jeff and Wanda made it clear that they would not help. Without them, my only option was to get my associate degree and search for lower-priced universities.

In the fall, I took accounting, business calculus, and another English class. Business calculus was by far the hardest class I had taken. The teacher introduced a math function, the derivative which was confusing. It took a long time to solve just one problem. Jeff once told me that he had failed this class twice back in college. I had not failed a class in years. I took his words seriously and knew I had to push myself once again to avoid failure.

Still, I often got low scores on quizzes. There were times I didn't even get to finish my test. On one exam, I left two problems unanswered and got most questions wrong. I received a 64/100.

I looked over my shoulder and saw an 85/100 on a guy's paper.

"You're pretty good at this," I said, "you think we can study together?" I put my paper down, hiding the score.

"I'm not that good," he said, "but yeah, sure. We can study."

"Sounds good. I'm Chamroeun, call me Cham."

"Adrian." We shook hands.

I was relieved making friends with someone that was smarter than me. Adrian and I often met up before class, going over the teacher's notes and doing problems together.

Our effort paid off. One time, I earned an 82/100 on the exam.

"Nice job, man," said Adrian, walking alongside in the hallway. "You're getting smarter." He chuckled.

"Thanks, bro. What did you get?"

"A 92. I thought I was gonna do better, but whatever." He shrugged.

I shook my head. "That's pretty good, man."

"It's all right, I gotta do better if I want to get into UW."

The word "UW" hit me. This was a university that denied me back in high school.

"Where do you want to go after this?" Adrian asked.

"I don't know. I was hoping Central Washington University, but we'll see," I lied. I didn't want to tell him that my family couldn't afford for me to transfer.

"Don't go to Central." He turned to me. "Go somewhere better. You're a smart guy and with your ethnicity, I bet you'll get into UW."

"I doubt that. I don't even know if I could pass this class."

"Bro, we'll pass this class. We'll keep helping each other." He stopped, looking at me in the eyes. "But you gotta apply to UW with me."

I thought about Adrian's words and didn't want to give up on the University of Washington. It would mean the world to me if I could continue my education there.

The next day, I went to talk to my business advisor. Sitting in front of her desk, I cut to the point.

"I want to apply to UW," I said. "What do I need to do to get accepted?"

"The University of Washington is a really popular school. It's most students' first choice." She rested her arms on the desk. "To transfer there, you need to have a really high GPA, but the school will look at other components, like your college essay and your background." She checked the computer screen. "Since you're an international student, you will have to take a TOEFL test, unless you apply to the Bothell campus."

"What do you mean?"

"The Seattle location is their main campus, but the University has three campuses. One in Seattle, one in Tacoma, and one in Bothell."

"Is the one in Bothell as good as the one in Seattle?"

"It's the same school." She chuckled. "The degree will still say, 'The University of Washington' on it." She continued to explain, all of which pulled my interest toward UW, Bothell.

I got up and shook her hand. Even if Thalen, Ryan, and Chai couldn't help, I still wanted to apply to the UW, Bothell. I wanted to prove to myself that I wasn't stupid, so I used UW as motivation. I told myself that *I belonged and was willing to do what was necessary to get accepted.*

My hard work and studying with Adrian helped me advance through all my classes, including business calculus. After finishing my fourth quarter at Bellevue College, I floated slightly above 3.30 GPA. It wasn't perfect, but I was glad to have progressed to the next quarter.

Reaching the middle of the winter quarter, it was time to apply for transfer. I submitted my application to Eastern Washington University because the school offered business programs on Bellevue College campus. This was a more affordable way. Thalen and Ryan didn't have the money to send me to the actual Eastern campus, located in Cheney.

I also submitted to Central Washington University. Just like Eastern, Central had business programs at Edmonds Community College which was close enough from our house. My last option was the University of Washington. I only applied to the Bothell campus because I knew this would be a better fit.

Months had gone by. I had been accepted to Central and Eastern. But I hadn't heard anything from UW. Reaching the end of spring quarter, I had to make my decision. I chose Central Washington University because Edmonds Community College was a closer commute.

I rested on the couch, turned the TV on and relaxed. The house was dead silent. It was a Friday afternoon, and everyone was at work.

While watching TV, my phone lit up. I saw an email from the University of Washington saying, "Dear Chamroeun, Congratulations!"

My jaw dropped. I rubbed my eyes to ensure I wasn't dreaming. I continued to read the letter while a wave of happiness hit me.

I rubbed my forehead with elation. I hadn't felt this proud since earning my first student visa. Excited, I drove to Chai and Ryan's house to report the news.

"I got into UW!" I said.

"Nice! Congrats, man," Ryan smiled.

"Good job, Chamroeun!" Chai gave me a hug.

"I thought I was going to get denied." I chuckled. "Then I got an email from them." I shook my head. "I can't believe it."

"I know you can get in," said Chai, "I'm proud of you."

"What does this mean?" I asked, glancing at Ryan.

"Well, I don't think it changes anything," he said bluntly. "Your sister and I still can't afford to send you there, I'm sorry."

I wasn't surprised to hear Ryan's answer. He had told me all along that he was incapable of paying for UW's tuition. Ryan, Chai, and Thalen had been funding my college tuition for the prior five quarters. Still, part of me didn't want to take no for an answer. I had worked so hard to get accepted at my dream school. I couldn't let this opportunity pass.

I left Ryan and Chai's house and drove to Bedrooms & More to meet Jeff and Wanda. "I got accepted to UW," I said, standing in their office.

"Wow!" Jeff's eyes lit up. "Congratulations! Good for you."

"Nicely done, Chamroeun!" said Wanda.

"Thank you." I took a deep breath. "I know you guys have helped me a lot in the past years." I put my hands in my pockets. "I know that you said you're done helping me with school." My heart was beating a hundred miles an hour. "But we all know that I can't go to this school without your help. This is my dream. I now have the chance to be the only person in my family to finish college. It would mean the world if I could earn a degree from the University of Washington." I cleared my throat. "If you could help me one last time, I promise to not disappoint."

Jeff had a sense of admiration on his face then turned to Wanda.

"How much is tuition?" he asked.

"For an international student, it's a little over 34 thousand dollars a year."

Wanda bit her lips.

"It's expensive, yes," I continued. "But this is a once in a lifetime opportunity. Don't you want to be a part of something special like this?"

"Well, aren't we a part of that already?" Wanda asked with a small laugh.

"You are. And I thank you both for everything you've done. My life changed because of your support, there is no doubt about it. And I think my life could get better if I could go to UW." I rubbed my chin. "Picture this, a kid from a third-world country holding a college degree. Wouldn't it be cool if that degree is from the University of Washington?"

Jeff and Wanda chuckled.

"It's really up to you," I added. "You both have the ability to change my path."

Wanda glanced at Jeff then looked at me. "We'll think about it, Chamroeun."

I nodded with a smile then left the room. The ball was now in their court.

Approximately one week later, Jeff called and asked me to come meet him and Wanda at their office after school.

"Okay, Chamroeun," he said in a calm tone. "Wanda and I will help you with UW tuition." A wave of joy hit me. I couldn't help but grin.

"We will do it under one condition," Wanda added. "If Thalen needs help with anything at work, you have to show up and help him. You need to make yourself available and be helpful at all times, okay?"

"Yes! I will."

"And if you could get Ryan, Chai, and Thalen to continue contributing with whatever they are paying," Wanda continued. "Then you've got yourself a deal."

"Yes, I will let them know. Thank you so much!"

I gave them a big hug. This was one of the happiest moments in my life.

Driving home, I couldn't stop smiling. The radio was playing "R.O.O.T.S" by Flo Rida. Listening to the lyrics gave me a chance to reflect on my past. I thought of my family in Cambodia. I thought of Thalen and Kesor's relationship. I then asked myself, *how did I get here?*

It seemed like only yesterday that I had left Cambodia to come study in America. Not in a million years would I have guessed a kid like me, who came from one of the poorest countries and an impoverished family, would be pursuing a degree from an American university. Thinking about it made me realize that I truly was "one lucky kid." It was a miracle how my journey had unfolded.

One thing was certain, anything was possible as long as a person had the will. I worked hard and believed in myself so I could keep pushing toward my goals. Thanks to all the support from both my Khmer and American families, I was now inches away from reaching the end zone.

In moments like these, I wished I could pick up the phone and call Father. I couldn't imagine how proud he would be. It was still shocking to realize he was gone. But in my culture, death wasn't the end. So Father, if you're out there listening, this one's for you.

# EPILOGUE

"WE ASSEMBLED HERE today are issuing a new decree to be heard in every city, in every foreign capital, in every hall of power . . . from this day on a new vision will govern our land . . . from this day onwards it is only going to be America first . . . America first!" said President Trump on inauguration day.

His words shocked the world. America was now changing her role from "world police" to focus on "America first." I remember listening to the news on the radio on the way home from school during my first quarter at the University of Washington, Bothell. The president's words didn't make sense. America was and still is the world's police. In American schools, I learned that this country was built by immigrants. The land of opportunity will always open her arms to anyone who is striving for a better life.

Now, the land of the free was turning her back on immigrants, wanting to deny any opportunity to those who came from third-world countries. Or, as President Trump called them, "shithole countries."

I came from a "shithole country" and I often wonder *how my life would have turned out if America didn't accept me?*

Sitting on a couch at Chai and Ryan's house, I watched the evening news reporting on immigrants being deported all over America. Universities around the country released statements, warning international students to not leave the country because of a possibility of being denied returning.

I called Jeff. "Hi Jeff, sorry to bother you. I was just worried about what's happening."

"What do you mean?"

"I was watching the news. Seems like everything is a mess right now. People are being deported every day." I swallowed. "I'm just worried about my status, you know."

Jeff sighed over the phone. "You're right. Everything does seem like a mess right now. But you're here legally. They can't do anything to you."

"Yeah, but I'm still afraid. Everything is different now. I saw a report of universities telling their international students to not travel." I bit my lip. "I was thinking about visiting home this summer, but I think this will make it much harder for me to come back."

"I'm sorry, Chamroeun. It seems like this president is doing whatever he can to reject immigrants. And yes, I think this will make it harder for you to come back if you were planning on visiting your family." He paused. "In this situation, my advice for you is to stay and finish school. But it's really up to you."

Once again, I feared being denied. I didn't want to make the same mistake as I did with my Father. But this time was different. The possibility of being denied was higher than ever. My only option was to stay so I could fulfill my promise to Father. To pursue my dream, I would disregard the president's hatred toward immigrants like I ignored people's criticism in the past. Now, I was positioning myself to become the first person in my family to graduate from college.

On a cloudy day, I parked my car in the lot, heading to my global business class. It was spring 2018. This was my last quarter at the University of Washington, Bothell. I had passed all of my classes in the prior year and was expecting to graduate in June.

Entering the classroom, I sat in the middle row next to my new friend, Nicholas.

"What's up, dude?" he asked.

"Yo!" I put my backpack down. "Did you watch the video that the professor asked us to?"

"No, it's our first class. I didn't even know we had to watch a video." He looked at me over his shoulder. "Do you think Professor Jagan gonna ask us questions?"

"I hope not." I chuckled. "Even if he does, it's the first day of class. How hard could this be?"

Nicholas nodded. "I hope you're right."

I pulled out my laptop and prepared for class to start. Every seat was taken. Students sat elbow to elbow and talked until the professor arrived.

I overheard a few girls talking near me.

"One of my friends told me that he failed a student in his class before," said one girl.

"No!" another girl snapped. "He can't do that! This is a capstone class. You can't graduate if you fail. You know that, right?"

"Oh god, that would suck." The girl rubbed her face.

I turned to Nicholas. "Do you think this professor is as bad as people say he is?"

"I've heard a lot of bad things about him. I've heard students who've been asking the head of the business school to fire him because he's a mean guy." Nicolas had a sense of worry on his face. "But we'll see."

Seconds later, Professor Jagan entered the room. He was a short Indian man, wearing a blue suit and a yellow tie. He placed his folders on the table then surveyed the room. The class was dead silent. I could see people around me looking at each other with fear on their faces. He checked his watch.

"Okay, everyone," he said with an accent. "It's time to start class." He walked toward the middle row. "You all have watched the video, right?" He scanned the room.

I among many others nodded.

"What do you think?" The professor continued.

I raised my hand. He pointed at me.

"I liked the video," I said, "I think the author tells a really compelling story."

"Why?" The professor asked.

"Well, throughout the film, the author shows a lot of evidence to support his theory. He went to many countries and studied those countries' markets to predict the world's economy."

"So, you're saying just because he went to a few countries, that makes him right?" The professor lowered his eyebrows.

"I think so."

"Why?"

"The video shows that he had a lot of experience studying different types of markets. He used accurate data to support his conclusion."

"And you believe him?"

I glanced at Nicholas then swallowed nervously. "Yes, I do."

The professor looked at me intently but didn't ask me anything else. His behavior reminded me of my first grade teacher. I could tell he thought I was "stupid." He then searched for a different student. To my left, I saw a brown girl staring at me with a smirk. Embarrassed, I looked down, shook my head and smiled. I thought to myself, *here we go again.*

# THEN

This picture was taken in 2008, four months before I received the opportunity to come study in the US. I was in seventh grade at Khmer school.

# AND NOW

This picture was taken in 2018, during the graduation ceremony at Safeco Field, Seattle, Washington. I received a business degree with a concentration in Marketing from the University of Washington, Bothell. I graduated with a 3.65 GPA and made dean's list four times out of six quarters. I am now the first person in my family to fulfill my father's dream.

# UPDATE

Thalen and Kesor's relationship continued to fail and they are now getting a divorce.

Chai and Ryan got married in Cambodia, which also allowed me to visit my family and come back safely. After the wedding, Chai and Ryan moved to West Seattle.

Mother and the rest of my sisters are still living in Cambodia in a small house in Victory Hill.

Jeff, Wanda, Blake, and Drew continued to manage Bedrooms & More. They have opened a new store on same block as their old building.

Ramsay transferred to the University of Washington, graduated, and got married in the summer of 2019. I was one of his groomsmen.

As for me, I worked for Bedrooms & More after graduation, using my education to help Jeff and Wanda's business grow. I wanted to give back in return for all of their help.

After finishing this book, I am now ready to reunite with my family and am looking forward to fulfilling my promise.

**To learn about this project, or to make a donation in support of impoverished children in Cambodia, please visit: www.fulfillingapromise.com**

# WHY I WROTE THIS BOOK

I wrote this book to honor the two million men, women, and children who perished during the Khmer Rouge Genocide (1975-1979). May their souls rest in peace. I may not know the victims' names, but I will never forget the tragedy that occurred in my country. I believe that killing isn't the answer to solving problems, and good will always defeat evil.

I also wrote this book as a symbol of keeping the promise I made to the US Embassy in 2008. Ever since I was young, I've had a passion for wanting to help my community. Living in an impoverished village, I realized that many people, including my siblings, didn't have an opportunity to finish school due to their family's financial situation. It breaks my heart knowing that education is so important, and yet many children are dropping out because their families can't afford school supplies. Studying in America made me feel guilty, knowing that I've been so lucky while many students in Cambodia are suffering. I knew that I had to fulfill my promise once I graduated from college. Furthermore, I knew that I had to do something to give back to my community.

I'm also hoping that my story will help open the door for more international students to continue their education, not just in America, but in other advanced countries around the world. I want people to understand how an opportunity can mean so much to a kid like me who came from a poor family in one of the poorest countries in the world.

My message to kids living in extreme poverty, desparately searching for an opportunity: don't ever lose hope, and keep pursuing your dreams. If you're committed, if you work hard, and if you are willing to do whatever it takes, you will achieve your goals. Let my experience show you that anything is possible as long as a person has the will.

# ACKNOWLEDGMENTS

First and foremost, I would like to acknowledge my father, Peng Pen, who believed in the value of education. My father loved me dearly and always wanted the best for me. He was the source of light, guiding me in the right direction. I am forever thankful that he was a part of my life. My love for him is immeasurable. To Connie Missimer, who has encouraged me to write this book. She has given me advice on how to write and how to construct a meaningful story. Connie has always been a mentor to me. I couldn't have done this without her guidance. To my brother-in-laws, Blake and Ryan, who have been supporting me with this project from the beginning. Blake and Ryan have edited my writing and have believed in my story. Above all, they have been such wonderful brother-in-laws since the day I met them. To Mitchell Kopitch, who has been an advisor, polishing my writing and my storytelling from the first to the last chapter. Mitchell has been a friend and was committed to helping me bring this project to life. To Cathy Suter, who has revised and sharpened my story. Cathy was intrigued by my story and has guided me all the way to the finish line. To John Hughes, who has given me excellent feedback on how to publish my story. I am forever thankful for his support.

I wish to acknowledge both my Khmer and American families, the heroes that helped and guided me to achieve my goals. To my parents, my brothers and sisters, who have supported and protected me since the day I was born. I love them all dearly and deeply. I thank them for shining the light in the right direction. To my sister, Chai, thank you for being my best friend since the day I opened my eyes. I love you so much and cannot thank you enough for all the things you've done for me. I wish to thank Jeff, Wanda, Thalen, and the rest of his family for providing the opportunity for me to pursue an adequate education. Despite the ups and downs, I still love them from the bottom of my heart and will always consider them as my family no matter where I end up. To my brother-in-law, Thalen, I love you and thank you for everything that you have taught me over the past years. You told me that my life would change when I came to America, but the truth is, my life was already changing from the day I met you. For my sister Kesor, I will always have love for you. Despite everything that went on in my journey, I am truly blessed to have a sister like you.

To the coaches and friends that have contributed to my journey, I thank you all sincerely. I am so lucky to have met you and have had you all as part of my life.

# ABOUT THE AUTHOR

Regardless of how much I've changed, and how much knowledge I've gained, I will never forget my identity and where I came from. I will always consider myself the son of an impoverished family from Prey Veng Province. Cambodia will remain in my heart no matter where I end up nor how successful I become. Seattle is home to me, too. Even if I'm not an American citizen, I've become Americanized and am thankful for the opportunity that America has given me. The lessons I've learned in American schools have allowed me to make my own decisions and strive to do what is right. Being an agnostic, I believe in doing good. I deeply respect the Khmer way of life. I always try to be on my best behavior and respect my peers, regardless of their skin color or religion.

Despite writing this book, I still consider myself a business person. I always wanted to follow in Jeff's footsteps by becoming an entrepreneur. After working as a tour guide in Cambodia and after graduating from the business school at the University of Washington, I'm inspired to travel and see more of the world and meet new people. I hope one day I can start my own touring business that will encourage people to visit places like Cambodia or other regions they've never seen. I truly believe that there is more to the world than meets the eye.

Made in the USA
Monee, IL
15 September 2020

42640623R00184